# NOT WHEN, BUT IF?

How Sacramento Republic FC Rose from the
Ashes of a Half Century of Failed Local Soccer
Experiments to Win a Championship, Galvanize the
City, and Become an MLS Expansion Favorite

# EVAN REAM

# Not When, But If?

## © Evan Ream, 2024

**Edited by Kim Orendor**

Kim is my friend and former editor at the newspaper for which I started covering Sacramento Republic FC. She's also an excellent author who has written two books. You can find her work at www.kimorendorwriter.com.

**Cover art and design by Dante Peri**

Dante is a senior in my journalism class at Da Vinci Charter Academy. He's better at creating art than I am at anything I'll ever do in my life. You can find his work on Instagram @dante.elephante.

ISBN 979-8-218-38057-1

*Honestly, I'm not up to speed on U.S. copyright law, but if you want to reproduce some sections of this book just keep it to like a paragraph and make sure to attribute it to me. I spent a decade writing this thing…at least buy a copy for a friend who isn't going to read it if you're going to steal my work. Also, get used to reading the footnotes.

*For Matt Ream,*

*The person most responsible for my addiction to this agonizingly beautiful sport. Soccer opened my life to a new world full of excitement, wonder, and pain. Neither this book, nor most of the things I do on a daily basis, would be possible without you.*

# Contents

Lady Bird: "I have to get out of Sacramento."
Friend: "Why?"
Lady Bird: "Because it's soul-killing, it's the Midwest of California."
Friend: "Isn't there a thing like, think globally, act locally?"
Lady Bird: "You feel that the person who said that didn't live in Sacramento."

   *-Lady Bird*

# ONE
# NOT IF, BUT WHEN:
# OCTOBER 21, 2019[1]

It's a typical late October scorcher the day Major League Soccer finally arrives to announce Sacramento Republic FC as the league's twenty-ninth franchise. The temperature tops out at eighty-four degrees, but it feels much cooler under the shade of the trees Sacramento's early residents planted to shield the city from the heat. The Republic debuted as a lower division club more than five years ago, in 2014, and made enough noise to earn a visit from MLS officials that same year. The city entered every conversation surrounding expansion from that moment on, but what once was seen as a done deal had turned into an excruciatingly long and drawn-out process that left Sacramento's sporting future up in the air. Sacramentans, especially those who watched the Kings flirt with relocation, wondered if today's MLS press conference would ever come.

In 2014, MLS sent representatives to California's capital during a USL[2] playoff run that captivated Sacramento and culminated with an inaugural season championship. In that moment, everything was gravy—the Republic couldn't make a mistake in a city plagued with sporting incompetence. In a few short months, Sacramento established itself as the most prominent lower league soccer city in the

---

[1] I originally began each chapter with song lyrics from one of Sacramento's four most famous bands: Cake, Deftones, Oleander, and Tesla. However, these lyrics proved too expensive to license, so instead of putting them on paper, I'm merely going to footnote each chapter title with a song that I feel pairs well with the content. First off, I recommend "Friend is a Four Letter Word" by Cake.

[2] Since Sacramento Republic FC kicked off its first game in 2014, the league it has played in has changed names from USL Pro, to the USL, to the USL Championship. For simplicity, this book will refer to it as the USL.

United States. Everyone, locally and nationally, *knew* that the Republic's future lay in MLS. It was just a matter of time.

In 2015, MLS, as expected, awarded its next franchise to Minnesota. The prominent voices in American soccer applauded the league's decision to expand into the Land of 10,000 Lakes. Like the Republic, Minnesota United FC featured a strong ownership group and played in front of large crowds that dwarfed those of the rest of the country's lower division sides. The announcement came shortly after the Twin Cities bid cleared its final hurdle: securing a tentative deal to construct a downtown soccer-specific stadium. While some less-informed league watchers described the Sacramento and Minnesota bids as competitors, the reality was that United benefitted from much different circumstances. The club formed all the way back in 2010 under a different name and enjoyed more sustained success in its short history. Rational Sacramento sports fans understood MLS's decision, especially given that the league had long stated that it wished to increase its geographic footprint across the much-ignored Midwest. Minnesota's inclusion increased MLS's current and future franchise total to twenty-three, one short of the twenty-four-team cap that its plans then called for.

After struggling to remain afloat for decades, by the mid-2010s, MLS thrived as ownership groups from across the United States and Canada lined up to bid on bringing top division soccer to their city. Smelling blood in the water, the league set arbitrary limits on the number of clubs it would accept in order to create artificial scarcity and drive up future expansion fees. MLS held its final spot open for Miami, a glamorous city that played host to the shortest-tenured of the three first division American soccer teams to fold in the twenty-first century. David Beckham served as the public face of Miami's bid, which was contingent on securing enough downtown property to build a stadium in an area with astronomically high prices and convoluted politics. Despite its famous figurehead, the South Florida proposal appeared to have made little progress since the 2014 press conference where MLS laid out its intentions to return to Miami. A perceived lack of local fan support didn't help matters either.

In 2016, one year after the Minnesota announcement, Garber and MLS outlined plans for the league to expand to twenty-eight teams. This development stirred up hope in several markets around the country–twelve different U.S. cities submitted bids for the next four spots. By that time, the Republic had two full, highly successful USL seasons under its belt. Sacramento wasn't one of the favorites to secure a spot in MLS, it was *the* favorite. Garber and Co. set a hard application deadline for February 1, 2017, just a few weeks before the Republic would kick off its fourth season of play. The cities of Cincinnati, Charlotte, Detroit, Indianapolis, Nashville, Phoenix, Raleigh/Durham, San Antonio, San Diego, St. Louis, and Tampa Bay/St. Petersburg applied alongside Sacramento.

By then, the American soccer community had long understood the criteria for earning a successful bid. In every press conference surrounding expansion, Don Garber detailed the same four key factors that MLS strived for. The league desired a proven soccer fanbase, a large TV market, an owner with deep pockets, and completed plans to construct a downtown, soccer-specific stadium. Most of the budding cities from the list of twelve checked at least one or two of the four boxes. A few ticked three. But in 2016, domestic soccer experts felt that only Sacramento met all four requirements—the Republic had set multiple USL attendance records, the club had negotiated its own local TV deal despite playing in the lower divisions, wealthy local businessman Kevin Nagle had compiled a strong ownership group with immeasurable capital and experience in pro sports, and Sacramento had already released renderings for a state-of-the-art downtown stadium just a few blocks away from the Kings' shiny, new Golden 1 Center. And not that it mattered to MLS, but the Republic consistently ranked as one of the top teams in the USL after capturing the title in its first year. Sacramento to MLS appeared inevitable, a shoo-in, a formality more than anything. In fact, much of the city didn't understand why the club hadn't already received the green light.

Nearly a year passed as MLS mulled over the bids, with the league declaring that it would choose two new franchises in late 2017. The odds-on favorites were Sacramento and Cincinnati, the latter of which made a late, but memorable, entrance to the party after two seasons of shattering all of the USL's attendance records previously set by the Republic.

Residents of both cities eagerly awaited the December 2017 announcement, but MLS sent shockwaves through the American soccer community by failing to include either in the highly anticipated press conference. Instead, the league awarded its twenty-fifth franchise to Nashville and neglected to choose the second team that it had promised. Cincinnati garnered its spot shortly thereafter and then Austin, Texas joined the fold in January of 2019 despite not submitting one of the twelve official bids.[3] Seven months later, St. Louis joined the fold as well.

In 2015, Don Garber told Marcos Bretón of *The Sacramento Bee* that, "It's less about 'if' and more about 'when,' the Republic joins MLS." After the league passed Sacramento over four times, Republic fans began to wonder whether their club's inclusion into top division soccer now qualified as more of an "if" rather than a "when."

It's probably an understatement to describe Sacramento's soccer supporters as "jaded" before October 21, 2019. The Kings, forever losers, nearly bolted to allegedly greener pastures less than a decade before. MLS already fielded three Californian clubs and reportedly preferred the San Diego market over Sacramento if it were to add a fourth in state. Locals painfully watched multiple clubs leapfrog the Republic in the expansion progress. Maybe MLS to Sacramento would never happen—an increasing number of fans grew tired of the league dragging them through this drawn-out process. Some supporters advocated for staying in the USL over joining "ML$," as it became known on social media. The die-hards threw in the dollar sign as a virtual eye roll towards a league that had raised its expansion fee

---

[3] Google "Anthony Precourt Columbus Crew" for some shenanigans involving MLS expansion.

from $100 million when the Republic entered the bidding process to more than twice that figure in 2019.

And who could blame the fans for feeling jaded? Their team had been passed over by FC Cincinnati, a newer club with less pedigree from a city best known for topping its spaghetti with chili. At least Austin featured hipsters and BBQ. At least Nashville enjoyed nationwide prestige as the "Music City." At least St. Louis counted as a nostalgic pick as one of the first true hotbeds of American soccer. But what was Sacramento known for other than serving as California's capital while occupying a location roughly a ninety-minute drive away from both San Francisco and Lake Tahoe? With the Kings in the tank for what felt like the one millionth year in a row, the only national sporting news to come out of the city either revolved around the ineptitude of a franchise that once took the Shaq and Kobe Lakers to a Game 7 or the latest scandal involving controversial former mayor and NBA great Kevin Johnson.

In hindsight, it's probable that MLS never actually wanted to set up shop in Sacramento, but the unexpected USL success of the Republic forced the league's hand during a strange time for soccer in the United States. If wealthy owners had created the Republic and provided even a semblance of a business plan in the mid-2000s, the bid would have been fast-tracked like Salt Lake City's in 2005. However, in 2019, MLS found itself surrounded by an embarrassment of riches. The league that spent much of its first decade fighting for survival, could now take its pick between the multitude of $100 million-plus bids in large cities located in states that didn't already field three "major league" clubs.

Yet on October 21, 2019, it appeared as if Sacramento had finally crossed the finish line.

## October 21, 2019

Anyone who's anyone in Sacramento packs into The Bank, a trendy downtown bar converted from a nineteenth century-constructed financial institution. The city prepares for the final formality of MLS's announcement and the inevitable party to follow. Warren Smith is here, of course, making the rounds in his familiar gregarious fashion. The face of the founding ownership group spends his time mingling with the various business partners and connections he cultivated during the Republic's early years. His successor, the pharmaceutical magnate Kevin Nagle, chats with important locals as well, though in a much more reserved manner. Also present are lead investor Ron Burkle and Hollywood producer Matt Alvarez, both new additions who recently joined the bid to provide much-needed capital after several of Nagle's previous partners dropped out.

A temporary stage has been erected near the bar's entrance and on it stands a podium with three chairs on either side. There's an Old Glory Red backdrop hanging where a curtain would in a movie theater. It features nine rows of MLS logos, each surrounded on one side by the words "Sacramento" and on the other by "MLS2SAC.COM." The stage faces two columns of temporary seating bisected by an aisle, sort of like you'd find at a wedding. And this *is* a wedding–in just a few minutes, MLS will exchange vows with the city of Sacramento.

Local dignitaries, reporters, and big shots in the soccer community occupy the ground floor while members of the Tower Bridge Battalion, the Republic's largest supporters' group, stand on the balcony at the back of the room. They pass the time singing songs while a fan keeps the beat using an empty plastic trash can as a makeshift drum. "It took a Republic," reads one supporter's sign. Despite the sheer mass of people packed inside, everyone can make out Kings general manager and legend Vlade Divac, who stands a head taller than anyone else while sporting his typical dress shirt, unbuttoned at the top. Former Sacramento coach Paul Buckle converses with youth soccer representatives near the back of the ballroom. Journalists from *The Sacramento Bee* and *Soccer America* sit in the front row just below the stage to cover the culmination of a story they've followed for the better part of a decade. Meanwhile, Republic co-founder Joe Wagoner, the original man with the plan, unassumingly hides by himself in a corner. Notably absent are former mayor Johnson and the club's current coaching staff, though the latter lead a training session on the other side of the city at the same time. The size of the crowd proves so large that the seating area more resembles the mosh pit at a punk show than the setting for this long-awaited announcement. There's an exuberant buzz in the air, one that continues to rise until it's time to begin the ceremony.

Former U.S. international and Fox Sports broadcaster Stuart Holden steps to the dais to emcee the event in what could very well be his inaugural visit to California's capital. Before he opens his mouth, the dapper former midfielder has already won over the crowd by sporting a tie in the same shade of red as the Republic's home uniforms. Holden even pronounces "Sacramento" correctly–the "t" is silent for anyone born north of Bakersfield. More than a decade ago, Holden sat in the stands as an MLS franchise played its first-ever home game. Then twenty-one and still a month away from his professional debut, the Houston Dynamo player watched in awe as his teammates made history. In front of more than 25,000 Texans in April of 2006, the Dynamo shot right out of a cannon and into the local sporting landscape, embarrassing the Colorado Rapids with a 5-2 thrashing powered by four goals from Brian Ching. Holden begins his remarks by harkening back to his local club's inauguration.

"That is a night that I will never forget, the city of Houston will never forget," he says. "Now, I just want everybody in this room that has waited so long for that moment to picture yourself now in a brand-new, soccer-specific stadium here in Sacramento experiencing that moment."

The crowd erupts with a level of noise not heard in Sacramento since the early 2000s Kings at ARCO Arena. The fans finally allow themselves to dream of a future that had long proven elusive to cement. The boisterous supporters crank up the volume to such a high level that Holden stops speaking for a few seconds to just take in the moment.

"Goosebumps," he says, the only word he can manage to utter. "Goosebumps."

Holden still appears moved when it comes time to introduce the bigwigs. Governor Gavin Newsom, with his trademark slicked-back hair, struts out first. He's followed by mayor Darrell Steinberg, commissioner Garber, Burkle, Alvarez, and, finally, Nagle. The only six people in the building who occupy their particular tax bracket take their seats before Garber inherits the podium from Holden. The commissioner's receding hairline is trimmed to an appropriate length as always, and it doesn't detract from his well-coiffed demeanor. He steps forward in a black designer suit, blue dress shirt, and dark blue tie–with a pocket square, no less. As he prepares his remarks, Garber flashes his well-known grin that's almost too pearly-white. He carries himself like a smooth-talking salesman, one who can convince you to buy anything even while you *know* that there are likely many parts of the deal you can't comprehend nearly as well as he. These expansion press conferences are the moments Garber lives for.

The nature of the vast majority of the tasks required of a professional sports league's commissioner typically render them unpopular figures in the public eye, figures subject to immense criticism. On days like today, Garber delivers great news to hopeful cities instead of answering mostly fair questions pertaining to the exorbitant MLS expansion fees, the league's lack of promotion and relegation, or its controversial and potentially outdated single-entity structure. Garber isn't the most powerful, wealthiest, or famous man on stage, but at events like this, his star far outshines those in his immediate proximity.

"It's hard to believe that it was over four years ago when I told Marcos Bretón of *The Sacramento Bee* that it was less about 'if' and more about 'when' Sacramento was going to join Major League Soccer," he says. "Well folks, 'when' is today, and your 'when' has arrived." Other than stumbling over a few words in his speech and accidentally referring to the governor as "mayor Newsom," Garber enjoys a flawless few minutes on stage. He continues with his remarks by mentioning California's other three MLS teams, sparking a "Beat L.A." chant from the Battalion. The commissioner invites Burkle to join him at the dais and drapes a red scarf that reads "Sacramento 2022" over the shoulders of the reclusive billionaire. "So now it gives me great pleasure," Garber says while burgundy streamers fly through the air, "to announce Sacramento as the twenty-ninth MLS team."

"This is our home!" the Battalion sings. "SAC-RA-MEN-TO, S-R-F-C, the club for me…"

The pair then turn their attention to the projector screen above the backdrop as the event's production team queues up a video. Clips of the commissioner flash up on the screen, each with him wearing a different expensive suit while standing at a podium. Present day Garber watches as just a few feet away his past self announces successful expansion bids for Minnesota, Nashville, Cincinnati, Austin, and St. Louis. The feed then cuts to a throng of dejected Republic fans, wallowing in the misery of MLS passing them over yet again. It feels like celebrating a wedding with your significant other by playing a video montage of each of your former partners. Somehow highlighting Sacramento's disappointment serves as the introduction for Alvarez's remarks, which come and go without controversy. Finally, Nagle, the man who led the expansion bid for the past four years, approaches the podium.

Not one for extravagance or ceremony, Nagle stammers over his first few words before gaining the confidence to speak calmly and clearly. His prepared speech loses some of its effectiveness by repeating the "not if, but when" mantra that Garber just made his key point. Either the two hadn't compared notes beforehand or they just decided to hammer home the same sound bite that originally brought comfort and hope to Sacramento fans but now caused pain more than any other emotion. "Earning an MLS franchise was personal to me because I wanted the world to see everything that I love and value about Sacramento," he says. "At our core, we are a local community. We take pride in being underdogs and proving the doubters wrong. But let me tell you something, those who doubt Sacramento simply don't know Sacramento. We're in the business of doing extraordinary things every day."

"EVERY DAY!" shouts someone from the balcony.

Nagle pauses and looks up, his radiant blue eyes piercing a room full of grown adults to whom he's become a hero. Before the smile appears on his mouth, you can already see it in his eyes.

"EVERY DAY!" he repeats.

The clean-cut and enthusiastic mayor Steinberg speaks next, taking more time than any of the other six men on the stage to deliver his remarks. His predecessor, Kevin Johnson, earned city-wide plaudits during his early years in office for spearheading the successful effort to prevent the Kings from relocating. In his later years as mayor, Johnson declared it a priority to help the Republic cross the finish line into MLS. But he's not involved today, gone from the public eye possibly due to the wide array of controversies and allegations that have followed him for more than two decades.

In Johnson's stead, Steinberg, the former leader of the California State Senate, organized rallies, spoke at town hall meetings, delivered speeches, and attended community events in hopes of bringing MLS to Sacramento. He may not have initiated the bid, but he still hopes to take it the short distance left to pay dirt. And his inclusion on stage tonight certainly can't hurt his political career—the image of Garber, Newsom, Nagle, Burkle, Alvarez, and Steinberg holding a Sacramento MLS scarf will live on forever. Sacramentans will remember who led the charge when the city's second top-division sports franchise arrived. He begins his speech by fanning the flames for the tortured sports fans in California's oft-overlooked city.

"I want to begin my remarks by saying that I know that being humble is important," Steinberg says, "but this morning, I have texted mayors Sam Liccardo in San José[4] and mayor Eric Garcetti in Los Angeles[5] expressing my condolences to them[6] on becoming the second-best MLS teams in California. Game on! The rivalry begins!'"

The mayor then switches to a more serious tone, thanking all the local leaders who chipped in to make this day possible. He mentions everyone who contributed to the bid at any point of the process. Well, everyone other than Joe Wagoner, who stands silently in the back of the crowd. When Steinberg brings up Wagoner's co-founder, Warren Smith, the noise levels rise to their highest point yet. After Steinberg finishes rattling off names, the stunned fanbase interrupts him.

"WAGONER! WAGONER! WAGONER!" the Battalion chants as the confused mayor halts his speech[7] for a second before finishing with the crescendo.

"Today's historic day in the Indomitable City of Sacramento puts a big punctuation mark on what we already know: Sacramento is no longer just becoming the next great American city, we are no longer just becoming, we *are*," he says. "We are proud, we are tough, we are resilient, and we will never settle for anything less than what our proud history, our culture, and our people know that we deserve.

"We know our work together is just the beginning," he says after another minute of dictating adjective-filled sentences intended to bolster Sacramento's reputation to those watching from other parts of the country. "We can never rest for too long when there is more to achieve and more people who want and deserve opportunity. But for at least one day, today, let us revel together in our great achievements. The beginning of decades of excitement and incredible memories and a result that shows that passion, persistence, and love for a city can combine to create a magic moment. May there be many such other magic moments at the state-of-the-art Major League Soccer stadium in our downtown Railyards. May we wave many championship banners. May we continue to say, with big smiles, when we are asked, 'so where do you live?' 'I live in Sacramento!' Este es un gran dia para Sacramento! Vamos los Rojos! Glory, glory Sacramento!'"

Following the closing remarks from an off-the-cuff Newsom and a video of celebrities congratulating Sacramento,[8] it's official. Finally. What began as an idea

---

[4] The crowd boos this statement.
[5] This crowd further boos this statement.
[6] This crowd goes wild for this statement.
[7] "Many people took bows on Monday," Bretón wrote in the next day's *Bee*, "But two people didn't get the chance and that's a shame: Warren Smith and Joe Wagoner came up with the idea of Sacramento Republic FC and first brought the team to Sacramento. They are no longer involved with the team and there were hard feelings when the team was sold to Kevin Nagle. That sort of thing happens all the time. But while Smith's name was mentioned briefly by mayor Darrell Steinberg, Wagoner's wasn't. Republic fans chanted Wagoner's name, but he and Warren deserved better than that. Nothing is lost by being gracious."
[8] An eclectic group of past and current soccer professionals, other athletes, actors, and comedians all chimed in. Taylor Twellman and Landon Donovan both joked about how long it took for the Republic to get in, while Michael Strahan, Tom Brady, Tim Howard, Mia Hamm, Carlos Vela, Steve Harvey, Steve Nash, Steven Gerrard, Erin Andrewes, Josef Martinez, Robbie Keane, David Spade,

in the mind of a soccer-hating minor league sports executive, birthed during late nights over Grand Slams in a San Francisco Denny's, would soon become a reality. It took a Republic, that's for sure. Hundreds of local fans, players, executives, employees, and politicians collectively dragged Sacramento to its desired goal of attaining a second top division sports franchise. In just over two years, Sacramento Republic FC would debut in Major League Soccer.

## Not When, But If?

Except that's not what happened. It's summer in 2022, the year Sacramento Republic FC was supposed to kick off its inaugural MLS campaign. The club still hasn't played a top-division soccer game and the supposedly done deal for the downtown, soccer-specific stadium still hasn't broken ground in the decaying Railyards. Three years ago, MLS welcomed the Sacramento market as its 29th franchise. But now, no one knows if the city will ever reach the promised land.

## Part One?

One of the first lessons I learned while studying journalism in college was to never insert myself into the story. But I've spent much of my adult life covering Sacramento Republic FC and feel like it's truly difficult for me to tell this story without contextualizing some details of my own life.

As an eager and ambitious young journalist for *The Davis Enterprise*, I pleaded with my editors to allow me to cover the Republic. They agreed, sort of. Skeptical of the impact a lower-division soccer team could have in the area, they assigned me to document the club's inaugural match in early 2014 but wouldn't commit to further coverage ahead of time.

Then 20,231 fans packed Hughes Stadium for that contest and my superiors decided to prolong my beat indefinitely. At the very least, they felt, Sacramento Republic FC could fill much-needed column inches during the summer months where there were no high school or college sports to write about.

The Republic won the USL title in style that year, breaking American lower-division attendance records all the way to the championship game that it hosted. During the club's first-ever offseason, I began writing this book. The project was no secret—almost everyone involved with the club, and many of its fans, knew that I intended to release a complete origin story for one of the most successful soccer startups in American history. I figured that it wouldn't take too much time to

---

Holden, and Charlie Davies also sent messages, with Spade's being the weirdest. "I don't know much about soccer," he said, "but I feel like you should get Messi, Ronaldo, Aaron Rodgers...actually I know nothing about soccer."

complete–the buzz around the team seemed to suggest that it would earn an MLS expansion spot as soon as possible.

However, Sacramento's MLS bid stumbled several times, postponing the club's entry into top division soccer on more occasions than I can count. While still working on this book in addition to my newspaper duties, I started a new job as communications manager for a youth soccer company. There, my priorities shifted.

Ahead of the 2018 season, the Republic first team hired the president of that youth soccer company as an assistant coach, and I stepped away from my coverage to avoid any possible conflicts of interest. By then, I'd already spent more hours than I'd like to admit documenting this incredible story, which hadn't been fully told before. Many of the chapters I'd written stood in a state of near-completion. The only problem: there wasn't an ending–I stalled my progress while hoping that the club's inevitable entry into MLS would provide the bookend, I needed to wrap up the project with a happy conclusion.

After years of covering the franchise and its constant battle to prove that Sacramento deserved a top-division soccer team, I felt like I was finally ready to finish writing the book when I walked into The Bank on October 21, 2019. For years, various members of the soccer community had asked me when it would be published, so I brought it back into the forefront of my life with the intention of releasing it to coincide with the Republic's 2022 Major League Soccer home opener.

But as I learned through this process, a "sure thing" is never a sure thing.

A once-in-a-century pandemic ravaged livelihood across the globe shortly after the MLS announcement, making my book project feel like an afterthought in comparison. Then, in early 2020, three of my four jobs laid me off on the same day and my personal life and well-being spiraled completely out of control. This development came just weeks after Rodrigo López returned to his adopted home after five years away. A sellout crowd of 11,569 welcomed "RoRo" back to the field for a 1-1 draw against FC Tulsa on March 7. That match would be the last the Republic played for more than four months and the final time in 2020 where fans were allowed to watch in person.

When the club returned to play in July, my coverage returned with it. Without regular work consuming me, I needed a productive way to pass the time. I enjoyed this; it felt nothing like the conclusion of the 2017 season when I almost welcomed my boss's hiring because I was so burnt out and jaded from covering professional sports. For so long, I'd spent all my free time working to perfect the incredible story that surrounded the foundation of Sacramento Republic FC. Free of most responsibilities, I now had time to complete a project that had once become the bane of my existence. It was time to prove that I could actually make good on a promise I'd made back in 2015 when MLS to Sacramento appeared right around the corner.

I completed all the chapters covering the club's formation way back in 2016. For four years they sat untouched and unread in my Google Drive, which bummed me out. It looked like everything was finally falling into place, though. Enjoying my first bit of prolonged free time during the 2020 season, I spent most of my days filling in the blank spots and finally polished enough of my work to feel ready to publicly release all the epic stories I'd been sitting on for years.

There are so many untold tales regarding Sacramento Republic FC, which were fortunately relayed to me, that deserve to see the light of day. There are dozens of individuals who gave everything for the club, but still haven't been properly recognized for their contributions to the city's sporting landscape. There are a plethora of people responsible for turning an afterthought of a soccer city in the United States into the odds on favorite to earn an MLS expansion spot, perhaps few more impactful than Joe Wagoner.

Whenever I thought about October 21, 2019, my mind conjured up the image of Joe Wagoner standing alone at the back of the crowd in The Bank and an invisible wave of sadness would crash into my body, overwhelming my senses. I'd think back to how Wagoner could only watch while a series of people less involved in creating that very moment accepted the praise he deserved. But the sadness would always wash away, replaced by a feeling of excitement brought on by the knowledge that I'd soon tell his story and the story of Sacramento Republic FC. This daily emotional roller coaster could only be brought on by a character like Wagoner, who is an absolute legend. So are most of the others responsible for the club's early formation and the upward trajectory they helped set it on.

While we all struggled during lockdown, the Republic announced in 2021 that it would delay its MLS debut by a year to 2023. *The Athletic* first reported that news the day before I moved to Sacramento (from nearby Davis) for the first time. My desire to garner a better understanding of the city's culture ahead of the book's release partially motivated my decision to relocate.

Then, of course, in true Sacramento fashion, the promise of ascending to the highest level of soccer in this country vanished into thin air. The moment almost felt instantaneous. The powers that be pulled the carpet right out from under the local, passionate fanbase. Yet again, the city snatched defeat from the jaws of victory. Burkle never paid MLS a single cent but threw down $22 million to purchase Neverland Ranch. MLS to Sacramento died, or at least slipped into a deep coma.

Charlotte would debut in 2022 with St. Louis following the next year. Aside from a random Garber comment during MLS Cup 2022, California's capital was no longer mentioned during discussions regarding MLS's thirtieth franchise. Las Vegas, Phoenix, and San Diego moved ahead of Sacramento on the shortlist of favorites, with the latter officially announced in May of 2023. The "Expansion of Major League Soccer" *Wikipedia* page now listed Sacramento under its "Failed or stalled expansion projects" section.

From an optics point of view, these developments made sense–all three aforementioned cities qualify as larger or flashier markets. Furthermore, either Vegas or Phoenix would help extend the league's geographic footprint. Objectively, considering Sacramento over any of the other three wasn't logical. Especially when it doesn't appear as if there's a viable owner who can front the ballooning MLS expansion fees, which now cost well over $300 million.

My jaded attitude returned alongside these setbacks, and I again put aside this project, no longer sure that I'd ever complete it.

But then something strange happened in 2022. As a journalist, I'm not supposed to have favorite players, but I'm also not supposed to insert myself into the story during the first fifteen pages of my Republic book, if at all. While on the clock for my youth soccer company that year, I bumped into my all-time favorite Sacramento player, Ivan Mirković. The former midfielder had retired after the 2018 season to pursue a full-time career in coaching and our paths crossed several times in the line of work. Whenever I ran into him, he would always ask me the same question: "When is the book coming out?"

I would always tell him, and everyone else who asked, the same thing: "No clue, I don't have an ending." I feel like that's a fair response, and it probably is, but Mirković would always counter with the same rebuttal. "You can always release an updated edition," he'd say.

For whatever reason, I finally agreed with his view after that chance encounter. Maybe he'd succeeded in wearing me down after all these years. But it doesn't matter because I think Mirković is correct. The only thing I can think of whenever someone mentions the book is that same image of Wagoner, who has gotten the crap end of the deal so many times without having his story properly told. And he's not alone. Most know about Warren Smith, but there are so many more who helped bring the Republic to town yet remain anonymous to this day. Everyone has heard of Ron Burkle, the franchise's false savior, but how many Sacramento fans know the names Erika Bjork, Kenny Cooper, Julia Jones, Brett Reitter, or Tim Stallings? And just wait for Jeremy Field, few people I've covered in my life have made me laugh as much as he while also providing sound insight into complex matters.

Every year I keep their incredible stories to myself is a year I prioritize writing the perfect book with a fairytale ending over shedding light on these hard-working, deserving individuals. When I first began this project, I imagined that it would jump start my writing career and help me achieve my goal of becoming a well-respected, mainstream soccer journalist.

However, that's not even what I want anymore and I'm not sure if it was ever what I desired. Now I just want to coach youth soccer, teach high school, and write during whatever free time I can find in between. These are the things that make me happy and because I feel that way, the text may include a few blind spots. It's an incomplete story, covering the origins of the club all the way through the end of the first season. But that's okay, because there's no such thing as a perfect book even if the Republic's 2014 campaign was nearly the perfect season.

It's finally time to tell this story. What follows is the first part of Sacramento Republic FC's incredible journey. I don't know if I'll ever follow this up with part two despite the fact that this text includes only about 80,000 of the 400,000 words of copy I've written on the subject.

I also truly have no idea what the future holds in store for the club. It's possible that one day the Republic will earn an MLS expansion spot for a second time. Maybe then it will actually get the chance to debut in the league. Perhaps the club will fold. Or maybe one hundred years from now, Sacramento will still fight for lower-division titles while dreaming of deep U.S. Open Cup runs.

However, it's clear to me now that wherever the club's final destination may lie, there are more consequential aspects of Sacramento's story. The Republic has proved a blessing for a city starved for sporting success. The important story isn't that of the club's product, but rather its beginnings.

And in order to tell that story, it's important to first understand the local "major league" sports culture and the history of professional soccer in the city. Both of which, like Sacramento's fruitless MLS bid, involve considerably more failures than successes.

# TWO
# LOVE FOUND A WAY:
# HOW SACRAMENTO SAVED
# THE KINGS[9]

"Hey, mom, did you feel emotional the first time that you drove in Sacramento? I did and I wanted to tell you, but we weren't really talking when it happened. All those bends I've known my whole life and stores and the whole thing. But I wanted to tell you I love you."

- *Lady Bird*

Grant Napear[10] struggles to fight back the tears. The longtime Sacramento Kings broadcaster–known for his fiery red hair, loud personality, and "If you don't like that, you don't like Kings basketball!" catchphrase–sees the writing on the wall. It's April 13, 2011, and moments earlier, Kobe Bryant's thirty-six points doomed the Kings to a heartbreaking 116-108 overtime loss in front of an overflow sellout crowd of 17,641 at ARCO Arena.[11] The result drops Sacramento to 24-58 on the

---

[9] I recommend pairing "Love Song" by Tesla with this chapter.
[10] Since fired by the Sacramento Kings for controversially tweeting "all lives matter" during the 2020 George Floyd protests. This book does not wish to analyze this situation, merely to acknowledge that at one point in his life, Napear served as the voice of the only major league sports franchise in Sacramento.
[11] The text will only refer to this facility as "ARCO Arena" even though its name was changed to Power Balance Pavilion in 2011 and then to Sleep Train Arena the following year before it was demolished in 2022. Everyone in Sacramento still calls it "ARCO Arena," which is also still the title

now-concluded season, but that's not why Napear weeps alongside longtime broadcast partner Jerry Reynolds.

Twenty-seven years ago, the franchise relocated from Kansas City to the capital of California in search of a fresh start. And now, if the Maloof Family gets their wish, the Kings will pack up and move yet again, this time to the allegedly greener pastures found 400 miles south in Anaheim. Not only will Sacramento lose the only top-division professional franchise that has ever called this place home, but it will yet again suffer a defeat at the hands of the more famous half of California. For most of its nearly two century history, Sacramento has lived in the shadows cast by Los Angeles and San Diego in Southern California, as well as nearby San Francisco and the Silicon Valley. Retaining the Kings is more than a fight to save a basketball team, it's a fight to retain relevance.

"Jerry, all I can say to you is thank you," Napear says next to the glassy-eyed Reynolds, a former Kings coach. "We'll try to make it off the air. Well, I'll tell ya...let me catch my breath here. There's a lot of uncertainty as we all know, but the one thing that we do know is the love affair between this team and this city. And tonight, we say so long with the music from Sacramento's legendary rock band, Tesla, and iconic memories from your Sacramento Kings.

"Folks, this is *Love Song*."

The broadcast fades into a five-minute montage of the few great moments in Kings history as the commentators look into the camera with thousand-yard stares. They have nothing left to give on a night full of sadness.

It's over. Outside forces will deprive the perennial underdog that is Sacramento of arguably its most-recognizable asset. The decision may produce a black mark that will prove impossible to erase—would the city ever be able to drum up enough interest for another top division organization of any kind? Just a few years ago, Sacramento hosted "major league" ambitions as a potential expansion or relocation market for MLB and NFL clubs. The rotting foundations of the failed multipurpose stadium next to ARCO Arena stand as a reminder of the city's optimistic mindset. Yet Sacramento never could put the final stamp on bringing home a second franchise. The city fumbled whatever opportunity it may have had with either of those leagues just as it now appears powerless to save the Kings from leaving.

In a couple of months, local pro sports fans might find themselves with just one team to satisfy their fix: baseball's Triple-A River Cats. The Kings had been stuck in NBA purgatory for nearly a decade, but everyone in the city would take NBA purgatory over permanently wiping Sacramento off of the country's sporting map.

---

for its *Wikipedia* page. Bonney Field (now Heart Health Park) and Raley Field (now Sutter Health Park) get the same treatment.

# Vagrant

Contemplating relocation hardly qualified as a novel idea in Sacramento Kings history. Previous owner Jim Thomas made similar threats in 1997, prompting the city to shell out a $70 million loan in hopes of maintaining its "Major League" status. And if there's one thing[12] that the franchise has consistently excelled at in roughly a century of its existence, it's relocation—the Kings are the NBA's version of an army brat.

Originally founded as the Rochester Seagrams in 1923, the organization joined the NBA for the 1948-49 season as the Rochester Royals. The club knocked off the New York Knicks in the 1951 NBA Finals, then later bolted for Cincinnati. The Royals lasted fifteen seasons in Ohio before traveling further west during a three-year period in which they oddly split their home games between Kansas City and Omaha. It was during this time that the club adopted the Kings moniker to avoid confusion with MLB's Kansas City Royals. In 1975, the Kings decided to solely play games in Kansas City, an arrangement that lasted a full decade. The club then relocated for what Sacramentans hoped was the final time ahead of the 1985-86 regular season.

"In the modern history of American pro sports dating from World War II, the Kings had no equal in professional basketball, baseball, football, or hockey. No professional sports team moved among as many cities as the Kings," wrote former *Sacramento Bee* columnist R.E. Graswich in *Vagrant Kings: David Stern, Kevin Johnson, and the NBA's Orphan Team*. "They were the nation's itinerant team, like a tumbleweed that wore the labels of five cities under two nicknames while blowing across the United States before landing in Sacramento in 1985."

A small group of Sacramento-based investors had bought the Kansas City Kings in 1983 and lost $3.2 million in two years in the Midwest, according to minority owner Frank McCormack in *Never Lose: A Decade of Sports & Politics in Sacramento*.[13]

As unlikely as it seems now, indoor soccer may have also played a major role in the Kings' desire to leave Kansas City. Competing for attention with the Leiweke

---

[12] Other than losing.

[13] A 2013 *Deadspin* article titled, "A History Lesson for Sacramento: How Kansas City Lost The Kings" claimed that when the Sacramento-based investment group bought into the Kansas City Kings, it never made a concerted effort to actually keep the team in Missouri. The owners missed several self-imposed deadlines regarding their claims that they would announce the number of season tickets that the club needed to sell in order to become profitable and stay in the city. While maintaining that the desire was to keep the Kings in Kansas City, McCormack wrote that that number was 5,000, and he was in charge of selling that amount of tickets to the people of Kansas City. According to *Never Lose*, McCormack stayed in Kansas City fewer than two months while trying to hit that number, before heading back to Sacramento to help the campaign of pro-sports mayoral candidate Ross Relles. The Kansas City Kings never sold those 5,000 season tickets.

brothers[14] run-Kansas City Comets, the Kings struggled at the gate, failing to average five-figure attendances in the first five years that the two franchises overlapped. At the same time, the Comets drew at least 11,000 fans per game each year, topping out at an average of 15,786 in the 1983-84 season, one in which they fielded an underwhelming squad.

According to Mike Gastineau's *Sounders FC: Authentic Masterpiece*, brothers Tim and Tod Leiweke proved instrumental in revamping the typical gameday experience for the Comets. The Leiwekes, who would later play a major role in several MLS franchises, turned pregame into a spectacle. Instead of just introducing the players with a monotone stadium announcer and moving straight into the match, the brothers decided to cut the lights and blast intense music through the PA system to pump up the crowd. Thanks to the duo's innovative efforts, the Comets quickly knocked the Kings out of the Midwest sports market, and forced them over to California's capital, where prospective fans widely celebrated their arrival.

# Home

According to the 2020 U.S. census, Sacramento ranks as the thirty-fifth most populous city in the United States and just the sixth largest in California. And for what it lacks in size, it doesn't particularly make up for in notoriety. Los Angeles's film industry has been the most influential in the world since its inception. San Diego's pristine beaches draw hordes of domestic and international tourists. San Jose continues to serve as one of the world leaders in tech commerce. And San Francisco qualifies a vibe of its own even to this day. Of those six largest cities, only the more populous Fresno fails to overshadow Sacramento in most meaningful ways. The state may have chosen Sacramento as its capital in 1854, but the California Gold Rush ended the following year, and since then, the city has mostly existed anonymously both nationally and internationally. The state government operates out of Sacramento, but many of its governors choose to live elsewhere. The first narrative feature film debuted in 1906, but it would be another 111 years before anyone released one mainly set and filmed in Sacramento.[15]

---

[14] Of the brothers, Tim would later become famous in soccer circles for signing David Beckham to the Los Angeles Galaxy in MLS, a tale famously captured in Grant Wahl's book *The Beckham Experiment.*

[15] That film, of course, was *Lady Bird.* In 2018, *The Ringer's* Riley McAtee wrote: "This isn't just a film people from the area enjoy–it's one many feel the need to actively defend. That intense reaction from Sacramento citizens may be a byproduct of the fact that Sacramento has never gotten a fraction of this much attention on the screen. IMDb lists just thirty-four feature films containing the word "Sacramento" in their plot synopsis, a number that–no surprise–falls far short of that for other California cities like Los Angeles (2,132 titles) or San Francisco (738). Sacramento can't compete even with similarly sized metro areas like Orlando (82), Portland (88), Pittsburgh (86), or Cleveland (105)."

The most notable, and some would argue only, aspect of Sacramento arrived in 1985 when the Kings became the first top-division professional franchise to set up shop in the city. Unlike Los Angeles (six), San Diego (two), San Jose (two), San Francisco (two), and even Oakland (three), California's capital hosted just one team in the five biggest major pro sports in the United States and Canada at the time of Napear and Reynolds's emotional sign off in 2011.

But the city loved its one team from conception–traffic piled up in Natomas as thousands of eager supporters lined roads leading into ARCO Arena for that first game in October of 1985. Though the Kings fell 108-104 to the woeful Los Angeles Clippers, the passionate fans created a boisterous home environment on par with any in the NBA. Sacramento had finally arrived as a major league city.

"The people, the fans, they made it incredible to play there and live there," former Kings player and coach Reggie Theus told *ABC News* in 2015. "They were bringing out white limos for us, and it was almost like they were having a parade...As pros, we do our jobs. But it was bigger than our jobs. This was something that was city changing. This was life altering for a lot of fans there in terms of having a professional team that they could cheer."

Added Reynolds in the same story: "It was just such an event, I think Sacramento and the fans were so pleased to be part of major league professional sports."

The fact that, by the end of the 2010-11 season, the Kings had made the playoffs just ten times in twenty-seven seasons since arriving in the city, mattered little. Such was the popularity of the franchise that it sold out the first 497 home games in its history, the fourth longest streak in NBA history when it ended in 1997.[16]

# The Boys

When the Maloof family assumed control over the Sacramento Kings around the turn of the century, it inherited a franchise that had compiled a 413-703 record since relocating from Kansas City. The first-ever major league sports franchise in Sacramento thanked the fans who showed up in droves to games with thirteen straight losing seasons. The flaccid Kings earned just two playoff berths in those relatively anonymous campaigns out in Cow Town on the West Coast. But the Maloofs appeared in the right place at the right time to catch lightning in a bottle. The family had made most of its fortune in the early half of the 20th century

---

[16] At time of publication, that streak is still good for seventh all time behind Dallas, Portland, Boston, Chicago, Miami, and Golden State. Each of the top six streaks came during a stretch in which that club won at least one title as the Mavericks (one), Trail Blazers (one), Celtics (three), Bulls (six), Heat (three), and Warriors (four) all were among the most successful teams in the NBA at the time. The Kings posted a 359-628 record (0.364-win percentage) during their run of sellouts.

through securing Coors distribution rights in the American Southwest but wished to enter the exclusive arena of professional sports ownership.

Almost instantly, the Maloofs' new squad helped locals forget about more than a decade of futility when the Kings began the lockout-shortened 1998-99 NBA season featuring a retooled roster that finally put the franchise on the right track. In the offseason, Sacramento aggressively acquired three key players in power forward Chris Webber, veteran Serbian giant Vlade Divac, and exciting rookie point guard Jason Williams. Future NBA MVP finalist Peja Stojaković also finally jumped on board, arriving from Greek side PAOK two years after the Kings originally drafted him.

A 27-23 record in the truncated season proved good enough to earn the Western Conference's No. 6 seed in the playoffs where the Kings took the John Stockton and Karl Malone-led Utah Jazz all the way to a decisive fifth game. The pair of future Hall of Famers eventually bested their Western Conference counterparts, but for the first time in its California history, a sense of hope surrounded the Kings. Shortly after the postseason exit, the Maloofs bought out then-lead-owner Jim Thomas, a Southern California real estate developer, and traded in their minority stake for a majority. Following the sale, the Maloofs hitched a ride on the gravy train alongside arguably the most exciting team in the NBA and one that would qualify for the playoffs in each of the next seven seasons.

If 1999 was the start of the upwards trend on the curve that was the Maloof era, 2001 was its peak. In addition to opening the Palms Casino Resort in Las Vegas, the Maloofs saw their Kings finish with a franchise-best 61-21 record in the 2001-02 season after the acquisitions of Mike Bibby, Doug Christie, and Bobby Jackson lifted Sacramento into a true contender for the NBA championship. This is the team every Sacramentan remembers with an ear-to-ear grin on their faces before the smile fades into a sigh of "what if?"

Playing some of the most aesthetically pleasing basketball in the league, the Kings advanced all the way to the Western Conference Finals one fast break at a time. There, they met a historically great Los Angeles Lakers side that featured an in-prime Shaquille O'Neal and Kobe Bryant. In what some have listed among the greatest NBA playoff series of all time, the Lakers cruised to an easy first game win before Sacramento grabbed the next two. Just seconds away from taking a commanding 3-1 series lead in Game 4, Kings fans watched Robert Horry's famous three-pointer at the buzzer breathe life back into the Lakers while simultaneously sucking it out of Sacramento.

After the Kings rebounded by taking Game 5 at home, the next match-up would become mired in one of the biggest controversies in NBA history. Game 6 produced a four-point Sacramento loss in L.A. in which the Lakers shot forty free throws, including twenty-seven in the fourth quarter alone, eighteen more than the Kings. There was such a disparity in calls that commentator Bill Walton actively bemoaned the officiating several times on the nationally televised broadcast. Years later, disgraced NBA referee Tim Donaghy[17] filed a court document through his attorney claiming that the game was fixed because it was allegedly in the best interests of the league for the series to extend to the maximum of seven games.

Missing a multitude of shots down the stretch, Sacramento then threw away the seventh and final game at home in overtime. The iconic moment that night came when the Lakers left Stojaković, a thirty-eight percent three-point shooter that year, wide open for a corner three with the Kings trailing by one and twelve seconds left to play. Earlier in the season, the Serbian collected his first of two Three-Point Contest titles at the NBA All-Star Game. Naturally, his potential lead-taking shot didn't even graze the rim. There would be no appearance in the Finals, but there was always next year.

Only there wasn't—while many thought that the Kings would continue competing for championships with their stacked squad, Sacramento's NBA star never shone brighter than in that series. Webber blew out his knee in the playoffs the following season, returning Sacramento to small-market anonymity.

But during the run, the Kings became a countrywide phenomenon. Sacramento's high-octane style of play drew plenty of eyeballs, leading to regular appearances on national TV and one of the franchise's few cover stories in *Sports Illustrated*.[18] Perhaps no one rode the Kings' coattails more than the Maloofs. In particular, the two eldest siblings, Joe and Gavin, who served as the *very* public operators of the franchise.

Sitting courtside every game, the brothers basked in the limelight of their own local celebrity. They pounded their chests after big plays, rented billboard space to recruit Chris Webber to re-sign with the team, and filmed Carl's Jr. commercials where they boasted of their alleged $1 billion worth and penchant for ordering twenty-four-year-old Bordeauxs.[19] In the early 2000s, the brothers were the toast of Sacramento and the NBA, with then-commissioner David Stern reportedly lovingly referring to the pair as simply, "The Boys." The mutual love affair between the city and the owners of its only major professional team continued through an improbable run of success all the way until shit finally hit the fan.

# Bursting the Bubble

With a roster that featured far less talent than its 2001-02 peak, the Kings qualified for the playoffs in the 2005-06 season and pushed the No. 1 seeded San Antonio

---

[17] Donaghy was sentenced to fifteen months in prison in a 2008 gambling scandal, where he was found to have bet on NBA games and knowingly influenced calls to favor his bets. However, his claims regarding the competitive aspects of the Kings-Lakers series have never been verified.

[18] The article was titled: "The Greatest Show on Court; Sacramento Kings: Basketball the way it oughta be."

[19] In the commercials, they drank those bottles while eating fast food burgers.

Spurs to six games in the first round. It was the eighth time in eight years that head coach Rick Adelman guided Sacramento to the postseason, but the club declined to renew his contract following the Spurs loss. It would take another seventeen NBA seasons for the club to return to the playoffs, breaking the Los Angeles Clippers' previous record drought of fifteen.

Over the next few years, as a rotating cast of new head coaches failed to yield results on the court with the mediocre group of players the front office signed, the United States plunged into recession. The economy tanked just after the Maloofs added a $600 million Fantasy Tower to the Palms in Vegas. By 2010, the Palms was failing to make payments on its loan for the Fantasy Tower, forcing the Maloofs to reportedly sell ninety-eight percent of the property in exchange for erasing $400 million of debt. Even "The Boys" weren't immune to bad market conditions and without a state-of-the-art stadium in Sacramento, they weren't recouping much of their losses from the Kings either. In response, the brothers massively slashed roster spending.

"The 2010-11 Kings had such a low payroll, they dipped more than a million *below* the league's minimum team salary after February's Carl Landry/Marcus Thornton trade," then-*ESPN* columnist Bill Simmons wrote in a scathing piece on the Maloofs in April of 2011. "How did they fix it? By getting money from the Celtics to acquire Marquis Daniels, who was only crippled with a season-ending spinal injury at the time. Any time 'acquiring someone with a season-ending injury' is actually a savvy move, you know your season didn't go well."

During that same season, when the Kings unveiled the slogan "Here We Rise," news broke that the city of Anaheim was courting the Maloofs' NBA franchise by offering promises for a new, taxpayer-funded facility. From a purely fiscal standpoint, the deal made sense for an ownership group that had failed in its multiple attempts to construct a new stadium in Sacramento. Boisterous fan support coupled with eight straight successful years rendered ARCO Arena iconic, but by the early 2010s it had long outlived its shelf life.

Constructed in the late 1980s, with few corporate suites and revenue-generating amenities, ARCO was simply not a viable NBA venue anymore. So out-of-date was the poorly located concrete elephant that the NCAA refused to consider Sacramento as a host city for March Madness. In addition, the Maloofs were already saddled with more than $70 million in debt to the city, one they inherited from Thomas when purchasing the team. As their poor business ventures[20] piled up, the brothers proverbial "get out of jail free card" lay in the greater-Los Angeles area. The duo went as far as asking Anaheim to pay the $75 to $100 million relocation fee that the NBA required to move the team.

---

[20] Simmons touched on the Maloofs' poor spending habits in that same column, writing: "Here's what we know about the Maloofs. 1. They inherited a ton of money. 2. At some point, one of them said, 'We like basketball, we should buy an NBA team.' 3. At a later point, one of them said, 'We like gambling, we should buy a casino.' 4. They no longer have a ton of money."

That same year, the Maloofs registered "Anaheim Royals" as a trademark while the Anaheim City Council voted 9-0 in favor of allowing the franchise to relocate down south. Only two obstacles remained for the Maloofs to navigate towards a successful move: pro-Kings mayor Kevin Johnson and the community of Sacramento.

## Not Without a Fight

A well-connected former high-flying NBA All-Star and native son of Sacramento, Kevin Johnson[21] immediately began working the league's back channels to scramble for potential solutions to save the team. Meanwhile, when the community caught wind of the situation, it banded together to form the "Here We Stay" movement, a grassroots effort to bring widespread attention to the community crises.

Local blogger and longtime Kings fan Blake Ellington, one of thousands of locals determined to hold onto their beloved franchise, coined the phrase. Ellington gathered the local blogging cavalry together with a simple message. "[I] reached out to them to say, 'we have an audience, the fans need to get involved in this fight because it looks like the writing is on the wall,'" Ellington said. "They're going to need to get an arena here to keep the team. So, I started a discussion with the guys at those sites. The concept of this 'Here We Stay' movement blossomed from that."

Many involved would later describe the efforts from fans like Ellington as some of the movement's most crucial components. "The grassroots campaign was what kept us in the game," Johnson said in the 2012 Ellington-produced documentary *Small Market, Big Heart*, which chronicled the city's effort to keep the franchise. "It kept our pulse beating. We had a heart rate because the grassroots community spoke so loudly. Being from Sacramento, you remember the city of Sacramento and the transcontinental railroad; we've had a pioneering spirit. It's been the everyday people who have fought to keep Sacramento relevant and whole."

---

[21] It has to be mentioned somewhere that Kevin Johnson has faced a multitude of allegations, including continued accusations of sexual harassment and assault that have followed him since his days in the NBA, allegations that he failed to report $3.1 million in campaign donations that he was required to report under the state law, allegations that he used public funds to fund his private pro-charter school agenda through his nonprofit organization "Stand Up," and allegations that multiple employees who claimed to be employees of the City of Sacramento were actually on the payroll of "Stand Up." According to *Deadspin*, Johnson also used his vast array of connections to financially cripple a national association of Black mayors after said mayors rejected his pro-charter school platform. During this attempt to take over the organization he had the audacity to title one of his PowerPoint slides "Annual Meeting 'Coup.'" Also, according to *Deadspin*, Johnson responded to a request for public documents by *Sacramento News & Review* by suing both that weekly publication and the City of Sacramento itself.

One of the first major organized efforts, titled "Here We Stay Night," took place during a sold-out home game against the Los Angeles Clippers. During the contest, in a manner similar to the type of support the Tower Bridge Battalion would later provide at Sacramento Republic FC games, Kings fans stood and chanted in an organized fashion for much of the gameplay. Movement leaders handed out reading materials prior to the game to raise awareness of the seemingly inevitable move. The night proved successful, garnering widespread media attention while the fans provided a level of enthusiasm that harkened back to the team's glory days a decade prior.

Carmichael[22] Dave, a scruffy, chain-smoking, opinionated radio personality, drove the momentum forward by starting the "Here We Build" movement in late March. After learning of the Anaheim City Council vote, a frustrated Dave wrote on Twitter that he would pledge $200 to help the Kings fund a new arena while calling on the citizens of Sacramento to follow his lead. After sending the tweet, he walked outside for a quick smoke before returning to a perpetually buzzing phone overloaded with notifications. Desperate fans latched onto the cause and promised more than $140,000 within twenty-four hours. This caught the eye of *The New York Times*, which reported on the story all the way back on the East Coast. According to *The Times*, the figure reached $575,000 in the following two weeks.

Matt Graham, the owner of twenty-five local Jiffy Lube franchises hopped on the bandwagon, offering $1,000 for each of his stores. Shortly after Dave's tweet, Graham woke up his graphic designer and tasked him with an emergency assignment. Thanks to an all-nighter from said designer, all six of Graham's local electronic billboards displayed the "#HereWeBuild" message by the next morning.

The money pledged always proved more of an abstract concept than anything Kings fans would ever actually be expected to fork over–$575,000 represented a value roughly one-thousand times smaller than the amount that it would cost to eventually construct Golden 1 Center. But the fans' efforts went viral, and the community responded. The campaign culminated in that final home game against the Lakers, where the fans formed a "Here We Sit" movement. Long after the contest concluded, thousands of fans remained seated in ARCO's stands, physically refusing to let their team leave. Those still in the building continued to chant and make noise in support of keeping the Kings in Sacramento.

Hearing the support from the locker room, a few players walked back onto the court to set eyes on their fans for potentially the final time in Sacramento. Led by promising young star Tyreke Evans, several Kings returned to address the crowd and thank the loyal fans for sticking with the team. Eventually the loyalists relented to allow exhausted stadium personnel to return home. As the fans exited ARCO, the Maloofs prepared for their scheduled flight to New York where they would meet with NBA executives. In fewer than twenty-four hours, "The Boys" planned

---

[22] Carmichael is a suburb northeast of Sacramento.

to inform the league of their intention to officially file for relocation the following Monday.

However, the Maloofs weren't the only Sacramentans with travel plans–Johnson hopped on a plane as well and as he strode towards the NBA's Midtown Manhattan office, fans holding "Here We Stay" signs greeted him on the street. The league listened to the Maloofs' case before granting the mayor an audience. Behind closed doors, Johnson persuaded the NBA to instruct the Sacramento owners to hold off on their filing until the head of the NBA Relocation Committee, Clay Bennett,[23] visited Sacramento to research the feasibility of keeping the Kings where its fans thought they belonged.

The movement then evolved to using the phrase "Here We Purple," in which locals could show their support by wearing the color of royalty the day Bennett visited. Coincidence or not, Bennett arrived sporting a purple tie and quickly decided that the Kings would remain in Sacramento for at least one more season. Should a stadium plan fail to materialize by the end of that season, though, the Maloofs could choose to move the team to Anaheim. It was merely a temporary reprieve, but few could doubt the power and drive shown by the supporters by this point.

"I can tell you right now, without the fan movement and the fan voice, there is zero doubt in my mind, not an ounce, not an inkling of doubt that this team has moving vans in Anaheim right now," Carmichael Dave said in *Small Market, Big Heart.* "The process had to be completed by the politicians and the suits in general, but the fans ultimately, they're the ones that turned the tide."

The Maloofs still lacked the assets to privately finance a new arena so either the city needed to pass legislation to provide public funding, or it needed to convince the family to sell the team to someone less broke. The Anaheim buzz fizzled out and in February of 2012 locals heard the news they'd been waiting for: the Maloofs, the city, and the NBA agreed to terms to construct a nearly $400 million stadium in the Railyards District of Downtown Sacramento. The deal was presented as a win for all parties–Sacramento would finally begin developing the largest urban infill project in the entire country, the Maloofs would receive financial support and a state-of-the-art facility, and Sacramento would keep the Kings. The terms stipulated that the city would contribute most of the arena's funding while the Maloofs would pay $75 million in addition to whatever they received for selling ARCO Arena. Furthermore, a 5 percent ticket surcharge would eventually provide an additional $75 million towards construction costs. The city council approved the deal one week later.

---

[23] In 2008, Bennett, the chairman for the group that owned the Seattle Supersonics, was instrumental in relocating the club to his home state of Oklahoma in a move that has widely been described as shady with many contesting that he never intended to keep the Sonics in Seattle. It was almost the exact same situation that the Kings found themselves in in 2011, the same month that Bennett was elected to head the Relocation Committee.

Then, in a move that surprised no one, "The Boys" backed out of the agreement one month after the council vote. The Sacramento Kings returned to square one.

## The End?

The lockout-shortened 2011-12 season came and went without much national attention as Sacramento continued its tradition of fielding a truly horrific abomination of a squad on the court. As always, the fans still packed ARCO despite a 22-44 record from a team that featured few marketable stars outside of DeMarcus Cousins.

As the following season began, though, frustrated Kings fans could have thrown in the towel when it was reported that a Seattle-based ownership group made up of Chris Hansen, Steve Ballmer,[24] and the Nordstrom Family had officially bid to purchase the Kings. If the deal went through, the team would move to Seattle as soon as the 2013-14 campaign.

The Maloofs announced the sale, pending the approval of the NBA Board of Governors, in January of 2013. One month later, then-NBA commissioner David Stern confirmed that the prospective ownership had filed for relocation.

The setbacks didn't faze Kevin Johnson, motivated by a love of basketball and his refusal to allow his political career to be defined by his home city losing hold of a professional sports franchise playing the sport he once excelled in.[25] Johnson used his near-endless supply of contacts to piece together a competing ownership group featuring supermarket tycoon Ron Burkle[26] and 24-hour fitness founder Mark Mastrov. The mayor also helped outline the framework for yet another attempt to construct that elusive new arena. Acting in the NBA's best interests, Stern announced that the Sacramento-based bid wouldn't be considered unless it was as large as the $225 million[27] that the Seattle group put up for a 65 percent share of the team.

Golden State Warriors minority owner Vivek Ranadivé then bolstered the effort after agreeing to become the group's third major investor. Amid a shroud of uncertainty, 17,317 fans arrived at ARCO in April of 2013, twelve days before the NBA Board of Governors was set to vote on the matter of which group to sell the Kings to. Again, faced with a potential final game in Sacramento Kings history, fans packed ARCO to the brim just like the good old days of Webber and Bibby. Carmichael Dave arrived at the game following the conclusion of a month-long nationwide road trip he called the "Playing to Win Tour." It was the culmination

---

[24] Ballmer wound up purchasing the Los Angeles Clippers in 2014.

[25] Instead, many media outlets would define it as controversial thanks to the multitude of crime allegations he faced alongside the dozens of reports detailing his shady behavior.

[26] Of Neverland Ranch fame.

[27] Ballmer later forked out $2 billion for the Clippers, a near tenfold markup from his Kings bid.

of all the "Here We" movements, one final push to raise more awareness in support of keeping the Kings in Sacramento.

"There's no room in my brain right now to contemplate this team not staying," he told a reporter from *Neon Tommy*, USC's student journalism website.[28] "If for some reason, that's what happens, it's still gonna hurt just as bad as if I contemplated it right now. They're not gonna leave. They're gonna stay. We're the good guys in this story, and that's the way it goes. You have to believe in stuff like that, whether it's impossible or feasible."

The other 17,316 fans at ARCO probably believed too, despite the deep pockets and heavy influence wielded by the potential Seattle-based owners. The Kings predictably fell 112-108 to a Clippers squad nicknamed "Lob City" for its awe-inspiring above-the-rim play. The Kings weren't cool enough or good enough to earn a similarly awesome nickname, but the mood in the arena couldn't have felt less different from that of the season finale two years prior. Many described the final game in 2011, the one that brought Grant Napear and Jerry Reynolds to tears, as a "wake." The conclusion to the 2012-13 season appeared more hopeful and joyous. After all the efforts from the fans and city leaders, there's no way the NBA could leave Sacramento, right?

Shortly thereafter, the NBA Board of Governors Relocation Committee voted 7-0 against the relocation of the Kings. During a playoff game that season, NBA Commissioner David Stern said he felt surprised that the vote was unanimous, but also added that: "They decided as strong as the Seattle bid was, and it was very strong, that there's some benefit that should be given to a city that has supported us for so long and has stepped up to contribute to build a new building as well."

That May the full Board of Governors met in Dallas to officially decide Sacramento's fate as an NBA franchise. In a meeting scheduled for up to four hours, the league's thirty team owners reportedly hotly contested both sides of the argument for nearly all the allotted time. Ultimately, the wealthy businessmen voted 22-8 against relocation, allowing the Kings to stay in their home pending the finalization of the sale to the non-Seattle based group. "I would say it's a victory for Sacramento, not a victory for the NBA," Stern said.

Added George Maloof, while on the verge of selling the franchise to a local ownership group: "We tried to find somebody that would buy the team in Sacramento, and we couldn't. That's the fact of the matter…that was our first choice, but no one stepped up."

Burkle,[29] Mastrov, and Ranadivé swiftly purchased the team, with Ranadivé replacing the Maloofs as the new majority owner of the franchise. "The Boys" were finally out, to the relief of hundreds of thousands of people who had once loved them.

---

[28] Shout out to my friend, Will Robinson, who conducted this interview.

[29] Burkle later dropped out of the group due to a conflict of interest with his entertainment company.

Ranadivé and Co. required less than a year to secure a new arena, for which the city agreed to foot roughly half of the bill. The 17,500-capacity, modern Golden 1 Center opened in time for the 2016-17 NBA season, bringing a sparkling new facility to Downtown Sacramento. Though the Sacramento Kings mostly continued to flounder on the court, their future in the city was at least secure for at least a few decades.

During the whole debacle, a group of six eccentric individuals worked tirelessly on a completely different project—but one that was still tied to the outcome of the Kings. The six labored day and night to plan what would come to be known as "Sacramento Soccer Day." Free moments for the group came few and far between, but when they arrived, the six's eyes stayed glued to the latest developments regarding the future of the city's lovable loser.

If the Kings relocated, what would that say about the health and prospects of the local pro sports market? Would outsiders take the city seriously if it lost its only major league franchise? This wasn't Seattle where the loss of a basketball team could be offset by the wild success of two of its other three[30] top division clubs. Without the Kings, what incentive would any investors have to buy into a start-up in what could now qualify as a town full of failures? Would Sacramento even maintain relevance in the country, or even the state, without the Kings?[31]

These were all questions the founding six pondered. But luckily for them, and the locals, the community rallied around the Kings. Mayor Johnson accomplished his goal. Dave's good guys won.[32] Love found a way.

# Elsewhere in the City…

Since 1985, the Sacramento Kings have dominated the local sports media coverage almost by default. Without any other top division professional franchises, any top college sports programs, or a strong high school football culture, the Kings have long ruled the sporting landscape. And the fear of relocation only compounded the amount of television minutes, radio segments, and column inches the city's media devoted to the cause.

So, when another professional sports franchise announced its arrival in Sacramento in December of 2012, the news hardly registered locally. Right in the middle of the city's fight to save the Kings, a group called "Sacramento Professional Soccer" held a sparsely attended press conference to relay that it had successfully bid to join the third tier of professional soccer in the United States. This budding entry held a vested interest in keeping the NBA in town, and though its authors

---

[30] And a fourth when the NHL's Seattle Kraken debuted in 2021.
[31] It's a fair question to ask if it even does with the Kings.
[32] In an interview Carmichael Dave said that he thought the Kings leaving would have helped the Republic's cause.

couldn't influence the outcome, they actively rooted for the Kings to stay where they belonged. After all, if the city retained its major league status, Sacramento Professional Soccer's lofty aspirations wouldn't appear so far-fetched. The plan called for the latest in the city's long line of professional soccer teams to begin play in the United Soccer League in 2014, but ideally just as a steppingstone. The goal from day one was to eventually compete at the highest level of the American game: Major League Soccer.

With the Kings' uncertain future, locals could be forgiven for feeling skeptical of this ambition, especially given that nearly every local pro soccer team that had come before had failed in spectacular fashion. Furthermore, the masterminds behind Sac Pro Soccer had only recently grown to love the sport. Its two co-founders grew up playing "traditional" American sports and had, importantly, detested the beautiful game. And the one bit of experience the pair had in the sport nearly involved them becoming the sole architects of one of the most disastrous and ill-informed decisions in United States professional soccer history. They both came into the project with decades of lower-division pro sports experience, but the vast majority of it revolved around baseball.

But by May of 2013, at least Warren Smith, Joe Wagoner, and four green hires could continue planning their startup in a market alongside an NBA franchise. Now all they had to do was to avoid repeating history—the grave mistakes prior soccer franchises had made in Sacramento were well documented at the time but had since mostly faded into the minds of a few individuals in a niche community. Countless ambitious, but naive, ownership groups had already tried to bring soccer to the city but had failed due to either a lack of funding, a lack of public interest, or general incompetence. Most crashed and burned thanks to a combination of all three.

Researching the clubs that had come before Sacramento Professional Soccer proved important, but also painted a bleak picture. However, Smith and Wagoner felt determined to succeed where all their predecessors had failed. The pair certainly possessed the intelligence, passion, business acumen, and creativity to pull it off. It was just that given Sacramento's soccer history, it would qualify as a minor miracle if the fledgling operation remained in business by the time the Kings inaugurated their new arena just three years later.

# THREE
# THE BEAUTIFUL GAME'S UNLIKELY, UNKNOWN, AND UNTOLD SACRAMENTO TRADITION[33]

It's easy to understand why many locals viewed Sacramento Professional Soccer's 2012 launch through a veil of caution accompanied with a heavy dose of skepticism. The drama and incompetence surrounding the nearly thirty-year run for the Sacramento Kings paled in comparison when judged against all prior attempts to establish professional soccer in the city. It's not like this qualified as a local phenomenon—prospective leagues and franchises proved a tough sell all over the United States for most of the twentieth century. But in Sacramento, ever since the first attempt to gain a foothold nearly forty years prior, promising soccer ventures created a habit of blowing up in their owners' faces in the strangest circumstances at the weirdest times.

Looking back on the city's professional soccer history never fails to shock or amaze. The phrase, "Wait, they tried *what?*" always feels appropriate. If Sacramento's latest pro soccer venture hoped to last more than a couple of seasons, it would become the exception rather than the rule in California's capital. And in order to understand why Sacramento Republic FC eventually succeeded, it's imperative to understand why every other men's team failed.

---

[33] I recommend pairing "Rock 'n' Roll Lifestyle" by Cake for this chapter.

Since pro soccer first arrived in Sacramento with the Spirits in 1976, the city has played host to seven different full and semi-professional clubs on the men's side of the game. Three of those lasted a combined seven years in the second division, while two played in the third tier for one season each. The first semi-professional side went under after five seasons, while its successor continues to operate well into its second decade. And then there was the indoor squad that captured the city's attention more than any of its outdoor counterparts, but still closed shop before its tenth anniversary. Along the way, Sacramento clubs have collected four championships, four runners-up medals, and posted the single worst record in American professional soccer history. Many started as ambitious projects, while a few took the field seemingly by accident. But the one thing that they all had in common: save for the NPSL's Sacramento Gold, each folded in the bizarre circumstances that only lower-division professional sports can provide. And while the four-time national champion California Storm have become a beacon of success on the women's side, surrounded by a graveyard of male-driven failures, each of the city's eight notable high-level soccer teams enjoyed some level of boisterous support from the stands.

These are the stories of Sacramento's past soccer clubs.

# The Beginnings

Up until the 1980s, the closest any major professional sports league would come to Sacramento was nearly ninety miles southwest in Oakland. Given that the city's 1970 population of roughly 250,000 ranked outside the top-fifty nationwide and just seventh in state, Sacramento joining the top level of any of the "big four" would have been surprising. After all, fewer people lived in the city than in Norfolk, Va.; Wichita, Kans.; Akron, Ohio; or Jersey City, N.J.

While the first division North American Soccer League emerged in the 1970s, during a rapid period of expansion that would eventually lead to its demise, only the second division American Soccer League would find its way to Sacramento. In 1976 the Sacramento Spirits became the city's first-ever professional soccer club and finished eleventh out of eleven teams in the ASL, winning just four games total. The next year the club qualified for the league's title game before embarking on a wild campaign in 1978. That season, the Spirits fell back to the bottom of the table and were expelled from the ASL midway through the fixture list, only to return as the rebranded Sacramento Gold. In the first full season under the Gold moniker, Sacramento qualified for its second ASL final with a 1-0 victory over the California Sunshine in front of more than 10,000 fans at Hughes Stadium. The Gold proved victorious in the 1979 title game and the city lifted its first soccer title after just four years of play.

Naturally, the side changed its name to the (singular) Spirit for the 1980 campaign, again qualified for the final, lost in it, and then folded.

Nine years later, in 1989, the Sacramento Senators arrived in the city to play in the Western Soccer League. In the short-lived entity's North Division, the Senators faced the likes of the Portland Timbers and a San Francisco Bay Blackhawks side that boasted Dominic Kinnear and John Doyle.[34] The Senators split time between a variety of different venues in the Sacramento area, including Sacramento State's Hornet Field and San Juan High school. Incompetent on the field, Sacramento churned through two coaches during the season en route to a 3-13 finish.

Hyping the team before the season began, *The Sacramento Bee* wrote: "The WSL, entering its fifth season, has adopted a fiscally realistic approach toward rebuilding interest in soccer in anticipation of the United States hosting the 1994 World Cup. Under a three-year plan, the players will receive only expenses this year, achieve semi-pro status next season, and by 1991 be part of a three-league regional pro soccer organization."

Eight months following that statement, *The Bee* reported that the Senators had folded. Plagued by financial woes from the start—the team reportedly didn't have to pony up the cash for an expansion fee to the WSL, instead inheriting a license from another defunct franchise. The Senators couldn't raise the $30,000 bond required for the 1990 season, nor could they prove that they had the finances to meet the estimated $250,000 it would require to run the team for a season. The following year, the WSL would merge with the ASL to become what was eventually the A-League, the precursor to the USL.

# The Light That Burns Twice as Bright Burns Half as Long

Seven years after the Senators burned to the ground, the Sacramento Scorpions arose from their ashes. Twenty-six-year-old former Sacramento State player Kevin Campbell joined his father, Burdon, in a partnership to bring professional soccer back to Sacramento. Playing in the United Systems of Independent Soccer Leagues, another precursor to what would eventually become the USL, the Scorpions

---

34 According to *The Mercury News*, the Blackhawks once threatened to move to Sacramento in 1992 because the offer given to them by Spartan Stadium at San Jose State didn't include guaranteed dates for games. The San Jose State University Foundation demanded that Blackhawks leadership sign a document allowing the university to bump scheduled matches with one month's notice should another money-making opportunity arise. The two sides eventually came to an agreement and the Blackhawks played their home matches at the 30,000-seat stadium that would later serve as the original home for the San Jose Earthquakes. Newspaper clippings from the 1990s and early 2000s that cover soccer in the United States are wild.

featured something that every other Sacramento-based soccer team had lacked up to that point: star power.

On hand for the press conference to announce the team in late February of 1996 was Nigerian defender Stephen Keshi. Two summers prior, Keshi helped his country to the round of 16 in the 1994 FIFA World Cup, captaining the side–despite a hurt knee–in its 2-0 win over Greece that clinched the top spot in Group D for the Super Eagles.

"Keshi said he had an offer to play with the San Jose Clash of Major League Soccer, but declined the invitation when he determined that the Clash's schedule would interfere with his marketing studies at Pittsburg's [Calif.] Los Medanos Community College," *Sacramento Bee* reporter Mark Billingsley wrote that August, showing the value that some international players found in an MLS contract at the time. "If I wanted to further my career, I would have taken the job with the Clash," Keshi told *The Bee*. "But I'm playing now more for the fun of it."

According to teammate Jeremy Field, the late Keshi served as a de facto coach for the Scorpions at the time in order to assuage the revolving door of managers that saw the original coach leave part way through the season, only to be replaced by a pair of co-managers who didn't last the entirety of the campaign either. After his retirement from the game, the defender would embark on a distinguished international coaching career.[35]

Keshi was joined in Sacramento by fellow Nigerian international Augustine Eguavoen. A towering, mustached defender who spent nearly a decade playing in the top- division of Belgium,[36] Eguavoen's California adventure proved short-lived. Both he and Keshi lasted just the solitary season in Sacramento, but while Keshi moved into semi-retirement in the Malaysian Premier League, his younger compatriot transitioned seamlessly into the starting XI of the mid-table Russian side Torpedo Moscow.

Eguavoen came to Sacramento fresh off that 1994 World Cup that saw Nigeria advance to the knockout rounds. In their round-of-sixteen loss to Italy, the defender marked Roberto Baggio in a close, 2-1 overtime loss. Back in Russia after the Scorpions, the outside back parlayed his success to a spot on the 1998 World Cup team where Nigeria repeated its knockout stage performance. Like Keshi, Eguavoen would later manage the Nigerian national team, winning a third-place

---

[35] He helped the minuscule West African nation of Togo qualify for its first-ever World Cup in 2006, managed Nigeria to the 2013 Africa Cup of Nations title, and led his country in the 2014 World Cup.
[36] According to *The Bee*, Eguavoen was actually under contract for Belgium's KV Kortrijk when he made the move to Sacramento. "[Eguavoen] said that while United States, South American and African players are not allowed by their European teams to travel freely in the off-season to play with whatever team they choose, he got a temporary release from his club and followed Keshi to Sacramento," Mark Billingsley wrote in *The Bee*. "'The European players can go wherever they want and make big money in the off-season but we can't and that's not fair,' Eguavoen said. 'I'm currently trying to get out of my contract with KV Kortrijk. Sacramento seemed to be a nice place to spend the off-season and stay in shape.'"

medal with his country in the 2006 Africa Cup of Nations and making the knockout stages during his third spell fifteen years later.

The third African superstar who joined the Nigerian duo was Zambian international Charles Musonda. The wiry midfielder, who at his peak pulled the strings for Belgian powerhouse R.S.C Anderlecht, represented a respectable Zambian side nearly fifty times in a six-year period. Led by the local ownership and the African trio, the Scorpions drew a modest 3,169 fans for their opener against the El Paso Patriots. That figure factored in as the largest attendance in the USISL for the opening weekend of matches.

Fortunes only improved for the Scorpions, who formed an affiliation with the L.A. Galaxy, receiving Sacramento-native Guillermo Jara on loan in one of the partnership's first moves. The forward would go on to make sixty-seven MLS appearances over four years, scoring two goals.

"[The MLS alliance] is an opportunity for young players to look for something else," Jara told *The Bee* in April of 1996. "They'll think that if Guillermo Jara plays for the Galaxy, maybe there is a passageway for me to the future." An official, and much more sophisticated, MLS-USL affiliation wouldn't come until 2013, but the groundwork for such a deal was laid in 1996 in California. The agreement also went both ways, as Scorpions player John Jones earned a contract with the star-studded Galaxy after a strong debut with Sacramento in that first season.

A young Greg Vanney also saw playing time in Sacramento. A left-footed defender, capable of playing multiple positions, Vanney springboarded from the Scorpions to the Galaxy first team, and then to the United States Men's National Team all in the calendar year of 1996.

Vanney, Jara, and Jones played alongside a host of local players such as former Sacramento State and Jesuit High School star Jeremy Field, who would go on to play for the Sacramento Knights before becoming the Sacramento Republic FC youth academy manager. "It was not the best, most professional organization, but it was probably one of the best teams that has ever been in Sacramento," Field said. "There were some good players on that Scorpions team."

Field recalled the absurdity of it all while sitting in a booth at Bonn Lair, one of the oldest soccer bars in the city. It was a weekday afternoon, and the man nicknamed "Worm" sipped on a tall lager in the dark and empty confines of the East Sacramento watering hole. He explained how he got his nickname–in the 1990s he sported a giant curly afro that shot out of his head as if he'd always showed up to soccer directly after sticking his finger inside an electrical outlet. Originally, he went by "Jerm" for short, but his hair styling quickly had others calling him "Perm." Then when *Friday* came out in 1995, it was changed to "Worm" after its iconic "Big Worm" character who proved to be one of many lasting pop culture references from that film.

Worm knew everyone and everything in Sacramento's soccer scene and wasn't afraid to share his opinion on a particular person or entity. Soul music reverberated off the scarf-laden walls while he quickly talked on a hot summer day. It only required one question to open a treasure trove full of information delivered in the form of tangent on tangent on tangent, all of which somehow proved relevant. Sometimes he'd speak for twenty minutes at a time without even breaking to sip on his libation. Much of Sacramento's soccer history has been lost to time, only existing in newspaper microfilm or the memories of people like Field, whom most youngsters attending Sacramento Republic FC games have never heard of.

Those who've been around the Sacramento soccer scene to measure it in decades rather than years hold Field in high esteem but locating any official mention of him outside of a few early 1990s newspaper clippings proves almost impossible. Even those only include a handful of offhand references to Field, whose name produces few Google results. Everyone says that Field was a great player, but there aren't any pictures of him on the internet. Despite the sparse midday crowd at Bonn Lair, it's hard to pick out which random patron might be Field–he turned out to be sitting at the bar sporting a five o'clock shadow and half-full lager. Unless you were completely ingrained in the local soccer community, you probably didn't know Field existed. And even then, it wasn't that likely. His biography page on the Sacramento Republic FC website also failed to feature his likeness, nor did it include any biographical details. If you clicked on the link to his name on the Wikipedia page for a U.S. Open Cup game he scored in, the online encyclopedia directed you to an article about a British evolutionary biologist with the same name.

"He refers to himself as a ninja," Joe Wagoner, the co-founder and vice president of the Republic, said before setting up the meeting. "Because he gets shit done and you never see him."

But the ninja, Worm, Field, who also served as a director at a local youth club, sat there to talk shop while dressed like he was about to hit the slopes. He wore a brown beanie with sunglasses on top, a winter jacket, and long pants. The booth he ambled over to appeared random until he pointed to a framed Sacramento Knights jersey hanging just above. Without his assistance, memorabilia from the city's most successful men's soccer franchise may have gone unnoticed among Bonn Lair's other eclectic decorations. A handful of Eastern European soccer scarves hung from the walls alongside flags from each of the United Kingdom's four countries.

The journey that led Field to the Scorpions began at Sacramento State, where he turned out for the NCAA team almost as often as he cut classes to play pickup games in the city. The sport wasn't his only passion, though, and the 1990s grunge scene called him north on a whim. "I went up to Seattle and fucked around for a little bit," he said. "Went to a lot of concerts, smoked a lot of doobies." Kurt Cobain died in April of 1994 and the allure of following Alice in Chains, Pearl Jam, and all the others faded away for Field. Especially after the United States hosted the World Cup for the first time later that year.

Originally, Field returned to Sacramento to attend a Deftones/Funky Blue Velvet concert, but when he drove back north, he collected his possessions and reported back to the Hornets' athletic department. He was playing the sport he loved at a high level, but something felt off–his heart would never find the same love for college soccer that it did for Nirvana. Field left school after another year-and-a-half to try out for the Scorpions. "For me, I just finally went, 'You're not really trying in school, so why not just try to do the soccer thing and see what happens?'" he said. "My parents were totally supportive. They were cool. They always felt it's better that you get this out of your system than to go crazy second-guessing yourself when you're older."

The experienced internationals and local stars like Field helped draw the strong opening day crowd and the local media reported positively on the whole experience of Sacramento's newest soccer club. However, the initial interest quickly faded and the Scorpions struggled to break the quadruple-digit attendance mark for home games, which took place fifteen miles northeast of the city at Woodcreek High School in Roseville. The more popular indoor Knights drew crowds ten times the size of the Scorpions' over at ARCO Arena. On the pitch, the African star-power was enough to drive the club all the way to the Western Conference Finals, where it fell to the California Jaguars of Salinas in a three-game series.

But while the Scorpions appeared promising both on and off the field, even if initial interest wavered, complications brewed behind the scenes as the club headed into its first offseason. "They never really had the money," Field said. "I don't know at the beginning how they were paying dudes, but by midseason, [if] you threw that check to the bank, it'd bounce right back to you. I remember there was a meeting where [management said], 'Hey, basically, we can't pay you guys anymore.'

"The first year, about halfway through, guys stopped getting paid, at least the scrubs," Field added. "I don't know if they ever stopped paying Stephen Keshi, who knows? I was always curious where they got the money. They didn't have any money."

After the first season, all three African stars departed and though the Scorpions received a then-unknown Ante Razov on loan from the Galaxy in 1997, neither Jara nor Jones returned to the squad. "The product may be downsized and the stadium older and less attractive, but the Sacramento Scorpions deserve some accolades just for surviving," future Sacramento Republic beat writer Bill Paterson wrote in his lede for *The Bee* in a Scorpions feature ahead of their second season. Due to large swaths of empty seats at their 5,000-seat high school stadium in 1996, the Scorpions changed home venues to Cosumnes River College,[37] a pristine playing surface, but an un-lit one with little room for spectators.

In 1997, the USISL merged with the A-League to form a new second division, a division that the Scorpions hoped to join. The club's lack of capital, however, ruled this out. Instead, the Scorpions remained in the forty-team "Division 3 Pro League."[38] General manager Kevin Campbell attempted to coax more talent to the

---

[37] The future training site for the Republic.
[38] This was its actual name.

club, but his labor failed to pay off as the Scorpions struggled both on and off the field.

"Kevin Campbell is an ambitious young man who hopes he isn't too early for the soccer boom that spawned a successful United States World Cup in 1994 and the development of a national pro league, Major League Soccer, last year," Paterson wrote at the time. "The former Christian Brothers soccer player and current El Camino High School boys coach is the team's general manager and all-around mover and shaker.

"In other words, he answers the phones, sells the tickets, and handles public relations.

"But he may also be like General Custer at Little Big Horn, waiting fruitlessly for reinforcements to arrive."

Paterson's prophecy panned out as the team unceremoniously folded after the 1997 season, becoming yet another small footnote in the long history of American soccer franchises. Only 1,743 fans attended the Scorpions' 6-1 first-round playoff loss to the Chico Rooks. *The Bee*'s recap contained six lines in the local briefs section. Ironically, Sacramento native Jake Gwin helped oust the club, lighting up an overmatched Scorpions defense, checkmating the hosts with a four-goal performance for the Rooks.

In a 1998 feature in the "Neighborhoods" section of *The Bee*, reporter Vince Vosti spoke to Scorpions attacker Tony Glover, who would later go on to play for the Knights. "...Glover was back in the USISL before the conclusion of the 1997 season," Vosti wrote. "The [Scorpions], which went bankrupt at season's end, helped Glover keep his skills sharp. But the team was in turmoil as it tried to play out the season, despite mounting bills and lack of play.

"He likened the experience to hell."

The Scorpions quietly fell off the map and Field signed with then-third division French side Dijon. Though rumblings of another team in Sacramento made their way over to Field in Europe, the defender elected to continue trying his luck in France, rather than join up with another debacle of a franchise.

Two years after the Scorpions folded, second division men's soccer came to California's capital for the first time ever. The 1997 Division 3 Pro League champion Albuquerque Geckos[39] were one of the clubs selected to join the second division A-League for the 1998 season before they relocated to Sacramento in 1999.

Anyone who described playing for the 1998 Scorpions as "hell" likely never suited up for the 1999 Sacramento Geckos, a franchise that made the Scorpions look like Real Madrid in comparison. "If you had to pick a business to start in Sacramento, you probably wouldn't pick a soccer franchise," team president Terry Fisher told *The Bee* before the Geckos had played their first game. "This market is littered with soccer failures."

---

[39] Future Republic Academy Director and assistant coach Rod Underwood was a player on that Geckos team but did not continue to play with the side after they made the move to California.

Like every other club before it, the Geckos' dream sounded great to the untrained ear. Management hoped to form a partnership with the indoor Knights in order to split contract fees while providing local soccer players the chance to play nearly year-round. "The Geckos partnered with the Knights and so I was going to have like an eleven-month contract, so I was like, 'forget Europe,'" Field said. "The Knights contract was going to be great for six months, but that's only six months. When you go to Europe, it's basically a year-round contract, at least ten months depending on the deal you do. [With] Geckos in town, you would play outdoor and then again in indoor, so it was almost like a year-round contract, and I didn't have to move away, so I signed up with the Knights.

"A month after that, we did a bunch of these outdoor exhibitions in preparation to be the Geckos," Field added, "and then it was found out that the Geckos owed a bunch of money and the Maloofs weren't going to take care of the debt, so that relationship split."

Or as Knights general manager Hubert Rotteveel bluntly told *The Bee* in August of 1999: "The Geckos had some huge financial problems and to join them would have forced us to put too much on the line. We'd be doing all the work but they'd own it. It wasn't a good deal for us."

Sans-Field, and most of the rest of the Knights players, the ill-fated Geckos played a total of twenty-eight matches, losing every single one of them. The club earned just a single point all year in a shootout loss,[40] finishing eighty-nine points behind the first-place San Diego Flash in the West, and thirty-nine points behind the San Francisco Seals in the Pacific Division. The Seals placed second-to-last. Sacramento managed to put the ball in the back of the net a grand total of sixteen times and finished with a minus-seventy-five goal differential on the season.

Fans, if there were any, saw the writing on the wall just four games into the season when the Las Vegas Soccer Development Corp., which also owned the Flash, purchased a ninety-five percent stake in the team.

"We were concerned about the Pacific Division [of the A-league] and the Geckos' survival," Flash and Geckos CEO Yan Skwara told *The Bee*. "The important thing is to remember A-League soccer is alive and kicking in Sacramento.

"We want a team in Sacramento," Skwara added in the same article. "People like soccer. There is a market in Sacramento. We think a team could draw 10,000 to 15,000 fans."

---

[40] In the late 1990s and early 2000s, the United States Soccer Federation frequently experimented with the rules in the different iterations of its second division. Some of these included awarding more points if a team scored a certain number of goals or increasing the amount of substitutions allowed. In the 1999 USL A-League season, regulation wins were worth four points and scoring three or more goals in a game earned each club a bonus point. Additionally, ties went to shootouts, where a player was given the ball 35 yards from goal and had five seconds to try and score in a one-on-one situation against the opposing team's goalkeeper. The winning team earned two points, while the losers recorded one.

A soccer team in Sacramento *could* draw 10,000 to 15,000 fans. Just not for another fifteen years.

One month after "saving" the Geckos, Skwara's group pulled out, citing losses of over $40,000. "There's the potential that this team may fold," head coach Ron Preble told *The Bee*. "We have no money to operate. We've actually contacted several businesses about potentially picking up the franchise, but nobody wants to touch us."

Lacking potential buyers, the A-League bought the club and rebranded it as "Team Sacramento." Team Sacramento stumbled to an all-time incompetent finish and folded before the turn of the century. High level outdoor men's soccer wouldn't return to the city for four more years.

## Meanwhile, A Storm Raged On

Major League Soccer began play in 1996 hoping to ride the success of the United States-hosted 1994 FIFA World Cup to bring back top division men's soccer to the country for the first time since the NASL folded in 1984. While the twelve-year gap between first division leagues proved less than ideal, at least precedent for the men's professional game existed.

Similarly, the success of the domestic 1999 FIFA Women's World Cup drove interest in forming a women's professional league in the United States. Just months after Northern California native Brandi Chastain famously scored the decisive penalty to clinch the United States Women's National Team's second victory, American investors began discussing plans for a women's professional league. The Women's United Soccer Association kicked off in 2001 as the first female entity in the world in which every player earned a salary as a fully paid professional. A few other leagues in northern Europe were also beginning the process of paying livable wages to female pros, but there were few options for women to play full time before the WUSA.

Before 2001, the only real opportunities to play stateside soccer at a relatively high level involved the W-League and the Women's Professional Soccer League, neither of which were officially sanctioned by U.S. Soccer. By default, those two leagues existed as the highest level of female competition in the United States. In a novel move for the time, United Soccer Leagues organized the W-League alongside its lower division men's competitions in 1995. Three years later, several clubs from the W-League's Western Division broke away to form their own league after becoming frustrated with several different factors. This new competition was the Women's Professional Soccer League, which the California Storm would play in and dominate just as they had in the W-League. While the Scorpions and Team Sacramento floundered during the late 1990s, the Storm served as the only constant in the city's high level outdoor soccer scene.

Founded as the Sacramento Storm in 1995 by local Democratic Party lobbyist Jerry Zanelli, the Storm reached the W-League's title game in both the club and the nineteen-team league's first season of play. The following year, Zanelli and Co. swapped "Sacramento" for "California" but failed to qualify for the postseason in a competition that grew by five teams. Another title game defeat in 1997 ended the Storm's participation in the W-League. Led by Zanelli, six California teams broke off to form the WPSL.

By the time the 1999 World Cup kicked off, Chastain and fellow champions Julie Foudy and Kristine Lilly all were Storm alums. Days after the tournament final, *Sacramento Bee* columnist Ailene Voisin wrote in support of a potential future pro soccer league in the United States, noting that even Chastain had to return to her day job as a Santa Clara assistant coach following the tournament. Zanelli offered hope of such a league but noted that it could just be a flash in the pan if not handled correctly.

"I'm fairly optimistic it can be done, but I'm just not sure there will be a structure that will allow it to happen," he told Voisin. "You would have to find a way to capitalize on the World Cup win, and there are a couple of dangers. One is not trying to run before you crawl. The ABL[41] was an example of that. And I believe you have to have teams involved with the central operations of the league."

The columnist's final recommendation: "Today's reality means that Chastain, Foudy, Lilly and teammates can further their careers by pushing for a new league while playing in an old one–the [WPSL], a nine-member league that includes the Storm and other West Coast teams. This is as good as it gets. Play for free today, hope for pay tomorrow."

Playing home games at Natomas High School, the Storm captured its first WPSL title that season after finishing 10-1-1 in the regular season with a plus-thirty-eight goal differential. No mention of the victory can be found in *The Sacramento Bee*'s archive. The club returned to the final in the 2000 season before losing in the semifinal round in 2001 as Chastain led the Bay Area CyberRays to the inaugural WUSA championship.

The next year brought local competition as local youth coach Danny Cruz[42] bought into the WPSL to form Elk Grove Pride, which would play at Cosumnes River College in Sacramento. According to Cruz, the Pride paid an expansion fee of $40,000 to join the fourth-year league, which now featured ten teams. While Cruz told *The Bee* in a May 2002 article that he'd be able to call upon some of his former youth players for select games, most of his roster would come from his Elk Grove United '84 squad, whose parents helped cover team expenses.

---

[41] The American Basketball League was a women's professional basketball league that was founded in 1995. It lasted for just two full seasons before declaring Chapter 11 bankruptcy and suspending operations midseason in December of 1998.
[42] A different Danny Cruz than the MLS journeyman turned USL manager.

One of the five players Cruz mentioned as potential standouts from that squad was sixteen-year-old Megan Rapinoe. Cruz also noted that he hoped to develop his squad into a feeder program for the WUSA. Elk Grove Pride lost its first-ever WPSL match 4-0 to the San Francisco Nighthawks on May 4, with the paper noting that it came fewer than two hours after Elk Grove United fell 3-2 in the U18 State Cup title game in Livermore.

Eight days later, Elk Grove hosted the Storm and the more experienced side took an early 1-0 lead. However, up stepped Rapinoe, who scored a goal and assisted on another as Pride rallied to post a 3-1 victory. "People took notice that these girls can play," Cruz said after the match. "We could have scored more. We were on fire."

Instead of feeling frustrated because of the loss to the local upstarts, Zanelli focused his post-game thoughts on the bigger picture. "It's important that they get a chance to play some competitive soccer against some older players," he said.

The result appeared to invigorate California, which improved its form ahead of the July 13 rematch at the club's new home, Davis High School. In a back-and-forth affair, Storm defeated Elk Grove 3-2 despite the visitors saving two penalties. Near the end of the first half, after all five goals had been scored, Rapinoe was shown a red card. The victory improved the Storm's record to 9-3-1 and kept their playoff hopes alive, while Pride dropped to 5-7-1 and out of contention. Following the match, Cruz told *The Bee* that his club hoped to return to the league for the 2003 season.

"We had such a good time this year. The kids have learned so much. It's the best thing we ever did," he said. "Financially, we struggled. It was hard to find sponsors. The parents footed most of the bill. We're hoping to get more support for next year. We want to establish this in Elk Grove for the next four or five years." Both clubs reached their goals: the California Storm qualified for the playoffs and beat Southern California Ajax in Davis to capture its second WPSL title and Elk Grove Pride remained active for the following season.

Even with the Women's World Cup returning to the United States in 2003, it was clear that the third-year WUSA had long been on life support. More than 90,000 packed the Rose Bowl for the 1999 World Cup final, but the WUSA struggled to draw five-figure crowds while hemorrhaging money.

According to *The Bee*, Zanelli also operated the Storm at a considerable loss. The owner and coach reportedly spent an estimated $50,000 per season to keep the Storm alive and thriving. "I don't think people know how much [Zanelli] spends, but they know without him, it wouldn't be possible," said Storm player Katie Tate. "I don't think any other [WPSL] team does that for its players." According to the paper, Zanelli paid out of pocket for the team's travel, hotels, meals, and other soccer costs. Sometimes this included Zanelli's offer to pay players their normal work salary at their day jobs if scheduling conflicts forced them to miss a shift or two.

Still, the Storm managed to avoid defeat in every game during the 2003 season, except for the one that mattered the most as the Utah Spiders pulled off an upset win in the WPSL title game at Kezar Stadium in San Francisco that June. In doing so, the Spiders became the league's first champion to hail from outside of California.

The result proved just the first in a series of unfortunate events in Golden State-based women's soccer that year. Five days before the World Cup began, WUSA suspended operations after reporting roughly $100 million in losses. Just a few weeks later, the USWNT played at the brand-new soccer-specific stadium in Carson that would host the tournament final but did so in the third place playoff after falling in a 3-0 shock result in the semifinals to eventual champions Germany. There would be no repeat of 1999–neither the third-place game nor the final sold out the 27,000-seat stadium four years after the title match nearly drew in the six figures.

The next top division women's professional soccer league in the United States wouldn't kick off for more than half a decade, opening the opportunity for a host of former WUSA standouts to help the Storm claim its third national title in 2004. While many WPSL teams continued losing money, the league expanded to twenty teams in 2005, a year that saw the Storm again qualify for the championship game. Its loss to F.C. Indiana would be the club's last final appearance for seventeen years. Zanelli always fielded a competitive squad, but the trophies dried up partially due to the pioneer's success in his main goal: growing the women's game in the United States.

Women's Professional Soccer arrived in 2009 before departing after three seasons like its predecessor before the more stable National Women's Soccer League debuted in 2013 to finally fill the void at the top of the pyramid. By then, the Storm had again moved homes to Cosumnes Oaks High School in Elk Grove as the city prepared a longshot MLS bid. However, the club no longer enjoyed local competition as Pride had closed shop three years earlier.

On March 14, 2013, the Elk Grove city council voted to explore constructing a soccer stadium on 120 acres of vacant land at a cost of $100 million to hopefully attract a top division men's team. Until then, local officials hoped that the Storm would help increase the bid's visibility.

"I couldn't be more thrilled that the California Storm has decided to call Elk Grove home," mayor Gary Davis said in a press release. "Elk Grove is a hotbed for soccer, with the largest youth soccer program in the entire United States. The city of Elk Grove is actively pursuing land for a potential soccer stadium site while also negotiating … for the financing of a stadium. The next two to three months will be critical in our effort to house a Major League Soccer team in Elk Grove."

Once notable for the pull it had with star international players, the Storm slightly faded from prominence while the NWSL prospered nationally, and Sacramento Republic FC began play locally. Zanelli passed away in 2018 at the age of eighty and willed club ownership to assistant Jamie Howard-Levoy. The Storm moved to

Bonney Field in 2019 and then to a new stadium at Davis Legacy Soccer Complex in 2021.[43]

California ended its lengthy title drought the following year, besting 134 other WPSL teams to lift the Jerry Zanelli Trophy and claim its fourth league championship.[44] For all the local franchises that failed, the California Storm have consistently stood out as a shining example of a club constantly moving forward. At time of publication, only three teams had ever lifted multiple WSPL titles, and the Storm are the only side to ever win the championship more than twice.

In Sacramento's pre-Republic era, only one other local club can match the Storm for prestige, though not for longevity. As all outdoor men's franchises failed throughout the city, while the women's outdoor squad just started getting its feet wet, something was brewing inside of ARCO Arena during Sacramento's summer months. Men's outdoor soccer may not have been viable in the capital at the time, but the bastardized indoor version of the game absolutely thrived.

## The Sacramento Knights: An Introduction

Sixteen years after they captured the city's imagination, winning the 1999 World Indoor Soccer League Championship, three Knights legends sat down at LowBrau in Midtown Sacramento to talk about the most popular soccer team in the city before 2014. On a bench outside of the German pub, Jeff Alcala, Paul Hanson, and Craig "Money" Huff joined Republic vice president of Communications Erika Bjork to reminisce on their glory years during the 1990s.

By this time, Alcala had chopped off the long, flowing, black locks that once helped make him a fan favorite. His smile revealed a pair of dimples partially concealed behind the stubble that matched the two shades of his hair. Only when he stood up did the chronic wounds suffered through the grind of 100-plus games a year on what passed for turf in the 1990s become visible.

Alcala walked in the labored manner of someone who had his hip replaced before he turned forty. Five knee and three ankle surgeries robbed him of the breakaway speed he once used to blow by defenders at ARCO Arena, but he still retained his chill NorCal vibe. When he opened his mouth, he spoke like a stereotypical Californian, where depending on the inflection and tone of his voice the word "dude" could mean ten different things.

Ever the extrovert, Alcala dominated the conversation, relaying joke after joke, constantly making everyone within earshot double over in laughter. He liked to tell people that he "used to be huge in his own zip code." Just as everyone wiped away the tears shed from cackling during the first ten minutes of the conversation, Alcala

---

[43] Disclaimer: I work for Davis Legacy.
[44] Shout out to my good friend Janae Gonzalez for co-captaining the Storm to this title while earning that year's Most Outstanding Player award.

made Hanson, Huff, and Bjork break again with just the mention of a single name: Andrew Shue. The Melrose Place actor, Elizabeth's brother, moonlit as a soccer player in the early days of MLS. Publicity stunt or not, Shue played five games for the L.A. Galaxy during its first two seasons. Two years before MLS kicked off, though, Shue signed for the Anaheim Splash, then one of the Sacramento Knights' biggest competitors.

Though the Knights and Splash were rivals, the mid-90s indoor soccer community was tight knit. Almost everyone knew everyone else in the league, especially given that their paths may have also crossed while playing during the outdoor season or for a team in one of the competing indoor leagues. According to Alcala's friend on the Splash, the club's coach took the rest of the team aside before Shue's arrival and demanded that they treat him just like any other player.

"Any other player?" Alcala remembered his friend saying, "We're going to haze him." So, when Shue took his shirt off after pregame warmups ahead of his first match, the Splash captain didn't waste an opportunity to completely ignore his coach's wishes. "The captain," Alcala said while snickering, "rubbed [Shue's] jersey on his butt crack."

Cackles erupted from the three former Knights and Bjork before Alcala could even finish. They'd heard this story's payoff hundreds of times before, but unlike them, it never gets old. It's memories like this, however immature, that lived on long after the once-successful Sacramento Knights folded. The group found it necessary to retell several other non-soccer anecdotes before the actual soccer memories emerged.

By the end of their careers, each of Alcala and Huff played in the back, having lost the quickness to score goals, but not the intelligence to prevent them. Hansen, however, was born to defend. Casting a hulking figure with a bone-crunching handshake, Hansen's taciturn voice came as a surprise. His ginger hair turning gray was the only sign of age in a physique seemingly more suited for football than *futbol*. During his indoor soccer career, he dominated both the penalty area and the hockey-style penalty box.

Of the three, Huff was the only one who didn't resemble a former professional athlete. A slight, balding man, it's hard to put a finger on what would have led him to success on the field–he didn't pass the eye test. "Craig's still probably one of my favorite players to play with," Field later said at Bonn Lair. "You know you're good when you have the nickname 'Money.'" Money let the others do the talking, constantly reading the situation just as he did as a player. When he moved to speak, revealing a boyish grin, his words were poignant and incisive. There was no breath wasted. Everyone listened.

Alcala, Hansen, and Huff made up the backbone of the Sacramento Knights, one of the few stable franchises who played in a series of various unstable indoor soccer leagues around the same time the Kings started finding success. With the Knights, they won Sacramento's first top division professional sports championship while drawing crowds of 5,000 to 10,000 from 1993 to 2001. Hansen and Huff were Knight lifers, while Alcala played all but the final year. All three grew up in the area. All three remained involved in the grassroots community after retirement. All three would become Sacramento Republic FC supporters.

"When Sacramento had word that there was this team, a lot of us came back to try out here," Hansen said of the Knights. "We were soccer gypsies. We were going to show up wherever."

## Soccer, But American (And Zebra Club)

Looking for a way to earn revenue from ARCO Arena during the NBA offseason, then-Sacramento Kings owner Jim Thomas brought indoor soccer to Sacramento in 1993. It was Thomas's second escapade into niche sports—the former owner tried arena football in 1992 but the Sacramento Attack played just one season at the facility before relocating to Miami.[45]

Indoor soccer enjoyed its heyday between the end of the NASL in 1984 and the beginning of MLS in 1996. The sport's backers attempted to "Americanize" the game, turning it into a spectacle that even the most ardent soccer haters could enjoy. In the years between the existence of first division professional outdoor soccer leagues in the United States, the indoor game provided one of the few options for domestic talent to earn a living playing the sport they loved. Or at least a version of the sport they loved—some found the rules nonsensical at best.[46]

The sport may have only been soccer-adjacent, but several well-known outdoor players provided a high standard of play in the country's various professional indoor leagues such as the Major Indoor Soccer League, the National Professional Soccer League,[47] and the Continental Indoor Soccer League. While likely an outlier in terms of the amount of talent he possessed, future Sacramento Republic FC coach Preki jumped straight from the Saint Louis Stars' MISL lineup to that of the legendary English club Everton in 1992. He would later make a similar move from the San Jose Grizzlies to Portsmouth.

Branded as the Sacramento Knights, the newest attraction in California's capital struggled in 1993, finishing 12-16 and missing the playoffs for just one of two times it would over a nine-year period. Most of the early coverage of the Knights in *The Sacramento Bee* involved explaining the rules to readers, while columns derided the

---

[45] It was reportedly determined that California's workers' compensation laws rendered the sport too costly for Thomas.

[46] For example, this is an actual sentence from a game recap that appeared in the September 17, 1995, issue of *The Sacramento Bee*: "[San Jose] Grizzlies sixth attacker Troy Dayak started to signal a timeout but did not have his foot on top of the ball in the goalie's arc, which is required."

[47] The indoor NPSL, consisting of teams mostly from the East Coast, played from 1984-2001 before folding, leaving it open for the current NPSL to use its name when it was founded in 2003. This is also not to be confused with the original NPSL, which existed in 1967 before merging with the United Soccer Association to form the original North American Soccer League.

supposedly poor crowds that 'only' drew an average of over 6,000 in 1993, a number that would have placed third in the USL in 2015.

League regulations required each roster to include at least 75 percent homegrown players, so the Knights signed Alcala, Hansen, and Huff. Sacramento State graduate Steve Petuskey, a Senators alum like Hansen, also joined the team. Within two years, Petuskey's strong play helped the San Francisco Greek-American Athletic Club capture the U.S. Open Cup, but opportunities were so limited at the time that he elected to retire while at the top of his game to pursue the more lucrative career of a full-time UPS delivery man.

"At night I usually practice on my own," Petuskey told *The Sacramento Bee* in 1994 while he was still attempting to juggle two careers. "When I was part-time [at UPS] there was no problem making all the games, but now I have to do some adjusting." According to *The Sacramento Bee*, Knights players made around $1,000 to $3,000 a month, but it was never about the money for them. Until it had to be.

The Knights caught Alcala, Hansen, and Huff at the right moment in their lives. Just a few years removed from college, the trio could afford to live on their modest salaries in the team-subsidized housing. During the offseason in the winter and spring, they looked for playing opportunities elsewhere to earn more funds. "It was very situational, you know, you had some guys who could come in and do certain things, and other guys had families, so they couldn't play because they had so much responsibility," Huff said. "Us, we didn't really have families until the end of our careers. The timing was perfect."

Or as Alcala put it: "We got to be kids as long as we could. That's the way I looked at it."

Alcala remembered receiving the phone call from Knights brass informing him that the club had drafted him. He thought one of his friends was playing a prank on him until assistant coach Jim Amos hopped on the line and asked Alcala if he could make a PR appearance at ARCO the next day.

With a roster filled with young adults who had a plethora of downtime and mostly lived together in the same apartment complex, it would have been stranger if the young bachelors didn't get caught up in a series of never-ending shenanigans.

"I don't remember a goddamn score. I couldn't tell you," Alcala said. "I remember the championship. I remember us making playoffs, but I can tell you about the hotels, or the traveling, just with the players. Being in the locker room when shit happened. You just remember the stories with the individual people that you had. Your teammates. That was the most important part of it."

A large percentage of those stories feature the same backdrop: Zebra Club, a local dive on the corner of 19th and P streets. Zebra Club doesn't pretend that it's anything other than what it really is: a cheap and dirty place to drink copiously. There, you're just as likely to find a crowd imbibing at 11:00 a.m. on a Monday as 11:00 p.m. on a Friday. Naturally, Zebra's regular 1990s crowd included most of the Knights.

"I started going there because one of my good buddies from college lived like five houses down from it," Field later said. "One point, we had the whole team down there. One of the dudes reached behind the counter and stole a bottle of whiskey or something and we all got in trouble. I don't want to say we all got in trouble, but those dudes got kicked out and my Zebra Club pass almost got revoked."

Zebra Club operated somewhat like a casino for the Knights players, in that its confines were so dark during the day that it became impossible to tell time accurately–and by the end of each stay, all left penniless. In the daytime, the bar featured a quiet ambience, a perfect place for a lunchtime meeting over a greasy hamburger. At night though, it transformed into everyone's favorite last stop–a centrally located hole-in-the-wall selling cheap drinks with not completely atrocious service. As Field liked to say, "if you want to go watch a soccer game, you go to Bonn Lair; if you want to go chasing tail, you go to Zebra."

The weeknight drinking sessions, partying, and pranks reflected the state of American indoor soccer in the early 1990s. The players possessed great skill but could only be considered professionals in name. Most indoor players and coaches relied on second jobs to supplement their somewhat-livable soccer incomes. Cost cutting proved just as important to the players' monthly budgets as it did for the Knights franchise. Everyone knew the deal before they first suited up in 1993.

To spend less on hotels for road games, the Knights flew its players in on the day of games, with planes departing as early as 4:00 a.m. in some cases. As soon as the final whistle blew, they jetted directly back to Sacramento. "When that changed to leaving the day before," Hansen said. "We thought we hit big time."

Added Alcala: "It was always shit like that. I mean, literally, you'd wake up, a guy's having a beer at the bar at like 6:00 a.m. Not going to say who. There would be an argument, there would be almost like a fight there."[48]

After that middling 1993 season, which included Sacramento setting a league record for single-game attendance with 10,043, the Knights turned around their fortunes on the field the following year. For the 1994 season, they brought back the majority of their local players–a luxury of continuity not shared by many of their CISL rivals.

As the Sacramento Kings remained typically uncompetitive, the 15-13 sophomore Knights season finally gave the city a professional team to be proud of. The fans showed up in droves as nearly 7,000 per game packed ARCO's lower bowl to revel in hungover twenty-somethings speeding around at 100 mph. That is until Hansen inevitably kicked someone and went on timeout in the penalty box.

---

[48] At some point during this reminiscing, Alcala, who is of Native American descent and sports a feather tattoo on his arm, went off on a tangent: "I had great hair, huh? I really did. I haven't grown it yet. I've been waiting for it to turn all gray. I think now is the time. I haven't told my wife yet. I want it to be like Injun silver…I swear to god. I'm growing it out. Put that in [the book]…my dream is to have silver hair."

# The dos Santos Brothers Grew Up Watching the Knights

The 1994 Knights exited the playoffs in the quarterfinals, but planted the seeds of success for what would become Sacramento's most successful top-division professional sports season to date in the following year. Only one thing stood in the club's way: Monterrey La Raza. Despite the natural exotic beauty that the away trips to Monterrey provided, traveling south of the border to play their CISL foes offered more nightmare than vacation getaway for Knights players.

For the most part, two giants of Mexican soccer have dominated the city of Monterrey for more than half of a century: Liga MX rivals C.F. Monterrey and Tigres UANL. However, the campus of Tec de Monterrey, one of the most-prestigious research universities in the world, played host to the Knights' biggest rivals. Monterrey La Raza was one of the few foreign teams in the CISL's history, forced to play *futbol* according to rules devised by American sports executives who'd never played soccer before.

Still, the club frequently sold out its 2,500-seat stadium during every Knights visit. Just as Sacramento's indoor soccer club filled ARCO during the Kings offseason, La Raza gave local diehards an alternative during Liga MX breaks. An affluent, intelligent crowd attended games at the gym, which featured a playing surface closer in area to a basketball court than the indoor-soccer standard hockey-rink sized surfaces that appeared north of the border. Most indoor surfaces measured around 200-feet long and eighty-feet wide. Monterrey's was reportedly 162-feet long and eighty-two-feet wide.

"It was like a high school basketball arena. But not that good," Hansen said. "They allowed smoking in there too. [The fans] were flicking cigarettes at us."

Added Huff: "They were throwing batteries at us."

As a college freshman, Bjork began her communications career interning for Capital Sports & Entertainment, the Jim Thomas-led group that operated ARCO, the Kings, and the Knights. Through her work, she quickly learned about the unique challenges Knights players and staff faced during their away trips to La Raza. "My understanding is that they literally put the broadcasters on a stairwell," Bjork said. "They didn't even have a press box. They made their own [seats] and that's where they sat."

The conditions hardly qualified as the Knights' only problem in Monterrey, though. La Raza bolstered its home-field advantage with a strong squad that included Brazilian attacker Zizinho. Like his most famous son, former Mexico international Giovani dos Santos, Zizinho glided through opposing defenses at will. During his five-year career in Monterrey, the dos Santos patriarch picked up the baton as arguably indoor soccer's best player once Preki departed for England. In seven of the nine seasons in which the Knights fielded a team, La Raza compiled a 12-7 record against Sacramento, and won titles in two different leagues.

In 1995, Sacramento and Monterrey squared off in the CISL's championship series. Foreshadowing his son's play style, Zizinho ran circles around hopeless Knights defenders. Named Playoff MVP, he capped La Raza's 23-5 season with two goals and four assists in the final game, a 10-7 victory. Having pulled out all the stops including owner Jim Thomas organizing a private jet for the team to fly to the match, the Knights felt gutted to return home empty handed.

This was as close as the CISL version of the team came to winning a title, an era managed by English head coach Keith Weller. In the days before the widespread use of the internet and satellite TV, most Knights players knew little of their gaffer's past. When asked about his former career, Weller told his players that he used to drive a truck. Which was true—he'd operated a TV broadcast van at one of his prior jobs. It wasn't until his health started to fail that the Knights players discovered Weller's true past.

What Weller neglected to mention were the details surrounding his first career. For a time, none of the Knights knew that their coach had played for England four times or that he'd accumulated nearly 300 appearances for Leicester City.[49] Weller even appeared in *101 Great Goals*, a popular pre-internet age highlight reel featuring some of the best goals in English soccer history.

"It [was] one of those VHS tapes that all of us watched," Alcala said. "He had a couple of goals [in it and] he never once mentioned that. He was bigger than any of us ever could be or would be and he never brought that up, you know what I mean?

"It was always about us, about what we were, what we did, our importance versus where he was and where he came from," he added. "[Whenever any of us made a play,] he literally could have been like, 'I've done that a million times,' but he wasn't like that."

According to several Knights players, Weller's quality as a coach was inversely proportional to his competency operating motor vehicles. The Englishman took it upon himself to drive the team van when needed, crashing it into stationary objects several times during his tenure in Sacramento. Following the second-place finish in 1995, Weller's Knights tailed off a bit and bowed out of the playoffs in the quarterfinals twice after two straight 14-14 seasons.

After the 1997 CISL campaign, Alcala traveled to Mexico City to play in the inaugural World Indoor Soccer Championship for the U.S. selection, which was dubbed "CISL America." Hoping to keep up with the news back home, he picked up a copy of *USA Today* and flipped through the pages, only to discover that the league had gone under. Fed up with the sport's amateurism, Weller quit the Knights shortly thereafter and moved to Seattle. He opened a coffee shop in the Pacific

---

[49] He also enjoyed stints at Tottenham Hotspur, Millwall, and Chelsea in England before crossing the pond to play in the original NASL.

Northwest and resumed driving a broadcast van until succumbing to cancer in 2004.

# Champions

With the CISL gone, four of its former clubs hastily formed a new competition called the Premier Soccer Alliance for the 1998 season. To replace Weller, the Knights promoted former New England Revolution and Canadian National Team defender Iain Fraser to serve as player-coach. Fraser had spent the 1995 season with the Knights before moving to MLS in 1996.[50]

Even without La Raza in the PSA, the Knights slumped to a .500 record during the regular season. However, that mark proved the second best in the league as Sacramento qualified for its second indoor championship match. The Dallas Sidekicks, one of the only other somewhat stable organizations in the sport, prevailed 6-2 to send the Knights back to the drawing board.

The 1999 squad retooled by adding a swath of talented locals and joined the new nine-team World Indoor Soccer League alongside the Sidekicks and La Raza. Former Dallas Burn midfielder Gerrell Elliott signed with the club after ironically reportedly growing tired of the lack of professionalism in MLS. Elliott abruptly quit the Burn to rejoin the Knights, which he'd starred for from 1993 to 1995.

According to Alcala, the Burn still owned Elliott's rights, but the midfielder negotiated his release by claiming that he was moving back to Sacramento to become a bike courier. Months later, Elliott donned a Knights uniform, perhaps only legally because indoor soccer wasn't technically "soccer," and therefore not subject to FIFA rules. For Elliott, this was something as the norm for a person that Alcala described as an "introverted goth." According to Alcala, Elliott was so shy about his professional soccer career, that his post-retirement girlfriend had to Google him to find out that he even had played the sport.

The other big-name signing was the ninja, Worm, Jeremy Field. The Geckos initially caught his attention, but Field elected to hang around and give indoor a try instead of accepting a contract offer in Germany. A chance encounter during a late-night pickup game with Fraser led the Canadian to extend a trial offer to Field. Ever the soccer purist—he even preferred free-flowing pickup soccer to the constraints of the college game—Field felt skeptical at first.

"To me, indoor soccer was fake soccer," he said. "If you're technical and athletic, it's easy because everything is so fast...you can't play a Barcelona style indoors. Indoor is like fast break basketball." Field tried out, made the team, and helped fill out possibly the finest roster in Knights history.

---

[50] Fraser returned to Sacramento after the inaugural Revolution campaign when he was reportedly blackballed from the upstart league after filing a lawsuit that challenged its single-entity status. For more information, look up *Fraser v. Major League Soccer*.

The biggest problem surrounding the Knights ahead of the 1999 season had nothing to do with the team's collection of talent–their issue was much less tangible. Nothing was set in stone, but a rumor emerged as soon as the Maloof family acquired its majority stake in the Kings and, begrudgingly for them, the Knights as well. The word around town was that the new owners preferred to shut down the indoor soccer club's operations after six successful seasons on and off the field.

"We feel that we have the best indoor soccer team in the world," Hubert Rotteveel told *The Bee* shortly before the 1999 WISL season started. That same article also buried this paragraph near the bottom: "At this week's media preview, the Maloofs were supposed to meet their team personally, but they couldn't make it. Instead, they got tied up in contract negotiations for the Kings." It appeared as if yet another professional soccer team in Sacramento might fold, though this latest potential former franchise could at least call itself a perennial winner that drew solid crowds.

Attendance decreased for the fourth consecutive year, but the Knights posted a 17-5 record, good for second best in club history. Despite a more intimate atmosphere Sacramento went 11-0 at home and capped the regular season off with a twelve-game win streak. Two weeks later the Maloofs joined 7,107 fans to watch the Knights secure ARCO's first-ever championship banner.

The 7-6 victory over the Dallas Sidekicks in a rematch of the 1998 final was homegrown, with Elliott scoring a first half hat trick to go with a brace from Chris McDonald, and Antonio Sutton's solitary strike.[51]

The win helped generate positive headlines, increase season ticket sales, and provide the Knights with a reprieve. "They were going to try and fold the team," Field said of the Maloofs. "But we won the championship, so they couldn't do that."

Back at LowBrau years later, mentioning the Maloofs turned the joyous mood sour in a heartbeat. Alcala, Hansen, and Huff solemnly shook their heads while recalling these bits of Knights lore. "You could see the end was near," Huff said. "[The Maloofs] didn't introduce themselves to us [following the victory]"

Added Alcala: "We never met the owners."

Hansen: "But we won the championship that year. They had to hang on for one more year. Bad timing for them."

Huff: "I remember the Christmas party. They didn't really say anything about anything. We won the championship on the ninth, the twelfth?[52] The Christmas party was two weeks later. They didn't really say anything."

The Knights ran it back for one more year in 2000, at the very least so the Maloofs could avoid potentially inviting their first-ever wave of negative press in Sacramento. Behind the scenes, ownership slashed wages, stacking the deck against

---

[51] *The Bee* match report only listed six of the seven Knights goals on the night.
[52] It was the twelfth.

Rotteveel, who departed the club shortly after the title win. It was the end of an era for a man who had contributed possibly more than anyone to the local soccer scene. Before suiting up during the lone Senators season in 1989, the Dixon native cut his teeth at UCLA, helping the school earn its first-ever NCAA title in 1985 under the guise of a young Sigi Schmid.

"Hubert Rotteveel, he was a goofy dude," Field said. "But if you look at it, he had a great relationship and kept the franchise going for forever, and then Iain came in, and two years later it was done."

Within the next couple of years, both the Knights and Rotteveel fell upon hard times. Fraser gave it his best at the helm but was powerless to prevent the popularity of the indoor game from waning or the penchant of his disinterested owners to cut operational costs.

Meanwhile, the well-liked, All-American boy from just west of Sacramento turned to desperation after hemorrhaging money from his real estate business during the late 2000s recession. In 2010, reportedly armed with a BB gun,[53] Rotteveel robbed a series of Sacramento-area banks while using a bicycle as his getaway vehicle. The police apprehended the former general manager when a dye pack exploded on his person as he cycled past a patrol car.[54]

Huff, enjoying his second IPA of the night, cracked a joke about Rotteveel needing to rob a bank one day after the Knights racked up $30,000 in copy machine expenses. "Too soon?" he asked.

"No, never too soon," Alcala quipped back.

"Facebook blew up that day," Bjork said. "I think it was the fact that he was robbing banks on his bike is really probably what got me."

# The Sacramento Knights: A Eulogy

With virtually the same team, Sacramento went from lifting the title to missing the playoffs with a 5-19 record the following year. Alcala described the 2000 Sacramento Knights season concisely: "[It] sucked nuts," he said. Alcala retired at the conclusion of the season, and a patchwork Knights team stumbled again the following year to an 11-13 mark before losing in the semifinal round of the playoffs. Afterwards, the WISL folded, and many of the existing teams such as the Sidekicks joined the fledgling Major Indoor Soccer League.

In their third year as Knights owners, the Maloofs had roughly one month to decide if they wanted to continue operating the franchise in the MISL for a 2002 season that would coincide with the club's tenth anniversary. In 2001 Sacramento averaged more than 5,000 fans per game, still a respectable number nationally, but

---

[53] Huff claimed that it was an airsoft gun.
[54] While serving his sentence for the robberies, Rotteveel was subsequently found guilty of mortgage fraud in another bizarre set of circumstances.

one that was the lowest in team history. The Knights' 0-5 start to the season didn't help. Neither did the September 11th terrorist attacks, which forced the club to reschedule two games.

But the fans returned when Sacramento started winning. One contest late in the season nearly drew 10,000 spectators. According to the Maloofs, that wasn't enough, though. "If people don't want to see the product, and you can't get decent crowds, then you start to wonder why are we in it?" Joe Maloof told *The Bee*. "There could be a possibility that [the Knights] won't be here next year, but that isn't for sure yet. We're going to look at the new league and see if we want to become a part of that. We want to look at all the pluses on one side and the negatives on another and see if it's something we ought to try to maintain."

After hearing the disparaging comments, the fanbase banded together to show their support for the indoor soccer team in the hopes of swaying the Maloofs. In just a few weeks a grassroots movement led by Judy Arnold, Rick Arnold, and Hank Bernard gathered more than 57,000 signatures in support of keeping the Knights in the city. "The Knights are the real heart of Sacramento," Arnold told *The Bee*. While MISL officials pleaded with the Maloofs to join the league, the owners expressed concerns over its longer schedule and September-to-April calendar that overlapped with the NBA season.

The Knights submitted an application to join the MISL just ahead of the January 31 deadline but asked to enter as an "inactive team" and go on hiatus for the 2002-03 season. "We studied the schedule from every angle," Joe Maloof told *The Bee*. "We haven't yet found a way to make it work."

While the Maloofs didn't officially dissolve the club, those involved with it read between the lines. "As a player and a coach, we're all devastated and shocked," Iain Fraser told *The Bee*. "Even if you saw it coming, to know we don't exist as a team—you're never ready for that."

That March, the MISL held its dispersal draft, and the Knights made every player available for selection for the league's other nine franchises. "We feel that, besides taking away our professional soccer team, Joe and Gavin Maloof have taken away our good friends," the Arnolds wrote. "We are truly stunned and devastated by this news. We do not feel that there was ever a real commitment to our soccer team. Why would you own a team and never come to the games? Why were they not promoted more? Those are questions you should ask yourselves, Joe and Gavin. You have taken away a positive force for our youth, and you have taken away our good friends.

"Shame on you, Joe and Gavin, shame on you."

Added Rotteveel: "Soccer can succeed in Sacramento. The Maloofs want this thing to go away. It's not."

Clubs from across the country selected each Knight, but only five elected to continue playing indoor soccer with the team that owned their rights. At the end of the inaugural MISL season, the Maloofs updated the Knights' temporary hiatus into a permanent one and removed the only championship banner hanging from

ARCO's rafters. Local fan-favorite and future Republic assistant coach Antonio Sutton was one of the five who continued to play by signing with the Sidekicks. The dreadlocked midfielder extended his career but yearned for the good old days in Sacramento to return.

"It's a bummer. Once the team was disbanded, I knew [the Maloofs] wouldn't do anything to bring us back. I would love to play there again," Sutton told *The Bee*. "We had wonderful fans in Sacramento. Most nights, we had 6,000 or 7,000 people at Arco. In this league, some places–like in Kansas City, for instance–there's maybe 600 or 700.

"It's not the same."

Added Hansen in the same article: "The team had a good run, but we died exceptionally quietly, just kind of disappeared. I really think [the Maloofs] missed a great opportunity. We could have been a much bigger thing if they had only thrown a few bucks our way."

The MISL felt disappointed with the Maloofs' decision but remained hopeful that another ownership group would step in to revive the Knights. The league wished to operate somewhere in Northern California but looked at Sacramento as its priority. "It's a great market in Sacramento, one of the best for soccer," MISL commissioner Steve Ryan told *The Bee*. "We really believe in Sacramento. But we need the right facility and the right marketing group."

Ryan and the MISL never found either–the indoor Knights were gone for good. The majority of the club's former players blamed the Maloofs for not fighting to save the team, Huff less-than affectionately referred to the family as the "Magoofs," fifteen years after the fact.

"The Maloofs are dirtballs," Field said. "It was funny, after they folded the team, I saw them up in Tahoe, like a month later. I was still fired up. I wanted to just punch them in the face and then take off running, but I didn't."

# Limbo

Under new ownership, the Sacramento Knights relaunched as an outdoor squad in 2004 in the fourth division NPSL, the Zanelli-founded male equivalent of the WPSL. Fraser returned as the club's head coach and the ex-Canadian international brought back former indoor Knights Chris McDonald and Jeremy Field. "I just like to play," Field said. "I started the first part with the outdoor Knights. It was fun, it was fun. A couple of days a week we practiced. It did start to grind because you're not getting paid and you're starting to go, well I could coach and make more money or go do this for free."

On the last legs of his playing career, Field jumped at the chance to travel abroad during the preseason when he scored several tickets to Euro 2004 in Portugal. "That was sort of the tipping point," he said. "I said, 'Hey coach, sorry, I hate to do this, but we're not really getting paid. I'm bouncing and going to the European Championships for three weeks. I hope you're cool with that.'

"I don't know if he was or not."

Field's last match with the club came in a first round Open Cup contest in which he scored a ninety-first minute extra-time golden goal penalty kick to give the Knights a 2-1 victory over the Spokane Shadow. Others involved in the game remembered an exhausted Field sprinting over a hill to the locker room to puke immediately after the match, possibly due to the hungover state he may or may not have been in.

Field remembers it differently. "It's funny how stories get changed," he said. "I never puked, but I had just watched an NBA game where the guy, I think it was Derek Fisher, made the winning basket at the buzzer and ran straight into the tunnel holding up his pointer finger. So I scored in sudden death OT, put up my finger, and ran up a big hill into the locker room. No surprise Chris McDonald had received a red card that game so he was in the locker room. I remember him asking me if I got red carded, and I think I said something like, 'Nah, I was just in a hurry to let you know I had it covered.'"

Field turned back the clock to Seattle in the early 1990s to rediscover his partying form over in Lisbon. Naturally, he didn't own a cell phone at the time, relying on his wife to relay messages when someone wished to contact him. He returned to Sacramento with an hours-long backlog of voicemails–while Field had been pounding beers at fanfests and in stadiums, Fraser and McDonald had quit. The Sacramento Knights had now severed all connections with their indoor past. Neither Field nor McDonald would play professional soccer again.

According to new owner Laureate "J.R." Gholar, Fraser and McDonald departed following a dispute regarding the club's future. "Our long-range plan is to build a solid foundation with an amateur status for at least the next three to five years," Gholar told *The Bee* in June of 2004. "We're not trying to grow too big too fast. Chris and Iain wanted to go pro right away, but it costs $750,000 for an A-League team, $35 million for Major League Soccer. I'm not Maloof Sports and Entertainment. I'm just a local guy trying to run a team in my hometown."

Gholar claimed that he mostly broke even with the outdoor Knights despite yearly operational costs that he said hovered around $165,000. He also said that the club was in the process of building a new soccer facility in Sacramento. Gholar told *The Bee* that the Knights drew up plans for a $58 million, 30,000-seat venue that would be constructed over a two-year period. The owner further declared that the initial stadium project would be followed by a $35 million, 110-acre soccer complex in Elk Grove to serve as the club's youth academy.

Gholar, Knights coach Ron Preble, and California Storm owner Jerry Zanelli all agreed that the stadium would help the local soccer scene, but Zanelli remained the most realistic of the trio. Though he didn't specify where from, Gholar told *The Bee* he had funding lined up, while Preble said a new facility would help the club draw the same kinds of numbers it did at ARCO. "I say show me the money,"

Zanelli told *The Bee*. "I've seen seven or eight different people come through here touting everything from a soccer complex at ARCO to building one in a gravel pit.

"I've seen a lot of grandiose ideas with no realities behind them."

The outdoor Knights won the NPSL championship in 2006 before folding following the conclusion of the 2007 season. The $58 million stadium never evolved past an idea mentioned haphazardly in the newspaper.[55]

In 2010, Ruben Mora Sr. and his son, Ruben Mora Jr., revitalized the Sacramento Gold moniker and set up shop at River City High School in West Sacramento. The club entered the NPSL and won the title in its first year. Unlike the outdoor Knights, the Gold never folded and still operated at time of publication.

Thanks to the two NPSL sides, Sacramento is one of just three cities with multiple league titles alongside Miami and New York. But while the Gold and the California Storm continue to draw solid crowds, play exciting soccer, and provide a place for young players to develop, true professional soccer died in Sacramento before the turn of the century. After Team Sacramento folded in 1999, every potential outdoor professional start-up failed prior to launch. According to former Sacramento River Cats executive Joe Wagoner, one group came close to setting up a team in the mid-2000s, but nothing concrete materialized.

This would all change because a group of three men began regularly meeting to drink beer and talk around a table in a Sacramento area garage. The two louder men were baseball lovers who frequently made fun of the third for sipping on drinks while kicking around a soccer ball. The ball, seemingly attached to this man's foot, became ubiquitous in their gatherings.

For years, the third man juggled the ball in a corner while imploring the other two to take the sport more seriously. This man claimed that a soccer team in Sacramento was destined to succeed, if only it were run correctly. For years, the other two men laughed off the third. They considered soccer a stupid sport, a communist, anti-American waste of time. The first two men were named Joe Wagoner and Sean Morrison.[56]

The third man, the soccer lover, the goofball, the outcast, was also the ninja. He was Worm, the one and only Jeremy Field.

---

[55] At time of publication, the "Sacramento Knights (2003-2007)" Wikipedia page still includes the following sentence: "It has been announced that the team will play its 2009 season at Folsom High School as part of the United Soccer League.

[56] Morrison would later become Sacramento Republic's director of club partnerships.

# Sacramento's professional and semi-professional soccer teams and their major honors:

**Sacramento Spirits/Gold/Spirit**
American Soccer League (Division 2) 1976-80
Honors: Champions (1979), Runners-up (1977, 1980)

**Sacramento Senators**
Western Soccer Alliance (Division 2) 1989

**Sacramento Knights (Indoor)**
Continental Indoor Soccer League 1993-97, Premier Soccer Alliance 1998, World Indoor Soccer League 1999-2001
Honors: Champions (1999), Runners-up (1995, 1998)

**California Storm**
W-League (Division 2) 1995-97, WPSL (Division 2) 1998-
Honors: Champions (1999, 2002, 2004, 2022), Runners-up (1997, 2000, 2003, 2005)

**Sacramento Scorpions**
USISL Select League (Division 2) 1996, USISL D-3 Pro League (Division 3) 1997

**Sacramento Geckos/Team Sacramento**
USL A-League (Division 2) 1999

**Elk Grove/Sacramento Pride**
WPSL (Division 2) 2001-2010

**Sacramento Knights (Outdoor)**
NPSL (Division 4) 2004-07
Honors: Champions (2006)

**Sacramento Gold**
NPSL (Division 4) 2010-
Honors: Champions (2010)

**Sacramento Republic FC**
USL Pro (Division 3) 2014, USL (Division 3) 2015-16, USL (Division 2) 2017-18, USL Championship (Division 2) 2019-
Honors: Champions (2014)
U.S. Open Cup: Runners-up (2022)

# FOUR

## BRANDING A CITY[57]

"I'll drink as many beers as you want to have, but I don't know a damn thing about your sport."

-   Sacramento Republic FC co-founder Joe Wagoner

Ryan Wagoner lies in discomfort in his normally comfortable Land Park home while his acid reflux flares up yet again. It's the fall of 2010 and the six-month-old Ryan doesn't know what's wrong with him nor can he articulate the pain he feels. He starts to cry. While Joe and Rachel Wagoner can't stand watching their son go through this, they've at least discovered the solution to calm him. One of the two packs the baby bag while the other picks Ryan up and buckles him into the car seat in the back of the Wagoners' early 2000s gold Acura RDX.

Joe Wagoner slowly drives through cozy streets lined with white picket fences and immaculate green lawns. Something about the moving vehicle calms Ryan and after cruising for a few blocks through the neighborhood, he silently nods off. Careful to avoid making noise, the Wagoners turn right onto Freeport Boulevard and then take a left on Sutterville Road–the usual route that no one in the family dares deviate from, especially with Ryan napping.

Either Joe or Rachel Wagoner (or both) make this drive more days than not. And when Joe's behind the wheel, he can't help but stare out to his left on Sutterville as he passes into Curtis Park. The massive Sacramento City College campus expands out into the distance at a right angle, but Joe keeps his eyes focused slightly farther forward. As his Acura continues forward, he remains transfixed on

---

[57] I recommend pairing this chapter with "Sheep Go to Heaven" by Cake.

the giant concrete horseshoe stadium that allows pedestrians on the adjacent overpass to stare into its vast confines.

As the car descends to the surface level, Joe shoots a glance in the rearview mirror to ensure that Ryan remains peacefully slumbering. Once confirmed, he steals one more glance back at the sporting venue before turning to face Rachel. "God, that's such a great stadium," he says. "You know what this town needs? A soccer team."

"Yeah, yeah, yeah, whatever," Rachel responds. She can't count the number of times he's told her this, but the drives all blend together at this point. It's a pipedream, Rachel thinks of her husband's words. She doesn't understand how Joe can focus on anything other than the fact that the slow, bumpy drive yet again put Ryan to sleep. Forget a soccer team.

"We have a sleeping baby," she says, "that's awesome."

The Wagoners take the same route every day for months. Once every 24 hours, they pass by the Sacramento Zoo, Sacramento City College, and the barred windows of the run-down watering holes that cry out for a modern makeover. But each time, Joe Wagoner develops tunnel vision on a solitary object: Hughes Stadium. Fall of 2010 becomes winter and brings in the new year. Winter turns to spring, accompanied by sunlight basking down on the apple of Joe Wagoner's eye.

Eventually Ryan Wagoner recovers, no longer requiring the afternoon drives to sleep soundly. But nothing can cure Joe Wagoner's obsession with the stadium. Three years before Sacramento Republic FC will take the field at Hughes for the club's inaugural match, the idea of creating a professional soccer team to take advantage of the stadium's vast confines constantly nags at Joe Wagoner. It's an idea born from all of those monotonous tours through South Sacramento.

"We joke in our house that the Republic was actually Ryan's idea," Rachel Wagoner later said.

Idea becomes research, research becomes business plan, business plan becomes reality. In the spring of 2011, with Ryan climbing all over him in their living room, Joe Wagoner types up the initial report that will serve as the founding document of Sacramento Republic FC.

Jeremy Field may have originally pushed Joe Wagoner to start a professional soccer team in Sacramento, but it was a sick infant who really helped hammer that idea home.

## The Sacramento River Cats

Fewer than 500 feet from Sacramento Republic FC's then-Land Park headquarters sits New Helvetia Brewing Co. Named for the 19th-century settlement that preceded present-day Sacramento, New Helvetia was one of the many up-and-coming craft breweries in the greater Sacramento area that became popular around the same time as the Republic. It was also the de facto after-hours meeting spot for the club's employees. Head over to the rustic, red brick building on the corner of Broadway and 18th Street after work back in 2015 and you'd be just as likely to find a front office staffer putting back a few in the bar's sleepy confines as you would in the Republic's office itself.

It was a typically hot and dry early summer Sacramento evening in the club's sophomore year when Republic president Warren Smith, Executive vice president Joe Wagoner, and vice president of communications Erika Bjork plopped down in a booth to discuss the origins of the Republic over beers. They attempted to give their undivided attention to a reporter, but constantly checked their phones, which wouldn't stop vibrating from incoming messages. As three of the most important staff members working for arguably the biggest club in U.S. lower-division soccer, they were always on call.

Smith sat ready in case an important contact reached out, one that could suddenly force him into negotiations. Wagoner laid back a bit in his seat but stayed attentive to his multitude of eclectic responsibilities that ranged from selling tickets to thanking corporate sponsors. Dozens of interruptions popped up during the most inopportune times of his congested schedule every day. Breaking news might have arrived at any moment, forcing Bjork into spin doctor mode.

All three hoped for radio silence as they focused on finalizing an agreement to bring storied English Premier League club Sunderland A.F.C. over for a friendly later in the year. Though the deal neared closure, it wasn't quite finished, but the trio still offered up a generous amount of what little time they had.

Someone at the bar hung a Sacramento Republic FC flag on the back wall next to a March 1959 map of the city. A 2014 team photograph, taken in front of the Capitol Building, covered another wall across from the window-side booth where staffers enjoyed their drinks. A poster told everyone who visited the bathroom that New Helvetia's beer, like the Republic, was "Built for MLS."

Wagoner, a quirky, laid-back Midwesterner with nearly two decades of experience in minor league professional sports, broke the ice. He explained how the trio of individuals, with the help of many more, first believed they could bring professional soccer to California's capital. Oddly, that dream started with the Sacramento River Cats, the city's Triple-A baseball affiliate of the San Francisco Giants.[58]

With the towering stature that helped him in a standout football career as an offensive lineman across the Causeway for UC Davis in the mid-1980s, one might have expected Warren Smith to possess a personality or ego that matched his gargantuan frame. But when the bald and clean-shaven club president opened his mouth, he spoke softly and thoughtfully. Every answer he gave arrived in a calm and collected manner and was delivered with direct eye contact.

---

[58] Formerly the affiliate of the Oakland A's.

Smith didn't speak like he was trying to sell anything, nor did he embellish his past or current achievements. It was like he had a product he felt so confident in that it spoke for itself and therefore allowed him to simply make objective statements about the club. When he talked about the Republic, he mostly stated facts in a genuine and truthful way that's rare among professional sports executives. Close friends and co-workers described Smith as a champion of Sacramento, a notion he'd always laugh off to retain the modesty that epitomized the community aspect of the Republic.

Around the turn of the century, Smith helped lay the initial framework that brought the River Cats to West Sacramento. Partially because of his efforts, the city landed its fourth professional sports franchise after the Kings, the ill-fated Knights, and the WNBA's Monarchs.

Smith initially appeared hesitant—he constantly fumbled with his keys while checking his phone every few moments. It was crunch time with the Sunderland deal, and it wasn't until he cracked a joke that he broke free of the stuffy sports executive stereotype. With a completely serious look, he told the table that Bjork dated a Maloof and then said he met Wagoner because his co-founder moonlit as Smith's "yard guy." Though he tried to hold a straight face, he broke when everyone else doubled over with laughter.

Smith's first smile, like all his others, reinforced his genuine nature—he smiled with his whole face, squinting his eyes to reveal crow's feet behind his trademark oval-framed glasses. During Republic games, Smith wandered seamlessly from location to location, mingled with fans, fellow staffers, and anyone else who wished to chat. He was the type of guy who seamlessly fit into any social situation. In the same hour he could nonchalantly drink beers in the supporters' section before popping into the VIP section to close a business deal.

Sometimes he dressed in one of the dozen or so tailored tan or gray suits he wore to press conferences. A betting man would guess, though, that he preferred the days when he wore khaki shorts, tennis shoes, and a tucked in polo to fade away from the public eye into a random Sacramento sports fan.

As the executive vice president of the Sacramento River Cats, Smith helped lead the successful grassroots effort to construct Raley Field, the 14,014-seat minor league baseball park that hugs the banks of the Sacramento River across the Tower Bridge from Downtown. The timeline from groundbreaking to completion of a venue that earned widespread plaudits for its design lasted nine months.

Raley Field quickly became a popular location for locals to spend an evening as most spectators could enjoy a ball game in full view of Sacramento's illuminated skyline while the sun set at their backs. Smith teamed up with the late local investor Art Savage to negotiate the terms to bring a Triple-A franchise to Raley Field—the pair acquired the Vancouver Canadians' franchise rights in 1999 to finally bring baseball back to Sacramento.[59]

Smith found a perfect partner in Wagoner when the latter joined the River Cats staff in July of 2002. The Illinois native possessed a creative mind that frequently produced ideas closer to the half-baked variety rather than the sort ready to pull out of the oven. By the time he arrived in California, Wagoner had built an impressive portfolio of absurd gimmicks and marketing ploys that he peddled at various minor league baseball clubs in random cities throughout the country.

His prior stop as a Sioux Falls-based front office executive required Wagoner to push the envelope to stick butts in seats in the Middle of Nowhere, USA. One of the more-notable involved creating the band Bitch Bergr[60] with coworker and future Portland Timbers VP of communications Chris Metz. The pair recorded a song called "Take the Cat Away," which they joked was the "smash hit" that they'd perform live after a Sioux Falls Canaries game.

When the members of Bitch Bergr discovered that only one other South Dakota-based band had submitted a song in the Post-Rock Experimental genre on the now-defunct mp3.com website, they uploaded "Take the Cat Away!" in that category. After pestering a few friends to download the single, they watched as it soared to the top of the chart. With the No. 1 spot secured, Wagoner and Metz advertised their group as "South Dakota's most downloaded band" on a flier promoting their post-game concert alongside a group named The Traveling Dingleberries.

"We were horrid," Wagoner said, unable to contain his grin. "We were absolutely horrid, so bad. But it's funny because now those guys are with the Timbers, and I made fun of them for being in soccer."

It didn't take Wagoner long to peel back the layers of his multifaceted personality. Like Smith, he frequently worked multiple sixteen-hour shifts in a row without batting an eye. He would start his day in the Sacramento Republic FC office and run back-and-forth between meetings during normal working hours before returning home for dinner and bedtime stories with the kids.

After he tucked everyone in, he would then race back to the dark and empty Republic HQ to catch up on emails, plan ticket sale initiatives, and finish whatever other miscellaneous tasks that had the tendency to pile up when no one was looking. It wouldn't be a stretch to guess that his mind constantly raced with an endless checklist of unfinished business but when someone else talked, he made it

---

[59] Original Sacramento Kings owner Gregg Lukenbill, a local developer, tried for many years to lure a baseball franchise to the city, going as far to construct the template and foundation of a stadium near ARCO Arena. He was ultimately unsuccessful in his efforts.

[60] "Bitch Bergr" has an entry on *Urban Dictionary*, written in 2009, that claims the band influenced the Rolling Stones. As of publication time, the entry has been liked twice and disliked five times. At the bottom of each page on that sophomoric website, there's space to write a sentence using the word in order to better understand its context. "Bitch Bergr rocked at Stu's last night," reads this entry. "I think I shit myself during their hit song, Take the Cat Away!"

clear that he listened back. He nodded with whomever he spoke to and held eye contact through his square-rimmed glasses.

But behind all the hard work, Wagoner was a wild child at heart, ready to drop everything in a moment for a beer. He brought both halves of the work hard/play hard lifestyle to the office and made it his purpose there to fulfill the latter half every Friday afternoon. No matter how much he had on his plate, Wagoner took a break at the end of every work week to walk to the store and return with shopping bags full of brews to crack open while shooting the shit with his co-workers. Even before the first sip, his booming cackle reverberated throughout the office to help lighten the mood for a stressed gaggle of employees. Sometimes during his night "shift" he busted out the very same bass guitar that propelled Bitch Bergr to stardom.

"That's where he does a lot of his thinking and planning," Republic vice president of merchandise Tim Stallings later said in an interview. "It's really loud in there...the guy playing guitar or bass upstairs is probably better."[61]

# Entertainment Value

As deep as the love of baseball ran through Smith and Wagoner, both conceded that the action could become monotonous during the annual summer slog. Triple-A baseball somehow managed to squeeze a seventy-two-game home slate for each team into a six-month period, forcing the pair to adapt to the lulls. In their baseball days, Smith and Wagoner constantly experimented with various forms of in-game entertainment to, at the very least, amuse themselves.

There were successes, like promotions that involved free food giveaways if a certain player on the other team struck out. There were also failures. Take for instance, the "genius" idea of "Who's in the Can?"

"Here's the deal, we'd take the mobile camera into the bathroom and show two feet [of an anonymous player] underneath a stall," Wagoner said in between sips of lager. "And we'd give three answers to who it is and then you'd, 'Guess who's in the Can?'" Wagoner and Smith roared with laughter and their collective stressed demeanor morphed into delight as they recalled the wild promotions that someone, somehow, greenlit.

After "Who's in the Can?" came "Make Kenny G Stop." To raise money for charity, River Cats upper brass sometimes replaced every opposing player's intro song with a track written by Kenny G. Until the fans scraped together $3,000 to "Make Kenny G Stop," the smooth saxophone of the oft-mocked jazz musician

---

[61] For the first few years after the Republic moved into their Land Park office, they shared the building with a professional musician. Sacramento staffers would often complain that said musician played too late at night, while the musician reportedly got annoyed when during the day Republic staffers loudly messed around with the foosball table or Skee-Ball lane owned by the club.

serenaded each player as they entered the batter's box. After the crowd inevitably pledged three large, the next hitter strutted out to the guitar riff from Joan Jett's "I Love Rock and Roll" to the relief of the 10,000-plus who typically packed the stands in West Sacramento.

"Remember the man-eating chicken?" Smith laughed more than asked. As with all the good stories, the Republic president ceded the floor to his more-animated co-founder.

"So we're getting towards the end of the season, we're so bored, we [needed] something to have a crazy ass time," Wagoner recalled. "So let's tell everyone that a man-eating chicken escaped from the zoo." The club planted a fake journalist down on the field during the first inning of a game to report that the city issued a warning regarding a man-eating chicken. Before the widespread use of cellphones and social media, no one at the game could easily verify the validity of the information, but most of the crowd shrugged it off anyway.

Two innings later, the "newsman" returned to announce that a credible source spotted the man-eating chicken just across the river on the opposite side of Tower Bridge. The Raley Field parking lot lies just a few feet off Capitol Avenue over the bridge–the first turn drivers can take after the golden structure leads to the ballpark's entrance. The report indicated that the wild beast inched closer to the River Cats game, but still roamed the streets of a different city in a separate county. There was no reason to panic, the "reporter" told the fans.

Somewhere around the eighth inning, the "journalist" made his third appearance, which came with a warning: apparently someone spotted the man-eating chicken inside Raley Field. Parents should keep their children in sight, he declared. One frame later, the camera feeding the jumbotron panned to a River Cats sales associate who, according to Smith, often drank on the job but also sold out stadiums in his sleep. The salesman wore a white undershirt smothered and stained with a wide array of various dipping sauces. The club dressed him as if he hadn't changed or showered in the past month or discovered the purpose of a napkin. The camera panned closer to the slob, who loudly and messily chomped down on some sort of snack like a toddler trying to eat spaghetti by hand.

There was no man-eating chicken, but rather, a man…eating chicken.

"That was having too many beers the night before and being like, 'Well, what are we going to do to keep this interesting?'" Wagoner said. "We played sixty-five games. I don't know."

## When Cooler Heads Prevail

Whether due to, or in spite of, the in-game promotions, the River Cats quickly became one of the most successful teams in minor league history, topping Triple-A baseball in attendance in each of the team's first eight seasons in Sacramento.

Meanwhile, the club's Pacific Coast League rival Portland Beavers struggled and declared bankruptcy. Beavers brass looked at the success story emerging 600 miles south on Interstate-5 and asked River Cats executives to take over operations in 2004. Smith and Wagoner were two of the higher-ups entrusted to right the ship in the rainy Northwest. "It came with this little problem," Smith said. "Called the Portland Timbers."

According to Smith, the Beavers/Timbers joint venture was hemorrhaging nearly $2 million a year as both clubs averaged just over 5,000 in their 15,418-capacity facility. The baseball executives devised a solution that they felt was obvious: dissolve the Timbers. "We could shore up 30 percent of the losses and focus on what we knew we could protect, and that was the baseball team," Smith said. "And that rabid group called the Timbers Army didn't let that happen."

Founded in 2001, the Timbers Army became one of the United States' first supporters' groups that acted and operated in a manner consistent with similar organizations in Europe and South America. Instead of showcasing fandom in the typical American fashion of sitting and reacting to plays on the field, the group stood, sang, and waved flags and banners behind Providence Park's north goal for the full ninety minutes. Even during the Timbers' lower-division years, the Army packed the stands to provide an intimidating home-field advantage.

At the time of the River Cats takeover, the Timbers Army probably ranked only behind D.C. United's *La Barra Brava*[62] in terms of sheer size and noise-making capabilities for supporters' groups in the country. Led by these boisterous fans, the Timbers enjoyed some of the strongest crowds in the three different second divisions they played in from 2001-2010—the club averaged more than 10,000 fans per game in its final season in the lower tiers. And in the latter part of the first decade of the new century, the Timbers easily out-drew the Beavers.

And it was the raucous support from the Timbers Army that convinced Smith and Co. to modify their original solution—they feared the public relations nightmare that would inevitably follow any potential Timbers dissolution. Instead, the River Cats executives chose to save the team that would eventually become one of Major League Soccer's iconic franchises.

On the baseball side of operations, Smith and Wagoner cut spending while elevating the team's average attendance to the middle of the pack in Triple-A. The city's renewed interest in the Beavers, combined with the continued success of the Timbers, convinced local investor Merritt Paulson to buy the two franchises and end River Cat involvement in Portland. Following the purchase, Paulson announced aspirations to bring MLS to the Rose City.

"I remember Art Savage telling [Paulson] that he thought [Paulson] was crazy," Smith said. "Well two years later, he applies to the league and buys in for $30 million and now his franchise is worth seven times that…[During our time in the Northwest] we learned that Portland is very similar to Sacramento. We learned

---

[62] Possibly Section 8, who support the Chicago Fire, as well.

demographically, economically, spiritually, logistically, there were a lot of synergies...we learned, in effect, it's easier to sell tickets in soccer than in baseball because you're selling a game every other weekend versus eight games in a row."

Smith paused and looked up before continuing. "The last thing we learned is we... missed an opportunity," he said with a hint of regret. "We thought [Paulson] was stupid, and at the same time he showed us how much we didn't know."

Following their work in Portland, Smith and Wagoner both departed the River Cats for new projects. The former left professional sports to become the CEO of the startup Clean World Partners; the latter accepted the role of senior vice president for the Sacramento Mountain Lions,[63] an upstart gridiron squad in the United Football League. The UFL abruptly folded in 2012, leading Wagoner to again switch sports and take over the operations for a minor league hockey team in San Francisco.

"The San Francisco Bulls: Act like you got a pair," were the actual name and official slogan for Wagoner's hockey team. It was bizarre branding to say the least since the team didn't play within the city limits of San Francisco, and there's no intuitive link between the city and Bulls.[64]

"It was thoroughly offensive to 75 percent of San Francisco," Wagoner said of the slogan for his ill-fated club in between laughs. "But thankfully there's only 3 percent hockey fans there, so we didn't piss off those people, but everyone else definitely let us know that it wasn't okay."

Wagoner joined the Bulls six months into franchise history and only needed one look at their books to determine they was doomed from the start.[65] He forfeited his title of CEO in December of 2012 while remaining on the payroll of a consultant—he wished to focus more on the idea he formed two years previously during those car rides with Ryan. Before he left the Bulls, Wagoner organized his personal capital and used it to open a bank account for his next sporting adventure: bringing professional soccer back to Sacramento.

## The Worm Returns

When Wagoner originally moved to Sacramento just after the turn of the century, he quickly befriended a pair of Jesuit High School alums in Sean Morrison and Jeremy Field. The duo had lost touch for years after high school until deciding to reconnect after a chance encounter at a local movie theater. Morrison worked in the River Cats front office with Wagoner and, according to Field, invited Wagoner over to his house one day because "he looked like he drank beer."

---

[63] Future actor John David Washington, Denzel's son, suited up for the Mountain Lions during all four of their campaigns.
[64] In fairness to Wagoner and the Bulls, they did play at an arena in Daly City called the "Cow Palace."
[65] The Bulls folded in January of 2014.

"I met Jer through Sean in 2002," Wagoner said during a 2016 interview at Republic headquarters. "We'd always sit outside and smoke cigarettes and drink beer. I might have smoked a little bit more than he did. So we're out there and he's just always kicking a ball. He always had his foot on a ball. I'm like, 'What's the fucking deal with the soccer ball all the time?' He goes, 'I'm a professional soccer player.' I'm like, 'that's the dumbest shit I've ever heard...like seriously, how hard is that?'

"At the time, I guess Jeremy was the best [soccer] player in Sacramento," added Wagoner, who was familiar with Field's time with the Knights. "I [have] made fun of soccer my whole life. [I] came from the Midwest; we didn't have it in high school. I'm from a small farm town in Illinois–this shit didn't exist. What was this thing that's not played on a baseball or football field? And around the late 90s, they started tearing down outfield walls and putting in soccer fields and I worked in baseball, like what? This is communist. This is horseshit."[66]

Wagoner's only experience with soccer prior to moving to Sacramento came after a two-year stint as a pitcher at what is now Midland University[67] in Fremont, Nebraska where he stopped playing after he "finally realized that [he] sucked." After quitting baseball, his friends asked Wagoner to join the school's club soccer team. Wagoner agreed, but only on the condition they would drink beers after the game, and he could wear jersey No. 55 in honor of former Major League Baseball pitcher Orel Hershiser.

"I ended up getting a concussion and breaking my nose less than forty minutes into my soccer career," Wagoner said. "I spent sixteen years of baseball with no injuries and with just forty minutes of soccer, my face will never work correctly again. It takes a few beers to tell the entire story. I'll spare you the gory details, but that was my first and last soccer match."

Still, during the Wagoner-Morrison-Field gatherings, Wagoner constantly threw barbs at Field and the sport Field loved that Wagoner lasted just over half an hour playing. "There were many, many drunken conversations where he'd be kicking a ball and I'm just making fun of him, like this is the dumbest sport I've ever seen," Wagoner said. "He says, 'I'm telling you, man, someday someone's gonna do it and it's gonna work. Why not us?' You fast forward to [Republic director of finance Brett Reitter] and I sitting in the Mountain Lions' front office like, 'Hey man, let's put a business plan together.'

---

[66] According to Wagoner, if someone had told him during his River Cats days that he would eventually co-found a professional soccer team, Wagoner would have called that person an idiot.

[67] When asked about his college experiences, Wagoner listed the following as "fun stories out of that place." Writing in an email, Wagoner said he "broke an eardrum jumping off a bridge after a party in the middle of the night and puked during a baseball team photo the next morning...got a tattoo on a drunken dare...started a really shitty band...about got kicked out of school three times–literally had to go defend [himself] three times in front of the college's adjudication committee...found a snake in my room and watched a cop battle it with a baseball bat...never slept in room again."

"There was actually a group of three or four people that were sitting in a garage for five years drinking beer, making fun of the sport while one guy was kicking balls at our head."

Field, who used to ride his bike over to the Mountain Lions games because his connections provided free beer,[68] was eventually approached by Wagoner after years of Field repeating the same message over and over again.

"We were over at Sean's house drinking Pabst," Field said. "Joe asked, 'Hey, do you think we can start a soccer team? That was literally how it started."

According to Wagoner, Field told him that, "When you get this thing started, people are going to come out of the woodworks telling you that they understand, that they know exactly what to do, that they have their finger on the pulse. My job is to tell you which ones are full of shit and which ones are legit."

Field's words quickly proved prophetic. "When we announced this thing, fucking people came out of everywhere," Wagoner said. "Two people claimed to have started the Seattle Sounders. We're like, 'No, we know [who founded the Sounders], and they're not you.'

"It's not like we're creating the iPhone," he added. "How hard of it is a stretch to say, 'Let's bring soccer to Sacramento?'"

Field also advised Wagoner on strategies to effectively market the team to soccer fans while also navigating the complex politics of youth club soccer. Field called it "uniting the tribes" of the "Big Six" youth clubs in the area: Davis Legacy, Elk Grove Soccer, Placer United, Sacramento United, San Juan Soccer Club, and Union Sacramento. In the 80s and 90s, each club was designated a pool of players it could choose from based on where each youngster lived.[69]

This changed in the early 2000s when NorCal Premier Soccer[70] arrived on the scene and made a series of sweeping changes, including allowing each player to choose the club they preferred. This began a battle between the "Big Six" for the top players in the area, spawning some feelings of bad blood and animosity between the clubs.

Field worried that if the Republic partnered with one youth club, it would alienate the other five. Securing good relations with all six became Sacramento's first step towards success. The second step entailed ensuring the club's finances. The only well-funded professional soccer team in Sacramento's history had been the Knights, who ended up in the hands of a family who, like Wagoner for most of his life, felt that soccer was a waste of time.

"The main thing with the Republic is, with Joe, I'd say, 'You gotta be able to get the money, you gotta find somebody that can get $2 or $3 million dollars that's just okay with losing it if it doesn't work out,'" Field said. "Or at least invest in

---

[68] "I hate American football, it's stupid," Field said in 2015.
[69] Field recalled once registering his grandma's house as his home address on a form so that he could play for a better club.
[70] Disclosure: I work for NorCal Premier Soccer.

marketing and advertising and promoting it over the radio and stuff like that. Getting the money is critical."

So, Wagoner turned to Smith, who may not have had the $2 or $3 million to lose, but definitely had the connections in the community to find someone who might.

"Joe then went on to be the president of the San Francisco Bulls, and oh god, he's acting like he had a pair," Smith said in jest. "He was driving home one night, and he said, 'You know what? What about soccer?'

"I said, 'Have fun!'"

Field: "Let's just say that Warren was a bit reluctant at first. He'd be the first one to tell you that. I think harassment by Joe and Brett eventually broke him down, and so, he just kind of went, 'What the hell? Go ahead, let's try it out.'"

Burnt out at Clean World Partners, Smith quit and moved into the market for something new. While waiting for that next opportunity, Smith threw Wagoner a bone and agreed to serve as a consultant for the upstart soccer bid. At the time Smith made this decision, Wagoner hadn't fully left the Bulls and therefore spent much of his time seventy miles west of Sacramento.

"I lived in a hotel from Monday through Thursday night because I lived in Sacramento and commuted," Wagoner said. "Then I'd work on [what came to be the Republic] from 9:00 to 3:00 in the morning for a year. There was a Denny's next to [the hotel]. I'd spend all night at Denny's because I could stay awake there."

While Smith opened inroads in Sacramento and Wagoner posted up in Denny's, a rival movement popped up just a few miles southeast of California's capital in the suburb of Elk Grove. Backed by a few prominent businessmen, the 170,000-plus strong city full of strip malls hoped to bring a Major League Soccer franchise to town. Wagoner and Field met the Elk Grove group several times at Bonn Lair to work out if it made sense to merge into a single entity.

"We tried to say, 'Hey, is there any way that we could sort of join forces? You know, I think we'd be better together than apart,'" Field recalled. "All we got out of that meeting is that, 'If we're not in Elk Grove, we're not interested.'"

Those meetings came during the same time period in which MLS publicly stated that it hoped to return to Miami with a David Beckham-led expansion franchise. However, the league said that it wouldn't pull the trigger until the former England international and his investment group had secured a downtown stadium deal in South Florida.[71] "MLS," Field laughed, "if they're not going to give David Beckham a stadium on the outskirts of Miami, there's no way they're going to put a fucking MLS team in Elk Grove, which those guys never understood."

With the Elk Grove distraction out of the way, Smith and Wagoner began discussions regarding which league they hoped the future team would play in. Their

---

[71] MLS ended up relaxing its stance slightly and Inter Miami CF debuted in the league in 2020, playing in a temporary venue on the former site of the defunct Miami Fusion 32 miles north of Miami proper in Fort Lauderdale. According to Inter Miami, the downtown stadium will open in 2025.

lack of capital–both had money, but not MLS money–ruled out the United States' top division. That left two options: the rival USL and NASL, which had split apart from each other over philosophical differences in 2009.[72]

"So, I called them both," Wagoner said. "Within 24 hours the USL called back–USL Pro at the time. I called NASL probably ten times and couldn't get a call back at all."

Wagoner placed those calls in February of 2012, ten months before officially departing the Bulls. Each day when he finished with the hockey team, he walked back to Denny's to work on a business plan to present to the USL. Wagoner signed a nondisclosure agreement with his team's future pro league to ascertain the finer details of a typical USL budget. What the league provided them left the pair shocked.

"It was nothing close to what we were looking to do," Wagoner said. "It was a quarter of the employees. It was 10 percent of the revenue. I'm not even trying to bag on [anyone else], but it was a fraction of what we were looking to do. So I'm like, 'Here's what we're looking to do, here's what I know we can do if we get the right people in place,' and they told us we were crazy. I mean, [the USL] told Warren, flat out, 'You're taking too large of a risk. You should never spend this money on the front office, you shouldn't do this.' I remember them telling [Smith], 'this is unheard of.'"

The NASL ignored Sacramento and the USL openly questioned Smith and Wagoner's sanity, but the latter still gladly pocketed the startup club's $250,000[73] expansion fee. Smith, Wagoner, and Reitter, immediately began working day and night on a project that wouldn't be publicly announced until December of 2012, more than ten months in the future. Everything had to be perfect. The name. The colors. The staff.

## Creating an Identity

Ten months later, Smith, Sacramento mayor Kevin Johnson, then-USL commissioner Tim Holt, and select members of the local soccer community gathered on December 3, 2012, for a press conference at Hot Italian Pizza & Panini Bar in Midtown Sacramento. There, a group called "Sacramento Pro Soccer" announced its intention to bring professional soccer back to California's capital. Already jaded by the consistently poor management of the Kings–and the multitude of past failed soccer franchises–the people of the city initially failed to

---

[72] The NASL ownership groups wanted to challenge MLS's certification as the top division of soccer in the United States, while the USL clubs hoped for smaller, but more sustainable, growth. Though the NASL was originally designated by the USSF as the country's second division with the USL as its third, the former imploded after just seven seasons.
[73] According to one Republic staffer who wished to remain anonymous.

show much excitement for a new soccer franchise that was going to be spearheaded by baseball lifers.

Still, from the get-go, the goal for Sacramento Pro Soccer was to eventually secure a spot in MLS, the league that many less-informed locals assumed would soon arrive in at a proposed soccer-specific stadium in Elk Grove. At that moment, MLS coming to Sacramento also didn't seem likely, but if the league ever decided to set up shop in the area, it would certainly choose somewhere within the city limits.

"Our job is to prove to the rest of the world [Sacramento can support an MLS team] and compete with those cities that are trying to lure a Major League Soccer franchise," Smith said at the sparsely attended press conference. Seeing the public's apathetic response to the announcement, the skeleton soccer startup crew realized that to capture people's attention, it needed a strong brand. But before they could brand a team, they had to brand the city.

"I loved Sacramento from the moment I moved here nearly twenty-five years ago," *Sacramento Bee* columnist Marcos Bretón wrote in 2014. "But as an outsider, I noticed the strain of small-minded thinking here. I would tell my friends that no community was perfect, and that Sacramento's issue was that Sacramento didn't realize how great it was."

A 2015 *Sports Illustrated* feature described the Kings' 1980s relocation in less-than-positive terms: "...the Kings had recently fled Kansas City under a downpour of boos for the pasturelands of Sacramento, the NBA equivalent of a witness relocation."

Furthermore, in 2015, *Deadspin* released a piece portraying Kevin Johnson as "an asshole."[74] *Deadspin* wrote that: "After securing hundreds of millions in public funds to pay for a new arena for the Sacramento Kings, [Kevin Johnson is] now the most popular guy in the least thought about city of half a million people in the country."

The national media painted a clear picture of Sacramento, one that showed that people who don't frequent the city can't describe anything about it other than the State Capitol. "We needed to help brand Sacramento, not just brand ourselves," Smith said. "The key thing we learned in our research is that yeah, everyone looks to the Capitol as that iconic thing, but what we learned about people, what they appreciate is the spirit of California started here, is headquartered here.[75]

"So, we started researching flags."

The startup agreed that it had found the perfect moniker for the team that tapped into the demographics and spirit of the city. Quiet for most of the

---

[74] The article's subheader: "Everybody Knows Kevin Johnson is an Asshole, but Nobody's Willing to be the First Person to Say That."

[75] At this moment, Smith paused because Fred Matthes, the former Republic VP of ticket sales and services, walked into New Helvetia, not knowing that several of his colleagues had already posted up with beers at the same location.

conversation in the bar, Republic vice president of communications Erika Bjork finally chimed in.

A tireless worker who sported a razor-sharp wit and the word "fearless" tattooed on her left forearm, Bjork was the confident head of public relations the club felt lucky enough to snatch up from the beginning. Her quick thinking and ability to comprehend the bigger picture gave the club a perfect mouthpiece to communicate the Republic's message to the public. Every moment felt calculated with Bjork, who would preemptively call reporters when bad news broke to get ahead of the story and make those involved available for comment to ensure everything proceeded as transparently as possible.

But Bjork wasn't so serious that she couldn't enjoy a pint and a laugh during the few moments when she could pull herself away from the grueling schedule that came from operating as the Republic's chief point of contact. While her work always put her behind the scenes, perhaps only Smith enjoyed a larger Rolodex of local sporting and business contacts. And though she kept a low-profile during games and events, preferring to let others take the spotlight, it was Bjork who fans, reporters, and players turned to for any issue needing a quick fix during the club's first few seasons.

"Sacramento Citizens is the name that Joe and I were absolutely sold on," Bjork said in the conversation previously dominated by the club's two co-founders. "We were convinced. It just plays right into the democratic nature of the government for the people, by the people. And so does Sacramento."[76]

While still officially called "Sacramento Professional Soccer," the startup began using "Sacramento Citizens" on all its internal documents. The group went as far as picking a color palette, deciding on navy blue, white, and green. After a few weeks, though, Bjork discovered issues with the entire plan.

"Part of my opposition to the Citizen[s] was, I hate to say it, but in the world of the internet and [search engine optimization] and everything else," she said before pausing briefly to consider her next words. "We literally did twenty million tests on things like Twitter handles and Facebook pages and when you Google 'Sacramento Citizens,' it's the hotel."

Overlooking Cesar Chavez Park and resting just behind the California State Capitol building, the four-star Sacramento Citizen Hotel stands out as one of the most recognizable buildings in the tree-laden city. The moderate influence of the structure, which is one of the highest-rated in the area according to multiple aggregators, was enough to convince the trio to drop the "Citizen" name. After a brief flirtation with the "Sacramento Magpies," the group looked elsewhere for its moniker.

---

[76] Smith and Wagoner also had contacts at Manchester City and initially hoped that the Citizens name could help them form a partnership with the EPL side. They were rejected after one phone call and would later discover that City was in the process of purchasing 2015 MLS expansion side New York City FC.

Oddly enough, Bjork, Smith, and Wagoner turned their eyes towards Seattle.

When MLS granted Seattle an expansion franchise, the club known as "Seattle Sounders FC" decided to hold a fan vote in 2008 to pick what the team's name would be at the top division level. "Fans who wanted to vote could choose from three MLS approved (cringe-worthy) names: Seattle Alliance, Seattle Republic, or Seattle FC," wrote Mike Gastineau in *Sounders FC: Authentic Masterpiece*. "But they'd also be given the fourth option of a write-in vote." After counting thousands of votes, it was a landslide victory—more fans had written in the name "Sounders" than had voted for all three of the other options combined.

"We started looking at the name Republic and started doing some research...and learned that it was actually owned by MLS," Smith said. "MLS owned the name 'Republic.' We called the league about it and came to find that it was [a proposed] name of the Seattle franchise. The owners said that [when] they asked the public what they wanted, the public said 'Sounders.' So, MLS walked away from the rights to the name. We scooped it up immediately, even before we knew we were going to choose the name. We had to spend like $5,000 to do it. For us at the time that was a lot of money."

Like the Sounders, Sacramento Professional Soccer organized an online poll to ask fans to suggest names and colors. They ultimately settled on the Republic moniker, which had been conveniently thrown into the pot by future Tower Bridge Battalion member Jacob Escobedo.

There was still work to finish, though: the Republic needed a crest and a slogan. The latter proved simple—an American River College student emailed Sacramento Professional Soccer, instructing Smith, Wagoner, and Bjork to research the city's history. The student pointed to *Urbs Indomita*, Sacramento's official motto, Latin for "Indomitable City." The city adopted the motto in its infancy after Sacramentans responded resiliently to a series of natural disasters that plagued the early part of the city's 20th century history. The locals simply refused to give up.

"There was this spirit back then, and going back to the whole spirit of California, there was something special in Sacramento that no matter what, we'll move forward," Smith said. "For some reason, it was taken off of the seal in the 50s, so we started to learn the words seeking a rallying cry. So, we'll never stand alone, whatever it is."

Wagoner then jumped in to elaborate. "We were tying into the 'Hey, guess what, this is the spirit of us back then,'" he said. "Now they're trying to take our sports teams, they're trying to take the Kings, the housing crisis, boom, boom, boom. We're not going to lay down. We're not going to let this happen."

Added Bjork: "It's ironic considering for so long we've been known as a state worker city. When we did the research, there was a conflict, and we talked about how we position ourselves as the capital in Sacramento because when you live here, you're very apologetic about it. But when you're outside of here, it's very much what you identify with. That goes back to the star in the crest and everything else we felt was really important to acknowledge Sacramento."

With the motto taken care of, Sacramento Professional Soccer commissioned a company to mockup a few sample crests, which the group decided should include a red star. Thus began the process that would result in an instantly iconic badge.[77] All of the market research suggested that Sacramentans strongly identified as Californian, while loving both the city and the state's relatively young, but rich, history. To harken back to these ideas, the club decided to pay homage to the state flag on the crest, and what better way to accomplish that than by using the California Grizzly Bear? Due to copyright concerns, the Republic couldn't use the exact same animal depicted on the state flag, but it could feature something similar.

The startup spent roughly a month trying to figure out how it could draw a bear indistinguishable enough for fans to not be able to pick it apart from the original, but different enough to not invite a lawsuit for copyright infringement. First, it folded down one of the bear's ears—on the flag, both stand aloft. Focus groups quickly noticed the difference, forcing the Republic back to the drawing board.

Closing the bear's mouth, however, seemed to work for the next set of unbiased evaluators. On the California state flag, a bear prowls over a field of green, mouth open, seemingly hunting for its next victim. Behind it, there's a white backdrop featuring a red star in the upper left corner similar to the one Sacramento Professional Soccer hoped to include in its final crest.

Sacramento Republic FC's bear, adorning the bottom third of the crest, appears much more docile with a closed snout. The pair of images resemble each other so closely that Republic management wasn't actually sure which one was theirs and which one the California government owned.

"The bear we have, is it an open mouth bear or a closed-mouth bear?" Wagoner wondered aloud.

All that remained to complete the logo were a few minor tweaks. Most notably, the club moved the giant red star from the top of the crest to the inside of the beige-colored badge. According to Bjork, focus groups felt that the original placement reminded them of Russian military insignia. Now, the group could focus on how to actually introduce all of their creations to the people of Sacramento.

"The specific things that [Bjork] chose to tie our brand to—bicycles, craft brews—none of our ads have a call to action on them," Wagoner said. "I mean, me, coming from baseball...very often you see, 'Buy now! Tickets start at fifteen bucks.' That's just what you do. And she said, 'No, we're going to take a different approach.' The way it was rolled out was more intelligent. It wasn't, 'Hey, monkey, here's a five-dollar ticket, go buy it or do something else.' It was, 'Hey, we're connecting here and if you want to connect further then [come to a game] because our games are a celebration of the whole community, not just a sporting event. It's more of a movement.'"

---

[77] The Sacramento Republic FC crest won the 2015 r/MLS Best Crest Award on the social media website Reddit, despite not being an actual MLS crest at the time.

Unlike when any of Sacramento's previous professional soccer attempts came on board, the new startup had an advantage in an already-established local movement like the one Wagoner described. Founded in Lincoln, Nebraska in 2007, the American Outlaws quickly ballooned to the largest of U.S. Soccer's unofficial supporters' groups, surpassing 100 chapters nationally in 2013. Its Sacramento chapter emerged in 2011 and when Sacramento Professional Soccer announced its USL expansion entry, the local AO setup featured the biggest number of organized fans anywhere in the city who spoke English as their primary language. The group held U.S. watch parties at Alley Katz, a dark, Midtown dive bar that counted PBR tall boys among its most popular drinks.

As soccer still mostly qualified as a foreign sport to Smith and Wagoner, the pair began frequenting Alley Katz to watch U.S. World Cup qualification games. "I remember, we went and had that first meeting at Alley Katz," Smith laughed. "It was like, 'Hey, there are two or three individuals that want to meet about creating a supporters' group.' And God love Joe, one thing he is, is honest. I think the first thing out of his mouth was, 'I know nothing about soccer.'" Wagoner proved so clueless that when AO members asked him who he was considering for the club's technical director, Wagoner queued up a list of IT professionals he knew.

"In American sports we don't...listen to our customers," Smith said. "What we typically do is say, 'I have an idea and I'm going to push it down on you, and you buy it or not.' And also, they've become very, very corporate. NBA, NFL–Major League Baseball less just because of the amount of attendance, the amount of fans.

"What the fans were saying in all of our interviews and all of our focus groups and all of our online [interactions] is listen to your support."

Added VP of merchandise Tim Stallings, whom Sacramento Professional Soccer hired in January of 2013: "You can say that Warren and Joe, maybe they didn't know [soccer], but you know what they did know? They knew enough to listen to people. They didn't understand soccer, but they understood people. So people, when they started to react to the demographic's real desires and the real motivation, then that's when we started to follow that path more."

Sacramento Republic FC had settled on a name, created a meaningful crest, and by listening to the local soccer fans, began building the foundations of a two-way relationship with those who would determine if the club succeeded or failed. All the workings left club leadership feeling confident about its early trajectory. However, there was still one aspect left to work out: a plan for how the Republic would unveil its name, crest, and colors to the Sacramento public. A simple press conference wouldn't suffice–the muted response from the previous December's announcement remained fresh in Smith and Wagoner's minds.

No, Republic brass felt they needed something bigger. If they were going to shoot for the stars, they were going to try to do so in the most extravagant fashion possible. The group's ambitious business plan showed the USL that the Republic wasn't going to operate at the same small scale as past USL expansion sides, so why should it unveil the franchise's identity in a similarly muted fashion? The Republic wanted and needed to make a statement.

So, Wagoner and Smith devised a plan. A plan involving a historic club from one of best leagues in the world, an impossibly famous former Mexican international, and an energy drink no one had ever heard of. Two of those three aspects of the plan wouldn't come to fruition, but in early July of 2013, the Republic made the kind of statement that neither the city nor Major League Soccer could ignore.

The minds that brought local sports fans "Who's in the can?" "Make Kenny G stop," "The man-eating chicken," and "Bitch Bergr" began working to stage the biggest soccer event in Sacramento history.

# FIVE

# SACRAMENTO SOCCER DAY: HOW A COMMUNITY ACCOMPLISHED THE IMPOSSIBLE[78]

"With any luck, this is the week MLS in Sacramento was born."

- Marcos Bretón, *Sacramento Bee*

Ask any U.S. Soccer fan to explain the story of how they fell in love with the sport and they're likely to point to a single World Cup moment that sparked the tinder to ignite the fire for their newfound obsession.

Landon Donovan's stoppage-time goal against Algeria in 2010 secured both knockout round qualification and the hearts of thousands of new supporters. Others might point to the 2002 squad which defied expectations in South Korea en route to a round-of-sixteen victory over rival Mexico. But some recall memories of the tragic and improbable 2-1 win[79] over tournament favorites Colombia at the Rose Bowl in 1994 as the moment they became converts.

---

[78] I recommend pairing this chapter with "Digital Bath" by Deftones.
[79] The first goal of the game was accidently turned into his own net by Colombian defender Andrés Escobar. Fewer than two weeks after the ill-fated strike, hitmen murdered Escobar in his hometown of Medellín in an attack that was rumored to have been provoked by the incident.

The victory, the United States' first in World Cup play since the legendary 1950 upset of England, propelled the Yanks into the tournament's second round for the first time since the inaugural edition in Uruguay sixty-four years earlier. Pandemonium erupted all around the allegedly soccer-hating country that packed the stadiums with record numbers no tournament has bested. The scorer of the winning goal, Earnie Stewart, became the first-ever American soccer player featured on the cover of *Sports Illustrated* after the victory.

By chance, then-*Sacramento Bee* reporter Marcos Bretón found himself in Southern California that fateful day—he'd traveled on assignment to fill in for one of the paper's court reporters. A lifelong soccer fan, Bretón was on his way to the airport to fly north after completing his final day on the temporary crime beat. First, though, he turned his rental car northeast towards Pasadena even though he didn't have tickets to the USA-Colombia match that served as a must-win for both sides.

"I was on my way back to Burbank Airport and I thought, 'I want to make a detour and I'm going to swing by the Rose Bowl. I just want to soak up the atmosphere,'" Bretón said. "I went to three or four games at Stanford Stadium. But I wanted to see what it was like [at the Rose Bowl]. It was an amazing scene. [There were] Colombians everywhere, and they had the Valderrama wigs on."[80]

After his brief sightseeing adventure, the reporter boarded the short, seventy-minute flight home and completely forgot about the actual contest that kicked off midflight. Back in Sacramento, Bretón found some of his co-workers huddled around the TV in *The Bee*'s Midtown offices.

"It's not like now where the whole newsroom would be fixated on it," Bretón said. "Back then, it was just a few people who were watching the game, and I joined them. And then when the U.S. won this game—this huge upset, you could argue at that point, the most important moment up to that point in American soccer—a couple of us [said], 'Well, this is a front-page story, right?'

"Our editors at the time, [who were] old-school newspaper editors, old white dudes from the city [said], 'No fucking way,'" Bretón recalled. "So there's like a mini-rebellion, led by me, a mini-rebellion in the newsroom...I got pretty salty, and I had people here screaming at me in the newsroom, saying 'You don't know what the fuck you're talking about,'"

Eventually the old school and the new reached a compromise. The editors agreed to run a photo of American defender Alexi Lalas on the cover, while burying the gamer deep in the inside pages of the publication.[81] "You think about that now, it's so preposterous, and so reflective of what the attitude was," Bretón said. "And understand, the people who I'm talking about, the leaders of *The Bee*, I love those

---

[80] The captain of the Colombian National Team, and arguably its best player, Carlos Valderrama was the most internationally recognized Colombian player of the time thanks to his distinct blond afro and crisp passing. He also somehow played the sport without ever really running.

[81] The bulk of the story, in which Stewart's name was misspelled, appeared on D8, the forty-fifth of seventy-nine pages.

people, I respect those people. They just reflected an attitude about soccer that was so pervasive for so long and still lingered."

## Countering Apathy with Enthusiasm

Eighteen years later Warren Smith and Joe Wagoner announced the formation of Sacramento Professional Soccer, the city's first pro soccer team in over a decade. But while optimistic soccer fans showed some interest to start, the mainstream legacy media—including *The Bee*—refused to spend much time covering the fledgling club. The December 2012 press conference announcing the team hardly registered among the establishment news sources.

The dearth of local media coverage from that moment on seemed to suggest that the current old school media bosses were betting on the newest soccer iteration following in the footsteps of the Knights, Scorpions, and Geckos. Sans a regular beat reporter covering the club, nor devoted columnists writing about the story, nor nightly news segments featuring the team, there were few ways for Sacramento soccer fans to stay in tune with the yet-to-be-named side.

These aspects coalesced to put Sacramento Professional Soccer behind the eightball, facing something of a Catch-22 situation. Without consistent coverage in the media, it proved difficult for the fans to keep track of the club's latest developments. Without documented fan support or any product samples, prospective investors felt hesitant to fork over their valuable dollars to support a soccer team in a city where every other soccer team previously failed. Without a stable incoming cash flow, Sacramento Professional Soccer couldn't spend as much money as it would like on new hires and marketing campaigns. And without additional employees to share the work burden or the finances to advertise, the media was less likely to pay attention.

And so on.[82]

Simply, Sacramento Professional Soccer possessed few options to bring in capital for the USL product that didn't yet exist, much less one whose goal was to catch Major League Soccer's eye.

"There wasn't the immediate interest that we thought there was going to be," Wagoner said. "We started talking to potential sponsors, and it was, 'Ah, we'll wait to see how it goes the first year.' We started talking to potential season ticket people...it was really skeptical...if everyone in this town is going to wait to see what happens in the first game, we're dead in the water because we've got no season-ticket holders, we've got no sponsors, we've got no media, we've got nothing, and then if that eats shit, we're done.

---

[82] Shout out to Kurt Vonnegut.

"So, we had to do something massive now and say, 'We're here, and it's serious.'"

The Sacramento Professional Soccer office now stood five strong in leading the nascent effort: president and co-founder Warren Smith, vice president and co-founder Joe Wagoner, director of finance Brett Reitter, the newly hired camps and clinics manager Kenny Cooper, and vice president of merchandise Tim Stallings.

Together, they brainstormed novel ideas, no matter how far fetched,[83] in an attempt to drum up much-needed support. The "five guys in shorts," as Stallings called the group, spitballed on how to bring fans on board and secure new funding. "Nobody wants to be the first person to invest in a company," Stallings said. "They want to see who else has gone in ahead of them to give them some confidence that it's the first real deal and somebody else has done their due diligence."

Smith and Stallings were tasked with securing those initial investments, but by February of 2013, two months after the original press conference, they had yet to convince anyone to open their wallets. Sacramento Professional Soccer knew it had a solid, well-designed product ready to unveil to a city starved for professional sports successes. The startup needed to *show* the investors and the public it shared little in common with its predecessors other than the city or sport.

The "five guys in shorts" scrambled to construct a strategy to unveil the brand they smashed out of the park in creating. To win over the public, the startup had to think big–it needed to create something that no one could ignore. The first idea, to host another press conference, was quickly thrown out the window.

Instead, the club dreamed of hosting a massive event that would demonstrate the passion of Sacramento's sporting fanbase and show wealthy financiers locals would spend their hard-earned cash on the Republic. The goal wasn't to draw a few hundred people and *maybe* earn a spot on the same inside pages of *The Bee* the USA-Colombia gamer had graced two decades previously.

"This has to be huge, like 10,000 people," Wagoner said. "Well, where the hell do you have that? A stadium. Well shit, as long as you're there, you might as well have a game." And thus birthed the idea for Sacramento Soccer Day.

Thirteen months remained before the new club was scheduled to contest its inaugural match in 2014, and there was still no sign of tangible progress in bringing in outside investors or building a fanbase. "From the time when we launched to the time of Sac Soccer Day, there were multiple meetings, including some very critical people who are now part of the organization, [who said], 'We'll believe it when we see it,'" said future Republic vice president of communications Erika Bjork. "[Sacramento fans] wanted it so bad, but they had also been let down so much in the past by people who had said they were going to bring an MLS team or wanted to start professional sports, or even to some degree, the Knights."

To headline their game–and to hopefully help draw in a number of fans large enough to earn significant media attention–the skeleton crew reached for the stars.

---

[83] Except for "Who's in the Can?"

The goal: entice the first-ever English Premier League side to play a match in Sacramento.

Sacramento Professional Soccer first entered negotiations with Swansea City, but those quickly fell through. According to Wagoner, they began talks with Everton next, but the Liverpool-based club increased its appearance fee demands from $190,000 to $450,000. Eventually Norwich City, a provincial club nearly thirty years removed from lifting its last major trophy, signed on to play a friendly at Raley Field in West Sacramento.

"Norwich City is not going to sell out Stanford Stadium," Bretón said. "But Raley Field, yeah that works. It's sort of a lesser team in the EPL, but still."

Norwich City would likely appear familiar in the eyes of the local English-speaking soccer fans, but the Republic brain trust agreed that it would likely prove prudent to engage more Spanish speakers by finding a Mexican club to serve as Norwich's opponents on the day. The startup possessed far fewer contacts down south and initially struggled to find a suitable team, until it finally convinced the little-known Dorados de Sinaloa to take part. If Norwich qualified as a "lesser team" in the crowded English soccer landscape, *Los Dorados* could be described as a complete afterthought in Mexico.

The club had yet to celebrate its tenth anniversary, and its dearth of history was consistent with the size of its fan base, or lack thereof. Furthermore, the Sinaloa side rotted in the anonymous obscurity of Ascenso MX, then Mexico's second division.

But Dorados de Sinaloa came with a quirk that guaranteed to attract hundreds, if not thousands, of curious soccer fans: in late 2011 it signed aging Mexican legend Cuauhtémoc Blanco. Blanco had served as a thorn in the side of American soccer fans for nearly two decades but remained a legend to the massive stateside *El Tri* fanbase. Gamesmanship comes to mind when one thinks about Blanco, who enraged opposing defenders, fans, and coaches as much as he dazzled. His controversial personality[84] contained both the guile to crumple to the ground at any sign of contact and the audacity to pass the ball using his butt in competitive matches.

Supporters not fortunate enough to wear the same colors as Blanco resorted to ridiculing his virtually nonexistent neck, rather than admit that no one on their team was worthy of sharing the pitch with the uneducated genius of a player. The

---

[84] A brief and incomplete list of Blanco's transgressions:
  - While playing for Real Valladolid in Spain, he punched a journalist who traveled from Mexico to interview him.
  - The United States Soccer Federation banned Blanco for two years from U.S. Open Cup play after the then-Chicago Fire attacker punched a player on the field and then tried to headbutt the D.C. United employee who attempted to usher him off the field.
  - After he retired, he became a politician where he has since been photographed alongside drug cartel bosses and been accused of bribery, money laundering, and orchestrating a murder.

polarizing attacking midfielder was just the type of star power who could sell tickets, even though he'd just celebrated his fortieth birthday while under contract for a club no one had ever heard of.

"There have been other instances where there were exhibition games of Mexican teams at Raley Field that get no coverage in the English media, and it doesn't matter," Bretón said. "16,000 people cram that place. It was a horrible place to watch a soccer game, just fucking horrible, but people didn't care.

"I [would park] at the Downtown Plaza and walked across the bridge and it was just like the Tower Bridge was a parking lot full of Mexican people coming to watch the game."

In practice, the plan appeared perfect–Blanco's presence would overcome the lack of notoriety that Sinaloa brought to the table and engage the local Latinx population, while the prestige carried by an EPL club would draw in the early Saturday morning bar-crawlers.

"This game will give Sacramento soccer fans the opportunity to see two distinct styles of football–the short passing, inventive Latino style against a more direct approach from the English Premier League," future Republic technical director and director of football Graham Smith said in a press release advertising the match. Positioned well above Smith's quote in the statement were the career accomplishments of Blanco, as if any of the serious soccer fans in the Western Hemisphere could possibly be unaware of them. Even if Norwich played in the EPL, Blanco served as the event's headliner.

A second friendly, the undercard, was added to the schedule ahead of the Norwich-Dorados match to provide further community engagement. In it, a team of Sacramento area all-stars would face off against the San Jose Earthquakes' Premier Development team. Between the two contests, Sacramento Professional Soccer planned to publicly unveil the Republic brand. The second that happened, the club shop would officially open for business.

# Filling Raley

With the plan set in stone, it was time to start moving tickets, and for that, two of the "five guys in shorts" couldn't help. Smith served as the majority owner of the team and its public face, requiring him to constantly chase after potential investors through an endless gauntlet of meetings with skeptical parties. Tim Stallings, who met Smith while coaching Little League against his fellow Land Park resident, took up the position as Smith's right-hand man during the process.

Stallings also lacked experience within the beautiful game but had at least served as the president of his son's youth soccer club for a time. His low-key temperament provided Smith with the methodical approach[85] that the club needed to compliment Wagoner's quirkiness. Stallings, only equaled in physical stature at the club by Smith, retained the rail-thin physique of his endurance-athlete days growing up in Colorado. His time as an engineer taught him to think in efficient terms, where before he took over the Republic merchandising department, he was tasked with consolidating documents for potential investors to eliminate unnecessary obstacles between the two parties.

While Stallings, with his familiar face, gray soul patch, and black-rimmed glasses proved a great deputy to Smith, his significant workload left just three Sacramento Professional Soccer employees to sell out the entire stadium. And only Wagoner approached the daunting task with experience in sales. Every day, Wagoner, Cooper, and Reitter arrived in the unfurnished Republic office by 8:00 a.m. to work nonstop until finally calling it a day well past 2:00 a.m. some eighteen hours later. The trio hoped the grueling shifts in these barren headquarters would help counterbalance their collective lack of manpower. The only decorations on the otherwise-empty office walls were the movie poster-sized sticky notes, which listed the group's various ideas and goals. Every day, the three would periodically scramble over to the walls to cross off an accomplishment or scribble down something new to strive for, adding to what felt like an endless list of tasks.

"There were a lot of late nights," Cooper said. "Joe kept on saying, 'Sleep is a great eraser of excitement.'"

As with most other early era Republic employees, Cooper didn't receive a paycheck for any of these taxing days leading up to the brand launch. Instead, the club compensated him with equity as rewards for his Herculean efforts. Clean-cut and soft-spoken, but featuring a go-getter attitude, Cooper would later be found on game days sporting bags under his eyes, still diligently working on project after project right up until kickoff. Once the Sacramento games began, he would finally be able to enjoy two of his very limited hours of free time during the week.

Like most of his coworkers, Cooper grew up locally and attended Jesuit High School, a Northern California soccer powerhouse. After school, he broke into the business world with Smith's previous venture, Clean World Partners, an L.L.C. that specialized in innovating advanced, high-solids anaerobic digestion technology. A 2012 trip to Spain only reaffirmed Cooper's love of soccer and drove him to send an email to Smith. In that email, Cooper explained that he thought professional soccer was viable in Sacramento. Smith replied that he, and a guy named Joe Wagoner, had already begun working on exactly that, and set up an introductory meeting between Wagoner and Cooper.

Always one to make a good first impression, Cooper donned his nicest suit, thinking that it might be his only chance to break into the grassroots stage of a

---

[85] During an interview, Stallings positively compared the excitement of watching soccer to the excitement of watching chess—he considered both riveting.

movement that had the chance to change the city's sporting landscape. Of course, Wagoner being Wagoner, meant the meeting would take place at Zebra Club.

"I met Joe at Zebra Club, it was probably like one in the afternoon," Cooper said. "I came in a suit, thinking this is the interview to get on board. He's in his Illinois shirt, Cardinals hat, with jean shorts on, just on his computer in the corner with two or three beers already done. I'm like, 'Wow, I'm way overdressed for this occasion.'"

The pair, along with Reitter, the club's then twenty-four-year-old Director of Finance,[86] were tasked with climbing Everest. The goal: sell out 14,014-seat Raley Field in under five months without a real advertising budget or a surplus of man hours.

"Joe's such a likable guy, it was pretty much like whatever he said, he made it sound like you could do it," Cooper said during a 2015 interview at Republic HQ. "You know, climbing Everest, just like, 'Yeah, I could do that.' I fell on a lot of his experience too because he's been there and done this. I'm sure he's tackled harder things before."

Sitting next to Cooper, the shy and quiet Reitter responded in an incredulous tone, raising both of his eyebrows to the ceiling. "Selling 17,000 tickets[87] with five people?" Reitter said. "I don't think so."

One month before the big game, reinforcements arrived in the form of Julia Jones, a tall, blond, outgoing twenty-something with no professional sports experience. Sacramento Professional Soccer hired her away from a job waitressing tables, recognizing her easy-going personality and ability to make connections as a potential asset for the final push.[88] Regardless of the future titles Wagoner, Cooper, Reitter, and Jones would hold, their collective priority leading up to Sacramento Soccer Day was to engage the community and sell as many tickets as possible.

"I thought I was just going to be answering phones," Jones said.

Instead, the group tasked her with helping secure corporate sponsors. Cooper assigned Jones her workspace, an office that would have been empty if it weren't for two folding chairs. She began her new job at Sacramento Professional Soccer by using her legs as a makeshift desk while furiously typing away on her laptop. "I ended up just sitting in this dark little room sending off emails," she said.

Reitter chimed in to elaborate on the challenges the startup dealt with during the days leading up to the event. "It's easy to think of the idea to do [Sacramento Soccer Day] and once you announce you're doing it, then you look around the room with five people and you go, 'How the hell are we gonna do this?'" Reitter

---

[86] Two years later, Bjork would refer to Reitter as the "oldest 26-year-old you'll ever meet."

[87] The official attendance for the match was listed as 14,014, but the Republic wasn't sure of the exact figure as it sold an unconfirmed number of tickets in Raley Field's standing-room only sections. Staffers involved with organizing the event would interchangeably refer to the figure as anything between 12,000 and 17,000.

[88] Jones would later transition into the role of the customer service & season ticket holder relations manager before moving on to club partner UC Davis Children's Hospital in early 2016.

said. "We really needed help from the community. We could come up with great ideas all day, but thankfully Joe was the idea man and he was able to come up with a great sales plan. Kenny was killing it on the grassroots, and Julia was going out in the community, really getting help out there."

Whatever it was, Sacramento Professional Soccer showed up–the budding entity didn't consider any event too small to be worth its while. Whether it involved mingling with fans at American Outlaws watch parties, talking to local youth clubs, or handing out flyers at Sports Authority on the weekends, Sacramento Professional Soccer was there. The crew *needed* to appear omnipresent in the Sacramento community despite operating with a staff so small that it couldn't legally play in a soccer game.[89]

Slowly, those community members began to take notice–local businesses eventually started purchasing corporate sponsorships, finally infusing the club with much-needed capital.

The first partner to sign on was Mikuni, a popular sushi chain in Northern California. "That was about all we ate besides Taco Bell," Reitter half-joked. Then came bigger corporations, culminating with UC Davis Children's Hospital, which agreed to sponsor Sacramento Soccer Day before eventually striking a deal with the Republic as the club's first-ever jersey sponsor. UC Davis gave Sacramento Professional Soccer instant credibility in the community, something it almost forfeited in a money grab featuring an obscure energy drink that shared its name with a trendy, bald pop singer from Miami.

"Pitbull was this energy drink," Wagoner said while trying to keep a straight face before a Republic game in 2015. "It's like the worst energy drink in the world. And we were just taking anybody's money. If UC Davis Children's Hospital hadn't bought in at the last minute, it would have been very hard to pull off the event at all because they were able to get on board and write a check right away. That's the main one. I mean, Pitbull? We looked even more amateur now at this event when Pitbull's the name of your deal. Hey, it's the biggest thing ever brought to you by Pitbull! You couldn't even buy the drink in Sacramento, but whatever."[90]

Added Stallings: "[Pitbull's] motivation seemed to be more tied into getting a smoking deal on naming the [future] arena or kit sponsorship or something like that. I don't really think they understood the scale of what that would cost, and also the type of partner we would be looking for. But yeah, they were kind of funny guys, Pitbull."

---

[89] To avoid incurring a forfeit, FIFA laws require seven players.
[90] According to Wagoner, the drink was not, in fact, available for purchase anywhere in the Sacramento area at the time of Sacramento Soccer Day.

# The List

Eight days before the game, Wagoner emailed his exhausted employees, urging them to pull through the final week of the lead up to the event that would make or break Sacramento Professional Soccer. Naturally, that message came in the form of a vintage Wagoner essay–he's not known for his brevity. He wrote:

> [I]t is the bottom of the ninth, the final minute, sudden death overtime, fourth and goal, the final round, the last leg...we are going to penalty kicks! This is crunch time and it ain't for the faint of heart. It's our time to turn our internal dials to eleven and deliver. In all seriousness, this is where we see how good we are...how solid is our foundation? Will we stand solid like a brick house or collapse like a house of cards? Let me answer that question...we are a brick house and we will not fall. There have been many curves thrown our way the last few weeks and this has not been easy. Know this...we will overcome and continue to press on successfully...this movement's time has come and our spirit cannot be subdued...URBS INDOMITA!
>
> I've attached a final to-do list[91] that will take us through the next eight days. DO NOT BE INTIMIDATED BY THIS LIST! WE CAN DO THIS. WE WILL DO THIS.
>
> "In order to get this done, here are some tips for you newcomers to the industry...
>
> 1.    Please don't make any plans for the next eight days. You are on call 24/7. That means past 7pm, before 8am. Saturday and Sunday, etc...we need to live, eat, and breath[e] this until midnight on 7/18.[92] It will take every waking minute you have to get everything done. Your evenings now belong to this effort.
>
> 2.    Do not leave anything until tomorrow. Get everything done you can possibly get done before you pass out for the day. Tomorrow will present its own set of challenges that divert you from your to-do list, so get it done today.
>
> 3.    Plan your day the night before. When you come in each morning, you should have a clear plan of the first five things to get done before the day starts to get hectic.
>
> 4.    Please stay calm. This is important. Tempers are going to fly and emotions are going to run high. The more pissed somebody gets, offset their

---

[91] That to-do list featured 36 different points, each with sub sections. It was five pages long in a Microsoft Word document.
[92] The date of Sacramento Soccer Day.

*'pissedness' by getting really calm and speaking respectfully and clearly communicating. If somebody starts to blow, calm down the conversation with your tone and your mannerisms. Deep breaths...in through the nose and out through the mouth.*

*5.    Stay hydrated...drink lots of water.*

*6.    Avoid Chinese food.*

*7.    Say goodbye to social media for eight days (unless you're promoting the game).*

*8.    Become incredibly resourceful. Find the answer. You are smart. If you were not, you'd be gone now or wouldn't be on this to-do list. You are a trusted and incredibly valuable member of this team. Will you make wrong decisions? Yes. However, I promise you I won't get pissed as long as you make the smartest decision you could based on the best information available. At this point, a bad decision is better than no decision 75% of the time. Batting .750 gets you into the Hall of Fame.*

*9.    Own your to-do list. Kick the shit out of your list! These are the tasks you've been trusted with because we know you can do them well. There is no time for micro-management, so it is up to you at this point. I'm always here to answer questions, assist where needed or take a bullet for you, but your list is on you until that point comes. Make hourly progress. Nothing creates momentum like momentum. Act fast, smart and take it personally.*

*10.    Don't let Kenny breathe on you.*

*11.    After saying all this...it is very important to know it's OK to raise your hand if you know something is not going to get done or is screwed up. It's infinitely better to know something is off BEFORE the event as opposed to when we have 12,000 people in the stadium.*

*12.    Support each other. We are a team. We need to have each other's backs. It's cliché, but we're honestly only as good as our weakest link. This is magnified 10X in a live setting.*

*13.    LAST ONE...get ready to run one hell of an event. There are few things as gratifying as creating something from nothing and convincing 12,000 people [to] pay their hard earned money to come see what it is all about...On July 18th...somewhere around 8:00pm...find a corner to take a moment to stare at the crowd...take it all in...it is pretty amazing. I do it during the National Anthem each opening or inaugural game...in this case we'll have 35 minutes worth of anthems,*[93] *so you'll have more than enough opportunity.*

*Sorry for the long list, but I promise it will prove helpful if this is your first professional sports event...GO TEAM!!!*

## An Assist from the Club They Tried to Fold

The big day approached quickly, but momentum continued to build within the grassroots organization. Three days after Wagoner's email, Smith took a group of potential investors to Portland to see his old friend Merritt Paulson about setting up a possible affiliation with the Portland Timbers, and to take in a game while they were at it. Facing the defending MLS Cup champion L.A. Galaxy, the Timbers trailed after an early Marcelo Sarvas strike before tying the game in the twenty-seventh minute via Jamaican international Ryan Johnson.

As the full ninety minutes passed and only stoppage time remained, the game appeared headed for a draw with Smith and the throng of investors watching from a Providence Park suite. The home side procured one last chance, as fan-favorite Diego Valeri whipped a corner kick into the box right in front of the famed Timbers Army in the ninety-fourth minute of the match. The out-swinging ball somehow found the head of defender Andrew Jean-Baptiste, who rifled it into the back of the net past decrepit Galaxy goalkeeper Carlo Cudicini.

Jean-Baptiste ripped off his shirt in celebration, running to the corner and exulting in front of the sellout crowd of 20,674 he sent into full party mode. That goal, and the noise that erupted from the crowd, couldn't have come at a better time for Smith and his entourage, who stood stunned in the rafters of the aging stadium. Originally not paying much attention to the game, the group eyed the endless wave of green and gold and began to envision a similar future in Sacramento.

"The place just erupts, I mean, for ten minutes straight, just hooting and hollering," Smith recalled. "The game had ended in that ten-minute period. And I looked across the room and not one person was talking, everyone's jaws were just [wide open]. They were finally getting it; they were finally seeing what was possible; they were finally understanding it. The next thing you know, within two weeks, three weeks, we had all the investment locked up, and we're off to the races to start hiring people."

---

[93] The PA system played the American, Mexican, and English national anthems before the game.

# Snags

Newton's Third Law of Motion states: "For every action, there is an equal and opposite reaction." And before Sacramento Professional Soccer could begin hiring people–before Sacramento Soccer Day–that opposite reaction reared its ugly head as a variety of different problems popped up in seemingly every facet of the operation.

First, Dorados de Sinaloa decided against renewing Cuauhtémoc Blanco's contract in June, leaving the Mexican legend to sign with Lobos de La BUAP elsewhere in the country. This ruled Blanco out of Sacramento Soccer Day, an event in which his likeness dominated much of the marketing.

"Blanco was supposed to be the draw," Wagoner said. "If you bring up his name in our office, everyone will start laughing hysterically because he was on the team, and then he was going to come to a press conference, and then he got sold, but then he [still] wanted to come."

Then there was the hiccup featuring the other side of the matchup in Norwich City. "We tried to do a press conference," Wagoner said. "But it was hosted by someone who didn't understand soccer. [Norwich] had a pretty prestigious coach at that point who was like, 'What the fuck are we doing here?'"

If the breaks trended downwards, they continued their trajectory the night before the match when Sacramento Professional Soccer discovered what happened to the 500 tickets they had allocated to be sold via consignment. According to Wagoner, 498 of those tickets were returned to the club. To compound their troubles, the startup realized at the last moment that Raley Field didn't have any soccer goals on hand.

"We never really thought about goals," Wagoner said. "I mean, we had, but it was kind of like a last minute, like, 'Doesn't Raley Field have goals?'"

Wagoner dispatched Cooper and Reitter to grab goals from Sacramento State University, over eight miles away. The exhausted pair rigged the goals up in a makeshift manner to the bed of a pickup truck and drove them back to the ballpark, an issue complicated by Sacramento's local flora. But before they dealt with that, obtaining a pickup truck proved an issue on its own, as none of the skeleton crew owned one, forcing Sacramento Professional Soccer to rent one.

"We had to rent it from Volvo Rentals, recently changed to Blue Line rentals," Wagoner said. "The rental place was located halfway to Rancho Murieta. It was probably ten miles outside of town...it felt like halfway to Nevada at that point in time."

# The City of Trees: An Aside

The first recorded instance referring to Sacramento as the "City of Trees" came in 1855, seven years after gold was discovered at nearby Sutter's Mill, and five years after the city's incorporation into the new state of California. The dream of unfathomable wealth brought settlers to the vast swath of land freshly won during the Mexican-American War. Manifest Destiny was well underway, and pioneers began arriving in the fertile grounds of Northern California where the Sacramento and American Rivers converged. What Sacramento lacked in size–its population hovered just above 10,000 at the outbreak of the Civil War–it made up for in foresight.

The long and hot summers drove early settlers to plant hundreds of trees to provide a respite during the many months when temperatures regularly approached triple digits. The first hints of the brutal heat often came as early as March and lingered well past October. To battle the elements, the citizens of California's newly declared capital terraformed Sacramento's landscape, planting enough saplings to ensure the city ranked among the highest in trees per capita worldwide.

The decisions made by the city's first American inhabitants continue to benefit Sacramento to this day as temperatures in the city proper typically hover 10 degrees below that of the region's less-forested areas. It's during these moments that locals, hoping to welcome in an early winter with plenty of rain, thank the city's founders for at least ensuring that downtown stays cool into the hot fall months.

The night before Sacramento Soccer Day, though, a pair of locals in Cooper and Reitter cursed the city's excellent foresight as they prepared to transport the goals from Sacramento's eastern boundary all the way across the river that marks its western border. The pair secured the 8-foot-by-24-foot metal frames to the back of the truck using rudimentary knots and set off through the forested streets.

"I tore down about every tree on 8th Street," Reitter said. "But I don't know if we want to get into that. I was too scared to take [the goals] on the freeway because they were sticking out of the truck, about ten feet above the truck."

Added Cooper in between laughs: "It could have been a ten-minute drive down the freeway. We didn't even have caution tape or the flag that you have to put on a Christmas tree to say that you can have it on the roof of your truck. We took a route that took forty-five, fifty minutes to get there.

"No trees fell."

# More Troubleshooting

With the goals safely delivered to Raley Field on the eve of the event, it was time to rehearse the brand unveiling. The six full-time employees, future head coach

Preki, and various other consultants began practicing for the big moment that would take place fewer than twenty-four hours later. The plan involved covering the Republic logo on the Raley Field jumbotron with a banner during the first game. Then gameday staff would slip it off during the intermission while members of what would become the Tower Bridge Battalion marched onto the field sporting a massive Republic tifo[94] they'd painted. Preki would then join in to pump up the crowd with a few words before Smith delivered a prepared speech.

"The funny thing is we had a dry run of the brand unveil the night before, and it was horrible," Wagoner said. "Preki didn't want to talk, he [said], 'I shouldn't be on a microphone.' Warren couldn't get his script down. We couldn't make the fucking banner drop." The banner would later prove easy to drop, maybe too easy, but first Sacramento Professional Soccer needed to finish the rehearsal.

"The biggest thing I remember about Preki was, we had written him a couple of talking points, real simple, real clean," Bjork recalled. "It was the first time we had worked with Preki on a major level. I remember...he said, 'No, no. I'm just going to speak from the heart,' which when you've never heard someone publicly speak before and they're going to do it in front of 14,000 people, you seem a little nervous. Especially when we're unveiling the brand."

Added Jones: "I think I was crying and zip tying things at the same time."

Eventually, despite the setbacks and unfinished work, everyone returned home well past midnight to squeeze in what little sleep they could manage before the big day. Strong walk-up sales pulled the event across the line and into sellout status, causing even the local media to take notice. The strongest presence in any medium came via broadcast, where several reporters delivered live pieces from Raley Field interspersed with aerial shots from a helicopter.

"It started very much with wow, we'd be happy with...I don't even remember what it was back then, but it was probably under 10,000 [tickets]...to the point of like, we were a little worried about it," Bjork said "And we literally ran out of tickets. We had no seats anywhere. We were making up seats and tickets on the way. Up until that point, that was the most people that ever attended a sporting event at Raley Field."

Midway through the Sacramento all-stars versus Earthquakes PDL undercard, yet another unexpected issue left club officials scrambling. In a match that would finish in a 3-3 draw with future Republic goalkeeper Dominik Jakubek[95] between the pipes for the locals, rising winds over the Sacramento waterfront began impeding the quality of play. Also compromised: the makeshift fastenings that held up the sheet obstructing the Republic's still-secret crest and name. Frequent gusts began challenging the decoration's integrity and the word "Sacramento" appeared

---

[94] As defined by the *Oxford Dictionary*, tifo is "(especially at soccer games) a choreographed display in which fans in a sports stadium raise a large banner together or simultaneously hold up signs that together form a large image."

[95] Despite being a well-known player from the area, the game recap on the Republic website spelled Jakubek's name incorrectly.

at the top of the club's logo in what the Sacramento NBC affiliate referred to as a "sneak preview." Or as Stillings put it: "She dropped her dress a little before dinner was over."

"I was in the elevator at the time," Jones said. "I got a text message from a partner saying, 'Your brand's being unveiled without the announcement.' And there was just so much emphasis put on [the announcement], so I kind of felt like the world was closing in, but it worked out great, people were like, 'Wait a minute, that's it!' You're like, 'No, there's an announcement that goes with it!' But it worked out okay. At the time I thought my life was over."

It was another setback that proved that Sacramento Professional Soccer couldn't possibly plan for every variable. But it also proved that the group that was soon to be announced as Sacramento Republic FC could successfully respond to any unforeseen variables. "I loved that that happened, I totally loved it," Stallings said. "It's who we are. We make mistakes. We fix them. We apologize and then people still love us because we're honest about our mistakes."

Added Reitter: "I think that reference to the duck, where everything looks calm above the water, but the feet are going crazy underneath, that was us. To the fans, everything looked like it was going off without a hitch, but we were pulling out our hair and going crazy behind the scenes. To them it was perfect. It looked like it was planned when the sign came down. No one knew."

With the first game in the books, the moment had finally arrived, and Preki gathered with the supporters carrying the tifo to communicate his desires for the group during his speech. "Preki, with his Balkan accent, was like, 'Hey, I'm going to run out guys, and you guys just follow us," the Creek Bear[96] said. "And we're like, 'Yo, Preki, we have this really heavy tifo here, just take it easy on us.' And he's like, 'Oh yeah, I'll take it easy on you.'"

"Preki fucking sprints out there as fast as he can go," the Creek Bear added. "We're just doing everything we can to keep up. It took me two or three minutes to catch my breath while he was doing his talk, but that's Preki I guess."

Meanwhile, a video titled "The Chant" played on Raley Field's gargantuan video board. With a six-figure budget that the Republic startup really couldn't afford, "The Chant" took fans through citizens playing the sport of soccer around some of the city's most recognizable landmarks such as the Tower Bridge and the State Capitol. The short film, which also featured Jakubek heading the ball through the net of a basketball hoop, culminated when former Sacramento Knight Antonio Sutton headed a corner kick into the back of the net at Hughes Stadium for a fictitious future Republic side. All the action came to the tune of the lyrics from

---

[96] The Creek Bear is a fan who, before moving to the East Coast, dressed up in the Workaholics bear suit for every game in homage to the California Grizzly Bear. He served as the decidedly unofficial mascot of the Republic, and official spirit animal representative of the Battalion. He asked that his real name not be used in the book.

the first-ever song that the Tower Bridge Battalion penned, "Glory, Glory Sacramento," written by member Chandler Cooper.

# Creating "The Chant"

The two-minute film[97] would go on to earn wide critical praise as one of Sacramento Soccer Day's standout memories, but according to those close to the project, it almost never materialized. Producer, director, and part-owner of Franklin Pictures, Rusty Prevatt, explained the story two years after the event over a Chocolate Hazelnut Porter from the local Heretic Brewing Co.

The stocky Prevatt sported a fashionable "faux-hawk" type haircut with the typical millennial look of designer jeans, a gray T-shirt, Converses, and a 5-o'clock shadow. He sat on one of the Bavarian style wooden bench seats at the Federalist, a decidedly hipster bar built from a repurposed shipping container. Behind Prevatt stood an artificial turf bocce ball court with the rules to the sport written on the wall inside a silhouette of California. Lights were strung down from every odd or end of the ceiling to give the place a trendy look that was reflected by its clientele. All beer at the Federalist was served in mason jars while, as was the norm in the booming pub business, employees took orders on iPads.

Prevatt spoke slowly and steadily in long, eloquent chunks, putting together extended thoughts in the same way he imagined the large budget films he's produced. Unlike most of the Republic front office members he hung out with, his vocabulary featured few, if any, four-letter words. Instead, he'd throw in a "friggin'" every couple of sentences rather than risk offending the passerby in the surprisingly spacious establishment.

"I found this video that Nike made, I think it was right after the 2010 World Cup," Prevatt said in between sips of his 22 oz. bottle. "It's probably my favorite sports marketing video ever created. It's longform, first of all, so it's not like a thirty-second video or whatever, and that's not what they were looking for necessarily, as far as the reveal. They were looking for something longer that tells a story. But this piece just inspired me. It was soccer-related because it was right after the World Cup. We kind of marinated on it and found some other things and put together a package and basically pitched the idea to Joe and Warren."

During the pitch, Wagoner and Smith interrupted Prevatt to ask an important question. The idea sounded great, they told him, but how much would it cost? According to Prevatt, accurately budgeting short films can be notoriously difficult and so he and his company turned the tables on Sacramento Professional Soccer, asking the upstart company what it could afford. If Franklin Pictures had a ballpark

---

[97] The video is still live on Sacramento Republic FC's YouTube channel.

estimate, it could work around most constraints. The Republic co-founders tried to explain to Prevatt that they couldn't really afford any major expenses.

"You know, it's a startup and all these normal things I guess, so we said, 'Okay,'" Prevatt recalled. "But [we] just kind of ignored all that and went straight to the top of it if you will and thought, 'You know what? We're going to talk them into doing something really unconventional for a startup, that's truly, it's not like a Google startup, like they're starting on a nest. It's a true startup. There's not a lot of money on the table.'"

Franklin Pictures began immediately, working tirelessly at the drawing board to ultimately produce a concept that correctly predicted the future excitement that Sacramentans would have for their soccer club.

"Basically, we wanted to paint a picture that's forward-thinking," Prevatt said. "[In the video] the city is already in love with Sac Republic, they already know about it, they're already fans, they're already going to games, they're already buying T-shirts, they're already buying hats, they're already buying scarves. It's a success. We're jumping forward five years.[98]

"Our kind of principle was, let's present the vision to the community that this is where it's going to be in five years, that everywhere you walk, you see somebody wearing a Sac Republic hat or Sac Republic shirt," he added. "And to really introduce our community to the sport of soccer, it shouldn't have this driving music beat, or whatever else, like an NBA video or NFL video would have. It's gotta be true to the sport, so we think it needs to be driven by a chant."

Wanting the chant to feel authentic, Prevatt reached out to R.J. Cooper, who had taken an early leadership role among Sacramento Professional Soccer supporters. Prevatt first asked Cooper to keep the conversation off the record to protect the integrity of the brand reveal and then if Cooper's group had written any club songs yet.

"No, not really, normally the chants stem from stuff about the goalie's mother," Prevatt recalled Cooper telling him. "But we actually have been working on one."

Franklin Productions asked Cooper to put together something by the following Monday and Cooper's then-wife, Chandler, delivered enough lyrics to satisfy the local filmmakers. When Prevatt presented his vision to Republic decision makers, the startup agreed to shell out a large sum of money it didn't possess. Sacramento Professional Soccer greenlit the film.

"They put it all in," Prevatt said. "It was one of these, we think this is going to happen, here's all of our chips, and I gotta respect people like that.

"You can call it bad business, you can call it carelessness, or stupidity, or whatever," he added. "I call it friggin' brilliance."

With forty-five days until Sacramento Soccer Day, Prevatt's crew began furiously preparing to film a project he said would normally require about three

---

[98] Noting the club's immediate success, Prevatt later said, "Or in our case, we're jumping forward one year."

months of work. Franklin Productions coordinated a nine-day shoot around the greater-Sacramento area in which every shirt, sticker, and scarf that featured the Republic's logo was constructed from scratch. The production company hired roughly 500 extras for various scenes of the shot, including the culminating crowd which watched their beloved squad in the football-line free Hughes Stadium. But more on that later.

With hundreds of extras on set weeks before the event, all of whom became privy to the club's future name and crest, Franklin Productions hoped to produce a quality product while somehow keeping the Republic brand a secret from the greater public. In addition to providing free food for the extras, Prevatt and Co. chose a deliberate path in incentivizing those to stay quiet. Before one of the first shoots, Franklin gathered everyone together to explain how important they felt the secrecy was, telling the mass of actors that the process they'd undergo was special and its discretion would ensure that the club made a huge splash. Additionally, the set was declared a phone-free environment, though one that was only enforced via the honor system.

"It was pretty incredible to have that many people there, and there wasn't a single leak," Prevatt said. "That's pretty cool. It was phenomenal. I'm still blown away by it. I think that people really got that this was something special."

## The (Disastrous) Impromptu Screening

Roughly three days before the big event, while busy Franklin filmmakers frantically finished their masterpiece, the Republic called on Prevatt for an advanced viewing of the film, which was not yet complete. Wagoner, who Prevatt lightheartedly described as a "Nervous Nellie," looked forward to a first screening to see what his company had borrowed money for. With the truncated shoot schedule, Franklin hadn't had the time or resources to screen dailies for the Republic staff, but Wagoner wanted to check in on the progress.

While preparing the studio for guests Prevatt was told to expect Wagoner and maybe Warren Smith–this showing was to be the first time anyone outside of the production company laid eyes on the short film. Bjork assured Prevatt that he didn't need to prepare for more than a couple of Republic staffers. Postproduction wasn't complete yet, but Franklin felt that it could explain the progress to Wagoner and one or two others once they arrived.

"[Franklin said], 'Hey, stop by the studio and check it out,'" Wagoner recalled. "I interpreted that as, 'invite everyone you fucking know and come see the finalized video because it's going to be awesome.'"

Someone knocked on the studio door around the prearranged meeting time that night and a nonchalant Prevatt walked over to let Wagoner in. When he opened the door, though, he wasn't greeted by Wagoner's face. Instead, gaggles of people he didn't recognize stood outside, eagerly awaiting entrance.

"We literally had friggin' twenty-five people in this room," Prevatt said. "There were supposed to be three people, the [higher ups] reviewing if there were any changes that needed to be made or whatever. And we just had gobs of people showing up at our studio because Joe got so excited about it that he called everybody that he knew to come see it."

A deep feeling of anxiety washed over Prevatt, who felt reluctant to play his unfinished film. He doesn't remember most of the exact details of what still needed to be fixed–it might have been color corrections, the final music mixing, or completing the transitions. The one aspect Prevatt does remember: Franklin hadn't finished digitally painting over the football markings at Hughes Stadium. And there's no chance the video could have felt authentic to soccer fans if it featured images of gridiron.

"We had three more days, and we were going to use every second that we had," Prevatt said.

Prevatt played the rough cut and watched as Wagoner and Co. took in what they thought was the final cut. A rush of excitement quickly disappeared into disappointment and despair. Wagoner had spent the week talking up Franklin Productions to his employees, who were left questioning their boss's sanity. Silence filled the room.

"When it got done playing, no one wanted to be the first one to say, 'What the fuck was that?'" Wagoner said. "But Graham decided to be that guy."

Never known to bite his tongue, Graham Smith took issue with the Hughes Stadium playing surface. "I don't like that there's football lines on the field," Smith said, breaking the ice.

"Then Graham had like five other things, [he was] nitpicking this thing apart like crazy," Prevatt said. "Things kind of started to unravel. It was exactly why we didn't want twenty-five people there, because you have twenty-five friggin' cooks in the kitchen, all thinking they have a say because one person has an opinion on it."

Amidst the commotion, Smith, a former professional goalkeeper, focused on one final detail from the end of the video: the age of the netminder Franklin hired for Antonio Sutton to score on. "You wouldn't have a goalie that young," Prevatt recalled Smith saying. "I mean, no wonder he missed the ball going into the net. The goalie's too young, you gotta replace the goalie."

Prevatt's response: "Replace the goalie? I don't think you understand what that means."[99]

---

[99] Prevatt would later laugh at the incident. "You gotta love Graham, I mean, the dude is solid," he said. "Love him. But he's up there in age and that sort of thing. He's definitely got his viewpoint of soccer and what soccer should be, or football as he would call it."

Working bell-to-bell, the Franklin Productions coffee-loaded crew finished the project with changes made from all the backseat filmmaker suggestions. Well, all the suggestions other than replacing the youthful goalkeeper. Franklin agreed to another screening just one day before Sacramento Soccer Day to calm Wagoner's nerves.

"Graham loved it," Prevatt said. "Keep in mind, the only [major] thing, the *only* thing that was changed [with the video aspect] was now there were no lines on the field. [Graham Smith] literally thought that we replaced the goalie. He goes, 'That goalie is so much better. You guys are amazing.'"

The mood from the first showing to the second flipped 180 degrees as Sacramento Professional Soccer felt justified in its major expenditure. "See, I told you these guys were good," Wagoner said to Smith.

Meanwhile, the Franklin Productions team could only stare at each other incredulously. "Are you serious right now?" Prevatt whispered to a co-worker. "He thinks we replaced the goalie."

# The Culmination

Back at Raley Field, the banner dropped to reveal the Sacramento Republic FC crest as "The Chant"–sans football lines–played to the wide praise of the capacity crowd. Wagoner missed the film's true premier. He ducked behind a corner to deal with a phone that wouldn't stop ringing the second after the reveal.

"We had like 1,000 likes on the unveil in ten minutes," Wagoner said. "So, I remember sitting down there on the field, and it was like 'wow!' And Warren's talking and Preki's talking, and you're out of [the line of sight] and no one's looking at you, and it's just boom. 1,000. And you're like, 'Holy shit, we might be onto something.' And then, we went on sale with season-ticket deposits a week and a half later, and we had 1,000 in the first day before noon, and it was just like, 'We need to hire a lot of people.' We went from four employees to thirty-two employees in about two months."

On the field, though, there was still time for further hiccups. As Norwich City calmly dominated its Mexican opponents with a 3-0 shellacking, an overflow crowd moved into the section the Battalion vacated during the tifo display. Raley Field's ushers, experienced with baseball fans but not soccer supporters, compounded the complexity of the problem. Likely unfamiliar with soccer etiquette, the stadium employees reprimanded the Battalion for standing and singing.

After the game, while Jakubek[100] returned to goal to allow a long line of kids to shoot on him, Smith finally earned the opportunity to pitch potential investors with

---

[100] The gregarious Jakubek is known around town to partake in situations like this to this day. There's no promotion or meet-and-greet that he won't do. Stallings calls him "the best spokesmodel who ever wore a beard."

a tangible product. Instead, he headed off to drink with the reportedly frustrated Battalion. "If they were pissed, I never saw it because I got there and we just started ordering beers and drinking with them and then they shared some frustration," Smith said. "I think they just wanted to be heard. But they were more excited about participating...it's their brand. They helped develop it. They got to unveil it and it's the best thing that could have been done."

Sacramento Soccer Day proved more successful than most could have imagined, but some remained unconvinced of its importance. *The Sacramento Bee* sent an intern to cover the game action instead of a full-time staff member. Marcos Bretón attended the match, but as a columnist, he enjoyed creative freedom to choose the topics he covered. Bretón was sold, but the same type of people who kept the story of the U.S. win in 1994 off the front page, remained in the power positions.

"[The Republic] never engaged in any sort of complaining about the sort of tepid coverage initially, because I think they realized that they had to build something and if they built it right, people would show up," Bretón said. "And they did. So, they avoided some of the mistakes that the PR folks that Sac State or the River Cats or whatever [made]. They're like, 'Why [isn't *The Bee*] covering it more?' I'm like, 'Guys, even with the River Cats, God bless them, I'm a big supporter of the River Cats, they're a huge part of Sacramento, but it's like guys, you know, people go to the games not to watch the games but to experience minor league baseball, so I think you need to market the team for that.'

"Whereas, even though it's minor league soccer [with the Republic], there is a competitive aspect to it that's much more pronounced than in minor league baseball, and the fact that people jump on the bandwagon so much," Bretón added. "I think the folks at the Republic just bided their time. They maintained good relations with the media and then when the media folks began coming to them saying, 'This is great.' 'This is fantastic.' 'We need to cover this!' Their response was, 'Yeah, that's a great idea.' Instead of saying, 'Yeah, fuckhead, we've been telling you this all the time.' They didn't engage in that."

Eventually the media would come around, with two local newspapers sending regular beat writers to practices and games during the debut year. Overall, three reporters covered nearly every game during the club's first three seasons, which featured packed crowds and nonstop winning. But according to the "five guys in shorts," along with Jones and Bjork, Sacramento Soccer Day was really where the Republic movement began from both an investor and media coverage standpoint.

"It had to happen to make this thing work," Wagoner said. "The effort of the group that we kind of banded to get that done, that's the hardest thing I've ever done...if that failed, we would have been fucked. A baseball guy in Warren, and me, a baseball guy who had his last two startups fail? Who's gonna believe us about soccer? It worked, thank God, but people have no idea how close this thing was.

"If we had failed, we'd be done. It would have just been, 'We owe a shitload of people money, and [have] no way to pay them.'"

Added Kenny Cooper: "I think it kind of accelerated the mindset that we all had, especially for Joe, Warren, and Brett, that we needed some more bodies in here. We had a ticket sales guy, me, just calling off emails and phone numbers that I found on the Internet. We started to get some more structure, and that's when we [hired] a director of ticket sales, a vice president of corporate partnerships. Those were all individuals who had a lot of different traits that just ended up working really well together. It was a good learning experience, especially for those of us who haven't really been in sports for too long. But...it just kind of exploded.

"We realized, 'Oh shit, we gotta start hiring for this thing and hiring for that, and getting some more structure in the organization.'"

Sacramento Soccer Day enjoyed so much success it forced the Republic to audible from its original long-term planning just minutes after its name had officially come into existence. "At that point, we had to rethink the business plan we had put together," Reitter said as the original plan he co-wrote called for three ticket sales employees and one marketing person. That plan allowed for eleven total staff members and a head coach once the club became fully operational, which Reitter expected to take three years. All these projections were based on securing 3,000 season ticket sales according to Reitter.

"[By 2015 we were] up to forty full-time employees with another 240 on the books," Reitter said. "We just couldn't imagine where this was going to go. Once we got through the first day of season-ticket deposits, and I think we had almost 1,500, we knew that we had something special. We sat there and we watched the numbers go up and up on that day. The wheels were turning just on how far it could go to that point. Before that, we had no idea. We really thought we were just going to be, I shouldn't say another USL team, but one of the more successful ones."

The success that drove the initial ticket sales following Sacramento Soccer Day boiled over into the investor group as the Republic quickly hit its pre-launch capital goal shortly after the event. "After Sacramento Soccer Day, they got it," Stallings said. "We didn't have to convince [the investors] that there was a fan base here. They didn't have to be convinced that we knew what we were doing as far as developing a brand and getting people excited and pulling off an event."

Bretón's memories of the day focused more on the media aspect of it. Before Sacramento Soccer Day, the *Sacramento Bee* columnist had pushed the sports department to cover the city's future expansion team. However, like in 1994, the older guard prevailed. According to Bretón, he was told that the team didn't matter because it was a minor league outfit with limited resources. "I don't think you realize how big this is going to be," the columnist explained to his co-workers, who ignored him.

Still, Bretón privately assured the Republic that the attention would arrive in due time. "You have to be patient with us," he remembers telling the Sacramento higher-ups. "You have to understand that we have to crawl before we walk and run."

That moment came sooner than the longtime scribe thought, arriving as soon as Sacramento Republic FC announced its brand in front of a sellout crowd at Raley Field before immediately selling thousands of season tickets for the upcoming year.

"I think that Sac Soccer Day is sort of an event that came out of nowhere for many people," Bretón said. "It wasn't until Sac Soccer Day that it began to open [the media's] eyes."

Back on the field after the event, it was well past midnight as the exhausted startup crew still occupied the confines at Raley. Their levels of fatigue could only be matched by their feelings of euphoria over a job impeccably done.

Kenny Cooper, Brett Reitter, and Joe Wagoner packed the goals back up on their rented pickup and clipped more trees on the return journey to Sacramento State. It was around 2:00 a.m. and their final task was to return the vehicle to a pitch-black parking lot and deposit the keys in a mailbox that Wagoner said felt "incredibly accessible to anybody."

After debating whether someone would steal the truck from its drop off point, the trio threw up their hands, left it, and made a note to call the rental company the following morning. Finally, they each drove back home, bailing on the plans they'd made to celebrate a successful event well into the night.

"We thought we'd be doing shots and keg stands at 2:00 a.m. after Sac Soccer Day. Instead, we were returning a truck," Wagoner said. "There were no celebrations, no time for reflections, no breather. We had shit to do. We got up early the next day and went to clean up Raley Field. We had a few beers at New Helvetia later that day with Warren, Julia, the crew from Franklin Pictures, and a few others, but we never really had the chance to celebrate the event the way we wanted. Our hope was full day of many, many beers, sitting on the patio at the Virgin Sturgeon[101] rehashing the stories and the photos of the event."

Instead, they put their heads back down and continued plugging away– Sacramento Republic FC would kick off in fewer than nine months, and it needed more than five guys in shorts and two women to prepare.

While Sacramento Soccer Day served as the public introduction to the city's newest professional team, the club figurehead who pumped up the crowd during the logo reveal needed no such unveiling to the local diehards. Even though no one had seen him in nearly three years, the legendary figure he cut was so ingrained in the American soccer scene that the Republic earned national praise just for securing his signature. As Smith and Wagoner moved forward with all the off-the-field aspects of the franchise, Sacramento brass chose the mysterious, enigmatic, competitive, brilliant, and stubborn Preki to take charge of the on-field product.

No one could predict how Sacramento Republic FC would fare in its inaugural season, but with Preki leading the way, it sure as hell wouldn't be boring.

---

[101] A riverfront Sacramento bar and restaurant.

# SIX
# BUILDING THE FOUNDATION

"Behind them eyes, there's a million things going on, and you were never really 100 percent sure of how much he was angling for something. Not in a Machiavellian way or a suspicious way, but you know, it would be like, 'It's alright, Preki, it's okay man. Just relax. For fuck's sake, don't take it all so seriously, just have a good time.'"

-     Famed soccer broadcaster and former MLS manager Ray Hudson

## The Famous Manager[102]

Even though soccer probably qualified as mostly a niche sport in the United States in 2013, the scene still managed to produce a handful of household names in the prior few decades thanks to Major League Soccer and both U.S. senior national teams. Preki's Sacramento Soccer Day cameo may have been his first public appearance in more than three years, but his name still carried weight in the local and national sporting communities. The mononyms former Kansas City Wizards attacking midfielder took MLS by storm in its early days, relying on his trademark cutback. Everyone knew it was coming, but no one ever figured out how to stop it.

Preki also made headlines off the field as a legendarily stubborn figure who butted heads with coaches, opponents, teammates, and media members. For all his quirks, the Yugoslav-born attacking midfielder starred in MLS from the league's opening kick and didn't look back well into his 40s. His intense work rate,

---

[102] I split this chapter into three different song pairings, one for each section. To start, I recommend "I Walk Alone" by Oleander.

competitiveness, and skill drove him to become the only two-time MLS MVP winner and helped earn him twenty-eight caps and a 1998 World Cup roster spot for his adopted country.[103]

When Preki finally called it quits on his yoga-prolonged career as a 42-year-old following the 2005 MLS season, he continued along the path of other soccer-loving former professionals whose competitive fires raged on after retirement—Preki turned to coaching. It took him just a single season as Bob Bradley's assistant at Chivas USA before the club promoted him to head coach in 2007 when Bradley left to take the national team job.

Preki quickly found success in his new role, leading the club to a 40-29-21 record that included three straight playoff berths. In his first season as manager, Preki won the MLS Coach of the Year award while guiding a squad that finished two points off the pace set by Supporters' Shield winning D.C. United. It appeared as if Preki had picked up right as he left off, even after he left Chivas USA following the 2009 season to join a putrid Toronto FC side.

Preki headed north of the border to become the fourth coach in four years for the cellar-dwelling Canadian neophytes. By that point in Toronto FC's tire fire of a short history, the club had managed a 25-41-24 record, good for an average of 1.1 points per game. Had TFC played in the vast majority of any of the other soccer leagues in the world, it would have been relegated.

Predictably, club owners Maple Leaf Sports & Entertainment pulled the plug on Preki in September of 2010, despite his relatively successful 7-10-7 league record and a Canadian Championship title. Toronto would cycle through four more managers before finally making the playoffs for the first time in 2016 with its ninth head coach.[104]

Out of MLS for the first time in the league's fifteen-year history, Preki faded from the spotlight of the American professional game, completely disappearing from the public eye. Instead of landing a role in the media like so many of his retired peers, the player-turned-manager returned to Chicago to live in relative anonymity alongside his wife and son. Doing things his own way had always been Preki's M.O. and, like in his playing career, this provided promising returns while also burning bridges. It was, perhaps, a lonely path to take, but one that allowed him to never compromise any of his beliefs.

---

[103] Additionally, at time of publication, only five players have earned more MLS Best XI selections than Preki's four and the former attacker remains Sporting Kansas City's all-time leader in goals and assists. He still ranks fifth on the all-time MLS assist charts and alongside Barry Bonds and Tom Brady is one of just three athletes to win an MVP award in a big five sports league after his 40th birthday. In 2005, MLS named Preki to its All-Time Best XI as part of the league's 10th anniversary celebrations. Preki also won MLS Cup, Supporters' Shield, and U.S. Open Cup titles.

[104] For context: at time of publication, Sporting Kansas City, the rebranded club Preki once starred for, had six managers in 29 years. Two of those were interim head coaches, who led the club while it searched for a long-term answer.

"He had somewhat of a sad demeanor too much of the time," said soccer broadcaster Ray Hudson, who coached Preki for one season in MLS. "I always felt as if he was in that sort of area where, as all the great players truly inhabit, a lonely place at times. I played with the greatest of the great in the likes of [Gerd] Müller, [George] Besty...and on and on. They all have had that share of loneliness about them sometimes. Not being overly dramatic about it, but I think those types of gifted players need some sort of solace about them and maybe it all becomes a little bit too much. [Preki] needs his walk in the desert for forty days sometimes."

Preki walked off into the desert after Toronto and planned to continue indefinitely until a familiar face rang to speak about a new gig in California.

When Warren Smith and the Sacramento Republic FC brass hired Graham Smith[105] as their first director of football, he arrived prepared with a one-name shortlist for the club's first head coaching role. The smooth-talking, jack-of-all-trades, English First Division veteran relocated to Southern California decades prior to start his second life and quickly built up an impressive Rolodex of contacts and clients.

It didn't take long for Smith to reach his hand into a multitude of different facets in American professional soccer–if there was a way to make money in the game, Smith was involved in it. The former goalkeeper began his post-playing career working in public relations for the sportswear companies Adidas and Le Coq Sportif before spending five years on Chelsea's Board of Directors. In 1990, he founded his own player agency, First Wave Management,[106] and began representing professionals before turning to coaching in 2007 with the fourth division Ventura County Fusion. And out of his entire list of contacts built up through nearly 60 years in the game, the man Graham Smith tapped to lead the Republic was Preki.

The only problem: the other Republic decision makers weren't interested in Preki, and Preki wasn't interested in the Republic. Still, Warren Smith felt determined to complete his due diligence regarding Graham Smith's suggestion. "I

---

[105] No relation.

[106] Now called First Wave Sports International, the organization came under public scrutiny shortly after its inception when it was involved in two controversial transfers, according to a 2002 article in *The Guardian*. That piece noted irregularities in those deals, one of which resulted in a £20,000 fine for Aston Villa and one which involved Smith's First Wave co-founder handing an envelope filled with £50,000 to a club executive to allegedly push through a deal. These events prompted the U.K. government to launch an official investigation into Smith's finances. Not only was he cleared of wrongdoing, but according to that article, he formed a friendship with the officer in charge of his case. This was all reported in a piece where Smith revealed that he pocketed a £125,000 commission for helping arrange a Croatian striker's move to Villa. "I'd never seen him play but I'd heard of him," Smith said in the piece. "There was a feature in *World Soccer*. He'd scored a lot of goals, looked like a great player. [Smith's contact in the Balkans said the player] wasn't registered with FIFA and asked me if I'd help him find a club for his player. I'm not in business to turn down work." That player played just eight league games for Villa and is often described as one of the worst signings in EPL history.

called everybody I knew in the sport and almost 100 percent told me to stay away from Preki," the Republic co-founder said.

Meanwhile, the prideful Preki reportedly scoffed at the idea of leaving his home in Chicago for a position he felt was beneath him given his credentials. After four years of coaching in MLS, the thought of moving halfway across the country to lead a third division club during its expansion season sounded less than appealing.

After all, this was the same man who suffered a broken fibula and dislocated ankle as a 40-year-old in a 2004 preseason game and returned to training just 130 days later despite undergoing surgery in the interim. This was the same man who then played another full season of professional soccer in 2005 because he wanted to "retire when [he] thinks it's right" and didn't "want to go out on an injury."

This was the same man who, ahead of his first playoff run as Chivas USA head coach, reportedly challenged star striker Maykel Galindo to a shooting contest that carried on for so long that Galindo suffered an injury, sidelining him for the postseason. This was the same man who still carried a grudge against former U.S. manager Steve Sampson for playing him for sixty-five of a possible 180 minutes during the 1998 FIFA World Cup.[107]

Preki wasn't about to end his self-imposed exile for just any job, he wanted to compete at the highest level, the level he felt he deserved. With both sides apprehensive, Graham Smith set out to showcase perhaps his single best skill: finding common ground between people with vastly different personalities from highly dissimilar backgrounds.

"I told him he needed to make a statement," Graham Smith would later recall to *The Sacramento Bee* in an article detailing how he helped change Preki's mind. "You need to get the best guy out there, even though [Preki] should be in MLS, not the USL. It was a little bit like pulling teeth initially because Preki's a guy with a lot of pride. He's a guy who achieved some of the highest things in football in the United States. I had to tell him this was a journey that, hopefully, would propel him back into significance in the U.S. game."

Graham Smith arranged a face-to-face introduction with Warren Smith and Preki and whatever concerns either party held coming into it quickly melted away. "Graham continued to make a case with me and brought him out and, to be honest with you, in our very first meeting, I just got to learn what a wonderful human being this man is," Warren Smith would later say.

One detail that helped sway Preki: the understanding that he and Graham Smith retained the final say on all personnel matters, the absence of which the coach felt impeded his pathway to success at Toronto FC. "That's something you want as a head coach," Preki would later tell *The Bee*. "You don't want people interfering with your job."

---

[107] Preki turned 35 during the World Cup, making him the tournament's tenth oldest field player out of 608.

The two intense personalities in Preki and Graham Smith somehow meshed to allow Preki the creative control that a perfectionist such as himself had always wanted. "At times, the relationship is good," Preki said. "At times, it's, you know, a hard conversation. But at the end of the day, to be fair to Graham, he's never interfered with what I try to do. He's always been supportive."

Or as Graham Smith recalled: "He'll be screaming at me, and I'll be screaming at him. And he'll stand up to me, and I'll stand up to him. I'll listen to him for five minutes, and he'll listen to me for five minutes.

"And then we decide I'm always right."

# The Marquee Player[108]

It's easy to imagine Graham Smith and Preki screaming at each other a few months after Sacramento Soccer Day when they began building Sacramento Republic FC's inaugural roster. When selecting the club's first head coach, Graham Smith had advocated for a personal contact he truly believed in, so it made sense to continue this line of thinking when signing the club's first player.

Both Graham Smith and Preki knew Rodrigo "RoRo" López well. Graham Smith's final year as head coach at the Ventura County Fusion ended with the club lifting the 2009 USL Premier Development League title behind strong play from López, who was in the second of his three stints with the outfit. Graham Smith had long served as López's agent and even though he brokered deals for his client to sign with the Portland Timbers and Orlando City SC, the midfielder's career trajectory proved far from linear.

The diminutive, but creative, López originally appeared on the fast track for stardom when left his Santa Barbara home at 16 to sign with the academy of famed Mexican side Club Deportivo Guadalajara in 2003. While he never suited up for the first team, he caught the eye of U.S. Soccer scouts, who invited him into the youth national team setup in 2005. Because Chivas then only allowed players eligible to represent Mexico on their books,[109] the club gave López a choice: move to a smaller team in the country or return home to Southern California to sign Chivas's American offshoot.

López picked the latter, joining the Chivas USA first team ahead of its inaugural MLS campaign. Despite coming into the season with high hopes, the expansion team immediately unraveled–it took the club twenty games to cross the ten-point threshold. The now-infamous play of the 2005 Chivas USA squad that finished 4-22-6 didn't exactly provide a nurturing environment for young professionals looking to break through.

---

[108] I recommend pairing this section with "I Wanna Live" by Tesla.
[109] A policy that has since been relaxed to allow anyone with Mexican citizenship to suit up for the side.

"It was tough, we basically ended up with the Tapatío[110] players from Mexico, which if you look at the roster, it's number twenty-two through thirty," original Chivas USA head coach Thomas Rongen said via cellphone from Tampa in 2015.[111] "We basically didn't have enough quality from Mexico that we were able to sustain anything positive in MLS, which is a very athletic league, just a very tough league in those days...for players like Rodrigo López, being able to flourish there was hard. It really was."

López played in one match in 2005 and two in 2006 under Bob Bradley before entering his third professional season under the tutelage of first-time head coach Preki in 2007. That year, Chivas USA posted a club record fifty-three points, but RoRo hardly played. Preki called his number five times over the course of the campaign but didn't see enough to justify keeping him on the team. Following its exit from the MLS playoffs, Chivas USA placed López on waivers.

None of the league's other eleven clubs claimed him.

"He was a young boy," Preki later said. "Some things were hard in those moments for him, the defensive side of things." Rongen put it much more bluntly, saying: "It's not easy for a young player to develop in this country. When you don't succeed early on...there aren't too many other opportunities in MLS."

Out of contract for the first time in his young career, López cold-called Graham Smith, who showcased him with the Fusion in 2008. From there, he bounced around North America in stints with Cuervos Negros de Zapotlanejo, Querétaro, the Fusion (again), the USL version of the Portland Timbers, the MLS Timbers, the Fusion (yet again), and pre-MLS Orlando City SC. When López signed with the USL's Los Angeles Blues in 2013, it was his seventh club in nine years of what looked like would become a journeyman career.

However, something clicked for López during that season. Not only did RoRo play in all but three games for the Blues that year, but he helped his side qualify for the postseason, and finished second in the league with eleven assists.

To Graham Smith, the now 26-year-old father had proven that he could pull the strings for a solid team in the USL, but Preki still stubbornly saw the same raw player he'd cut ties with more than half a decade previously. With the inaugural Republic season fast approaching, Graham Smith called López against Preki's wishes.

The director of football hoped to sign his client, but in typical Preki fashion, the head coach made López try out first. Graham Smith told López to suit up at a combine in Ventura and even though he played well, the new Republic boss remained unconvinced.

"Preki liked what he saw, but he didn't want to sign me," López said. "He was like, 'look I know you can play, but this isn't really an environment where I can see

---

[110] The Guadalajara reserve team.

[111] Rongen was then serving as the head coach of the NASL's Tampa Bay Rowdies. Shortly after the interview, the Rowdies fired him in a controversial move.

much–you're playing a lot of guys who are just coming to play and aren't really that good.'"

With a serious girlfriend and child to think of, López offered Graham Smith and Preki an ultimatum: sign him or stop wasting his time. If Sacramento wasn't in the cards, he'd need as much time as possible to find some semblance of stability for his family. The two senior Republic decision makers likely argued before Preki eventually relented. Graham Smith offered López a two-year contract, which would be the only multiyear deal Graham Smith handed out ahead of the inaugural campaign that was entirely guaranteed.

"I said, 'Okay, I've gotta do it. It's my last chance,'" López said. "Obviously Graham told me that it was my last chance as well. Knowing the city was so into it and the fanbase that we were going to have, it seemed right."

On the one-year anniversary of their sparsely attended USL expansion announcement, Republic brass arranged a second press conference in Midtown at local chain pizza joint Hot Italian Pizza & Panini Bar to unveil López. "It's a significant signing because it's our first signing," Graham Smith told the small handful of reporters on hand. "What is great about RoRo is I have been privileged to work with him over the years and see his talent only improve over the years. I know he will flourish at Republic FC with his passing skills and as a set piece specialist."

Dressed in a slick gray suit, sporting gelled hair and a clean-shaven face, López aimed to introduce himself to Sacramento in the most professional way possible. Though calm and collected in front of the media, RoRo anxiously awaited debuting in his new home. But the USL season was still four months away and the ear-to-ear grin he sported at the conference faded the moment he set off to return down south.

While the rest of the Republic's soccer staff scrambled to fill out a roster, López worked construction back home to earn an extra buck or two while counting down the days until training camp. Even with the day job, he always found time for twice-daily individual fitness sessions. If López failed at the Republic, it wasn't going to be because of his effort level.

"They were long days," López said. "Obviously, with a family, you think about everything twice, the way you go about things outside the field, the hard work you need to put in to provide the support. It's tough getting into preseason, but once preseason began, I think Preki opened his eyes and said, 'This guy's worked hard, this guy showed me that he can play.'"

# The Team[112]

With Rodrigo López signed, Graham Smith and Preki drew on their vast connections to begin filling out the rest of Sacramento Republic FC's inaugural roster. Center back Mickey Daly, a Ventura County Fusion alum who spent the 2013 USL season with the Wilmington Hammerheads, became the club's second player. While the Graham Smith-inspired signing of the little-known Daly came without much fanfare, the next deal excited many of the diehards who had already pledged their support to the Republic. And unlike the previous two signings, Preki's fingerprints were visible all over the move.

While preparing for his second season at the helm of Chivas USA in 2008, Preki attended an amateur tournament at his club's home stadium in Southern California. Always on the lookout for even the tiniest of advantages, the sophomore boss liked something he saw in one of the players on the pitch, a towering center forward named Justin Braun. The 20-year-old Salt Lake City native had only turned out for his local community college, but Preki felt he possessed the size, strength, and skill to succeed in MLS and invited Braun to preseason.

The forward made the team that year and had suited up for MLS clubs ever since, scoring twenty-six goals in 131 games for Chivas USA, Real Salt Lake, the Montreal Impact, and Toronto FC. Braun's goal output had slowed down over the past few seasons, but at 27, the Republic felt he still had plenty in the tank and inked him to a deal six days before preseason was scheduled to begin. "I knew when I first saw Justin play in 2008 that he was a player with great potential," Preki said in the release announcing the deal. "Now it will be even better to work with him due to his experience of playing in MLS for five years."

That same release also unveiled the signing of 18-year-old prospect Gabe Gissie. Sacramento increased its number of players under contract to six three days later when it announced the additions of Northern California natives Max Alvarez and Emrah Klimenta. Both players earned Preki's trust after strong performances in invite-only combines, which the club invited Klimenta to after seeing him at an open tryout. Like Preki, Klimenta hailed from the former Yugoslavia and, alongside preseason signings Ivan Mirković and Nemanja Vuković, gave Sacramento a Balkan sporting presence that the city hadn't seen since Vlade Divac and Peja Stojaković turned out for the Kings.

Graham Smith's international relationships then helped secure the signatures of Northern Irish striker Thomas Stewart, Brazilian midfielder Gilberto, and Australian defender Harrison Delbridge. The Republic rounded out its roster with local products in veteran goalkeeper Dominik Jakubek, former Chico State midfielder Octavio Guzmán, and forward Chad Bartlomé, a Sacramento native who'd spent the last eight years playing for five different clubs in Switzerland.

---

[112] I recommend pairing this section with "Comfort Eagle" by Cake.

Overall, Graham Smith and Preki green-lit twenty signings in the months leading up to Sacramento Republic FC's March 29 franchise opener at fellow USL expansion club L.A. Galaxy II. While the club could expect a few more acquisitions and a slew of loan players through its new affiliations with the Portland Timbers and San Jose Earthquakes, the core of the roster was set.

It was time for Sacramento Republic FC to start playing games, the first five of which would take place away from home.

# SEVEN
# ROAD TRIP[113]

If the level of play Sacramento Republic FC showcased during its preseason matches provided any indication of how the club would fare during its inaugural season, local soccer fans were in for a long year. After defeating Sacramento State and UC Santa Barbara in closed-door matches to open the 2014 slate, the Republic traveled south for another private game, this time against the Ventura County Fusion. The hosts defeated Sacramento 3-2 before the Republic returned to Northern California to make its public debut.

On March 5, 1,105 fans packed Warrior Field on the campus of Cal State Stanislaus in Turlock to support their club for the first time. Facing the top-division San Jose Earthquakes, Sacramento fell 2-0 on two late goals. The result didn't surprise many, just as the 2-1 victory over Chico State ten days later also failed to turn heads.

On March 16, the Republic traveled a few miles west to take on UC Davis in front of a sellout crowd at Aggie Soccer Field. The 1,375 in attendance appeared split between supporting the NCAA side and the upstart USL club. Forty-five minutes in, the latter group of fans cheered loudest when a UCD player fouled Republic captain Justin Braun in the box. Rodrigo López elected to take the spot kick, only for reserve Aggie goalkeeper John Piasta to save. A Sam Hoeck header in the sixty-fifth minute gave UC Davis a lead that it held to claim an improbable victory.

Still, Preki relayed positive thoughts after the game and both coaches appeared pleased with the support in the stands that included an entire section occupied by the Tower Bridge Battalion. "I hope everybody continues to support, not only UC Davis soccer and athletics, but also that we all drive across the Causeway and

---

[113] I recommend pairing "What You Give" by Tesla for this chapter.

support the Republic for every home game and sell that place out," UCD head coach Dwayne Shaffer said after the match. "It would be awesome to watch a game on a warm Sacramento night and be able to enjoy a high-level professional soccer game."

Three days later, Sacramento closed out its preseason with a scoreless draw against Saint Mary's College of California.

Ongoing construction of the Republic's new stadium forced the club to begin the campaign on the road for its inaugural five fixtures. First up: L.A. Galaxy II, an MLS reserve side and fellow 2014 USL expansion team.

On the morning of March 29, roughly fifty Tower Bridge Battalion members packed into a bus heading south on Interstate-5. Just a few seconds in, the first crack of a beer can radiated throughout the vehicle—the party was on. Fans dressed in red and gold blasted music, poured mixed drinks, and sang songs as they motored down the freeway. Grown men and women steadily became more and more belligerent and by the time the bus parked in Carson—four hundred miles later—several fans had already passed out.

Those still awake crammed themselves inside a hotel room for more music and drinking—one of the first chapters in Battalion history was written somewhere in a stuffy hotel room in an unglamorous part of Southern California. Fifty fans weren't a particularly large number, but it was a start.

"Even the Timbers Army only had seven people for their first game," Battalion president R.J. Cooper said. "People see the Timbers Army on TV and they think that they can just show up and that will happen, but it's a lot more work than that. You don't become the Timbers Army by being meek."

Cooper and a small handful of other local soccer fans had created the supporters' group the year prior, mostly by bringing together members from the local American Outlaws chapter. While Battalion vice president André Barnes continually joked about only drinking Miller High Life, "the champagne of beers," the group prepared to support the club in its first competitive game. After a few issues with security, who tried to prevent one supporter wearing a Workaholics bear suit from entering the gates, the Battalion marched to the match for the first time before ahead of a USL fixture.

The small group of traveling supporters entered the StubHub Center's Track & Field Stadium and joined up with Republic front office staff members and a few Chivas USA fans who arrived to root against the Galaxy. Just over 1,000 spectators occupied the 10,000-seat facility and the supporters' sections for both clubs appeared roughly equal in size. The racing track surrounding the field separated the fans from the action, providing the icing on the cake that rounded out an underwhelming atmosphere.

With most of the diehards, and almost all the club's brass on hand to support the club, Sacramento Republic FC hoped to make a good first impression back home for those who couldn't attend. The front office staff scheduled three watch parties around the city at de Vere's Irish Pub, Hot Italian Pizza & Panini Bar, and

Field House American Sports Pub. The upstart USL didn't have a TV deal but had arranged to broadcast each contest live on YouTube, free of charge. The league tasked the hosts of each match with the responsibility of producing its own streams, which the Galaxy II accomplished without any hiccups during its inaugural game the week prior.

However, fans crowding all three of the Sacramento watering holes quickly noticed something was wrong when the announced kickoff time came and went without images from Carson. Instead of viewing the first minutes of Sacramento Republic FC's USL history, those attending the watch parties stared back at blank screens.

Just as the game was about to start, Joe Wagoner's phone buzzed in his pocket as it had hundreds of other times that day. After ignoring the first few messages in hopes of spending a calm ninety minutes watching the culmination of nearly two years of work, Wagoner finally checked his unread texts. In Sacramento, gaggles of fans publicly gathered in anticipation of the Republic's first-ever game. Only the YouTube stream the USL promised wasn't working.

Potential new supporters began flooding Sacramento's social media accounts with complaints regarding the issue. Sacramento Republic FC only had one chance to make a good first impression and through no fault of its own, it was already failing. Vice president of communications Erika Bjork and vice president of corporate sponsorship Brent Sasaki spent weeks organizing the three gatherings while communicating with the Galaxy about the technical aspects that would help ensure a stress-free stream. Republic leadership went as far as physically double checked the status of all the required systems in Carson.

But back in Sacramento, impatient bar managers began switching their empty screens to channels with working broadcasts.

"I ran to the L.A. control room and calmly, politely shared the news," Wagoner later said in a text. "They didn't seem to be overly concerned. My memory is fuzzy about what happened next. The nice guy in me wants to believe that we joyfully worked together to solve the challenge and then high-fived. However, if witness accounts are accurate, I apparently lost my motherfuggin' mind, threatened them and all of their current and future family members, and swore I wouldn't rest until each of them regretted the day they dropped the ball on the most important event in the history of the world."

Accounts differ on whether or not the Galaxy ever fixed the issues, but it hardly mattered–fans back home had already lost interest in what appeared to be the city's next incompetent professional soccer franchise.

Back in Carson, the match started slowly. Both sides looked tentative and when the first goal came, it wasn't exactly highlight reel quality. In the thirty-third minute, Galaxy goalkeeper Brian Rowe punched Max Alvarez's corner kick out to the top of the box, right to Rodrigo López. The Sacramento midfielder headed the ball towards the target and, though it may not have been on its way to the back of the net, an L.A. player cleared it upwards in desperation.

The ball traveled so high in the air it left the frame of the broadcast that no one up north could watch.[114] As it floated for seemingly an eternity, three defenders and Rowe gathered underneath in a hopeful attempt to again clear the ball, but Republic captain Justin Braun fought his way into the middle of the scrum. Like a power forward boxing out for a rebound, Braun thrust his hips into the mass of white shirts, using every inch of his 6-foot-3 frame to rise above the crowd and nod home his club's first goal.

As his teammates attempted to tackle him, Braun cut back and forth between them while racing towards the Tower Bridge Battalion. The forward then kissed the Republic crest over his heart and pointed to the traveling supporters. Sacramento fans embraced each other, some so forcefully that a few tumbled down on the metal bleachers.[115]

With few ideas going forward, the Republic attempted to hold onto the one-goal lead and did so all the way up until the eighty-first minute. Finding a pocket of space in the final third, Galaxy playmaker Raul Mendiola played striker Chandler Hoffman through on goal. Hoffman, one of the Galaxy's many first team players who the club hoped to develop in the USL, faked shooting the ball with his left foot and instead cut back onto his right. The threat required an intervention from the visiting defense, but Republic defender Mickey Daly bit on the action and slid harmlessly by. Hoffman then moved the ball back onto his left foot and tucked it inside the near post past onrushing goalkeeper Jake Gleeson.

The netminder pounded the turf in frustration, personifying the mood of his teammates—Sacramento would have to settle for a point. "I thought, on a better day, we walk away with the three points," Preki said after the match. "There is still a lot of room for improvement, and I know that as the season goes we will get better and better."

While the team remained a work in progress on the field, the Battalion and other Sacramento fans made an impression off it. For ninety minutes the group sang and cheered, sometimes louder than the contingent from the Angel City Brigade on the other side of the stands. "It reminded me of MLS," Mike Fucito, a forward on loan from the San Jose Earthquakes, said of the support. "They seem to be very passionate fans and we really appreciated it, and we enjoyed having them there."

The Republic would have to wait for its first three points, but the times called for a celebration regardless as Warren Smith invited the Battalion to a nearby Mexican restaurant and bar. During the match, the supporters sang "Happy Birthday" to Smith, but the club's co-founder wasn't the one who received free drinks that night. To thank the fans for making the trek, Smith announced he'd buy the traveling supporters a round or two while they partied well into the night.

If Sacramento Republic FC's USL journey began in underwhelming fashion in front of a sparse crowd, the club's second game made the L.A. Galaxy II contest

---

[114] The full, uninterrupted stream was somehow later uploaded to YouTube.
[115] You know who you are, Republic front office staffer who shall not be outed.

look like the World Cup final in comparison. Sacramento returned to the same field on April 7 to face the Chivas USA Reserves on a Monday shortly before noon. Unlike L.A. Galaxy II, the Chivas USA Reserves didn't compete in the USL. Rather, the league scheduled its squads to play against the second teams of all non-Galaxy[116] MLS sides twice during the 2014 season.

Few top-division outfits took these games seriously, especially Chivas USA, which would fold at the end of the year. An aging Adolfo "Bofo" Bautista lined up against the Republic, but it had been more than two years since the 34-year-old former Mexican international had scored a league goal. Instead, Fucito and Braun made the difference as no one in Sacramento watched the Republic pick up its first USL victory.

Because Chivas didn't operate in the USL, it wasn't required to broadcast the match, meaning to this day, the second, third, and fourth goals in Sacramento history only exist in the memories of those participating. Fucito scored the opener, Braun hit for the eventual winner in the twenty-fifth minute, and substitute forward Tommy Stewart added an insurance strike in stoppage time of the 3-1 victory. "I'm proud of my guys, they worked really hard and worked for each other and they were very disciplined for the most part," Preki said. "When you do that, good things will happen."

Five days later, Sacramento returned to Southern California for a much different type of challenge: back-to-back road matches. While unheard of in most parts of the world, the USL sometimes scheduled games on consecutive days to minimize travel costs. To compensate for the quick turnaround, the league allowed clubs five substitutions in each game.[117] The USL also believed that this rule would incentivize its teams to travel with more players on road trips rather than cut travel costs by departing with skeleton squads.

Though Daly opened the scoring in the eighth minute of the first contest, an April 12 match at the Orange County Blues, the lead proved short-lived. Just 683 fans watched as OC captain Allan Russell equalized with a penalty in the nineteenth minute. Fifty minutes later, the referee showed Sacramento defender Harrison Delbridge a straight red card for pulling down Blues forward Gibson Bardsley just outside of the box. Stephen Okai's ensuing free kick provided the winning goal in the seventieth minute. The on-field actions went from bad to worse for the Republic after the winner as a collision forced starting goalkeeper Jake Gleeson off the field. In stepped Dominik Jakubek, who last played professional soccer in 2011 as a center back in the Polish third division.

The game ended around 9:00 p.m. and at 3:00 p.m. the following day, an exhausted Sacramento side took the field against L.A. Galaxy II. The StubHub

---

[116] In 2014 the L.A. Galaxy was the only MLS club that fielded a reserve team in the USL.

[117] Allowing five substitutions per game has been commonplace since 2020, but in 2014, the USL was one of the only leagues in the world where this was permitted. The USL adopted the normal FIFA-approved amount of three in 2017.

Center Track & Field Stadium, emerging as a difficult place to play, hosted the Republic for the third time in four USL contests. Through three matches, the Galaxy had already compiled seven points at home and unlike its opponents, hadn't played since the previous week. Preki elected to start four players on eighteen hours of rest: Braun, Daly, center back Nemanja Vuković, and defensive midfielder Ivan Mirković.

Somehow, Sacramento left L.A. with three points. Daly scored his second goal of the weekend in the thirty-third minute before winger Max Alvarez hit the back of the net for the first time in his professional career just before halftime. With fifteen minutes to go, substitute forward Dakota Collins sealed the victory with his first USL strike. Jakubek, making his first start for the Republic, only faced one shot on goal and earned the first clean sheet in club history. Sacramento required the backup netminder as they only brought two goalkeepers south—Preki designated Emrah Klimenta as Jakubek's reserve if needed. In all, nine players featured in both games, with Daly, Vuković, and Mirković playing the full 180 minutes.

The grueling, twenty-one-day road trip finally concluded on April 19 as Sacramento traveled out of state for the first time in its short history. While the Republic had four USL contests under its belt, fellow expansion side Arizona United SC had played one disastrous match in club history. The prior Saturday, 2,888 fans flocked to the 12,339-capacity Peoria Sports Complex to watch Arizona's second attempt at operating a USL franchise after Phoenix FC's league license was revoked the previous year due to a multitude of violations.

Playing in a stadium that primarily hosted MLB spring training games, Arizona appeared ready to follow in the footsteps of a Phoenix team that finished 5-14-7[118] in 2013, while only managing to defeat one playoff-bound side. The week before Sacramento arrived, Arizona United SC hosted another 2014 USL expansion team, Oklahoma City Energy FC, for its franchise opener in a match that remained scoreless heading into the break. Two minutes before halftime, though, Arizona defender London Woodberry received his second yellow card in six minutes and was sent off. In the first twenty-six minutes of the second half, four different players scored for the visitors in what was then the USL's most lopsided contest of the season.

A repeat performance looked on the cards when Rodrigo López opened his Republic account twenty-seven minutes in after playing a one-two with Stewart. However, eleven minutes later, Arizona caught the Sacramento defense ball watching as Brandon Swartzendruber ghosted in at the back post to equalize the scoreline with a finish past Jakubek. Then, for the second time in three games, the referee sent off a Republic center back.

This time it was Daly, who was judged to have denied a clear goalscoring opportunity in first half stoppage time. Jakubek saved the penalty from Arizona

---

[118] Two of the victories came against Antigua Barracuda, which finished 0-26-0 and folded.

captain Matt Kassel, but Sacramento now had to play the final forty-five minutes down a man. The club nearly pulled out an improbable draw only for FC Dallas loan player Jonathan Top to slot home the first winner in Arizona United SC history with just five minutes remaining.

The five-game road trip concluded with Sacramento compiling a respectable 2-2-1 record, good for seven points. However, in games in which the Republic finished with eleven players, that mark was 2-0-1. "We have to, as a team, be disciplined and smart with the fouls that we commit," Klimenta said after the match. "We have to dig deep and show a lot of character, poise, and heart to keep playing and keep creating chances which we ultimately did. Unfortunately, the team that created more chances, even with a man down, lost tonight."

It was still early in the season, but Sacramento had shown it could at least compete during the first five games. Even with the loss to Arizona, the Republic still stood in a tie for third place in the USL standings with the Dayton Dutch Lions. Only the L.A, Galaxy II (ten points) and Orlando City SC (eight) had more points than Sacramento, but those clubs had already combined to play eight home games. Furthermore, the Republic's nine goals ranked second in the league, and its plus-three goal differential was tied for the best in the USL.

In trademark fashion, head coach Preki mostly refused to point out any positives when speaking to the media. "We have done a decent job," he said. "In saying that, we felt we have allowed quite a few points to skip away from us. We should have four to six points more. But we always knew that this was going to be a long, hard process."

Despite the streaming debacle, the club's moderate on-field success assured that Sacramento would return home with plenty of buzz surrounding it ahead of the April 26 home opener against the Harrisburg City Islanders. While an injury ruled Braun out of the match, the San Jose Earthquakes readied a like-for-like replacement to loan to the Republic. Coming off a solid rookie campaign in which he ranked fifth in goals among first-year professionals in MLS, Jesuit alum Adam Jahn arrived in Sacramento the Wednesday after the Arizona loss. A Davis native, Jahn provided a towering presence up top with his 6-foot-3 frame, but his clean touch on the ball earned him the nickname "Pillow Feet." However, he'd found playing time scarce so far in 2014–his solitary appearance for the Earthquakes in 2014 lasted three minutes before he was shown red.

Jahn, 23, and the Earthquakes hoped the club's affiliation with the Republic would help earn him regular minutes in order to continue developing, and it appeared as if he'd earn his chance right away. "I think it's going to be amazing," Jahn said of the upcoming home opener. "I mean, it's perfect timing, the first home game for the team. I'm blessed enough to be a part of it. I'm really excited to play in front of a lot of old friends."

With the squad coming together on the field, the front office continued preparations off it ahead of the Republic's Sacramento debut. "For our staff and for our team, it's very exciting to open our doors and show the people of

Sacramento the experience we're trying to create," Smith said. "I think we've done a pretty good job in developing a plan and a business model that will eventually work. [We're excited] for people in Sacramento to enjoy the sport at a pretty high level…I've been waiting for this day for a long time and look forward to the outcome. Win or lose, we ultimately hope to create a special entertainment opportunity for the people of Sacramento.

"Hopefully they'll have smiles on their faces when they leave Hughes Stadium on Saturday night."

Smith's confident proclamations, combined with ticket sales data and local Republic brand recognition, finally helped capture the local media's attention. *The Sacramento Bee* sent an intern to cover Sacramento Soccer Day in 2013 and hadn't bothered to cover the Republic's opening game at the Galaxy. However, the paper's soccer-loathing editors finally reluctantly agreed to free up column inches for the new club. *The Bee* recapped each of Sacramento's previous four games and featured the Republic eight more times in the nineteen days leading up to the match. Furthermore, *The Davis Enterprise* assigned a reporter to the Sacramento beat after feeling the club's buzz from across the Causeway.

Just over twenty-four hours before kickoff, Sacramento Republic FC announced that it had accomplished its mission. At 4:13 p.m. on April 25, club brass officially sold its last seat for the game, a feat made easier thanks to the nearly 5,000 who had already purchased season tickets. The USL's previous record attendance stood at 10,697, a mark that Sacramento looked set to nearly double. Professional soccer teams had come and gone in the city for decades, but this one finally felt different for those around long enough to see it all.

"I'm very excited," longtime Sacramento State coach Mike Linenberger told *The Bee*. "I feel a majority of the groups in the past tried to do things on the cheap, so they didn't last very long. This group is very different. They haven't been afraid to spend money, so I see a long-lasting situation in Sacramento."

Added winger Max Alvarez: "Knowing that there is the possibility of 20,000 people coming to watch us is pretty special, not only for the team but for the city. I know Sacramento soccer fans have been waiting for this moment for a long time. As long as we get results, we'll get the fan support. Then I expect nothing less than one day being in MLS."

Mentioning Sacramento Republic FC's ambitions to join Major League Soccer this early in club history may have appeared naive to some, but the sellout announcement piqued the interest of soccer fans and media around the country. Before the opener kicked off people began taking notice of the upstart sports market previously best known for basketball futility. When Sacramento Republic FC took the field at Hughes Stadium, it would mark the first fully professional men's outdoor soccer game in the city since Team Sacramento lost the fourteenth of its fourteen home games before folding in 1999.

The dawn of a new soccer era in Sacramento would begin on April 26, 2014. All the club had to do was take the field and deliver the fans a product worth returning for.

# EIGHT
# WE'RE ALL DOROTHY:
# A SELLOUT AT HUGHES[119]

As a wave of emotion washes over him, Joe Wagoner breaks down. He nearly collapses but manages to regain his composure despite his surroundings. After nearly two years filled with long nights, endless meetings, and frantic preparation, it's finally time. Two hours before kickoff, Wagoner nervously approaches the front gate to Hughes Stadium, the 20,231-seat monstrosity that he once dreamed would host professional soccer matches. As he strides down the concourse on the campus of Sacramento City College, he witnesses a sight he'll never forget: the fans arrive in droves.

Two officers clad in blue "CSC Security Supervisor" jackets stand in front of a seemingly endless line of locals that stretches all the way back to the SCC parking garage a quarter of a mile away. Running ten people wide, the mass forms less of an orderly queue than a peaceful mob. A peaceful mob of Sacramento Republic FC fans.

"I started crying," Wagoner would say in the Republic team headquarters eighteen months later. "I was just like, oh my God, people are here. I couldn't believe it. I still get teary thinking about it. I just couldn't believe it. They were there. They had their kits on."

The capacity crowd of raucous supporters cheers on the Republic, at the edge of their seats all night as they watch the action unfold. Witnessing the first fully professional outdoor soccer game in Sacramento in more than a decade, the crowd gasps with every half chance, oohs and ahhs at every bit of midfield wizardry, and

---

[119] I recommend pairing this chapter with "Love you Madly" by Cake.

groans when Robbie Derschang of the Harrisburg City Islanders scores just five minutes into the match after a defensive lapse from the hosts.

Local high school product and San Jose Earthquakes loan player Adam Jahn refuses to let the game go without a fight, though. Just after the half-hour mark the towering striker, who's just arrived on loan from the Quakes earlier in the week, heads home an in-swinging free kick delivered by midfielder Max Alvarez. Tens of thousands of fans in the 86-year-old concrete bowl leap to their feet as Jahn sprints to the corner flag to celebrate in exuberance alongside the teammates he's just met.

There will be no Cinderella story for the Republic, though. Longtime City Islander[120] attacking midfielder Morgan Langley nutmegs Sacramento backup goalkeeper Dominik Jakubek seven minutes into the second half after spinning past left back Jack Avesyan on the slick Hughes turf. The visitors claim a 2-1 victory, ruining the on-field result the Republic dreamed of for its first-ever home match. But off the field, the contest makes headlines nationwide.

## The Data

Twenty professional soccer matches took place in the top three divisions of soccer in the United States and Canada on the weekend of April 26 and 27 in 2014. In all, those matches drew an announced total of 209,307 fans.[121] Roughly one in every ten fans who watched a live professional soccer game north of Mexico in the Western Hemisphere that weekend did so in California's capital city. The Republic crowd bested the average MLS attendance of 19,051. It topped the *total* five-match NASL figure of 19,760. Sacramento fans represented over half of the 37,142 spectators who watched USL games that weekend. Overall, the Republic's crowd was the third largest, behind the Seattle Sounders FC (38,582) and Houston Dynamo (20,558).

Not bad for a brain trust whose original goal stood in the low five figures, a number that could potentially challenge Orlando City SC's USL regular season record crowd of 10,697, set the prior August. "I always said 10,000," Wagoner recalled of the ambition at the time. "If we can get 10,000 in Hughes, that would be great."

---

[120] Part of the fun covering this game: learning that "Harrisburg" was the location of the Republic's opponents while its club name was the "City Islanders." Like what? (For those die-hard USL fans, yes, I am aware that the team played their home games at a place called "City Island.")
[121] All attendance data was gathered from the official website of each respective league.

# 10,000

The success of Sacramento Soccer Day generated roughly 2,000 season-ticket deposits on the spot so the Republic front office figured the final 8,000 wouldn't prove too daunting of a task, especially given season-ticket sales continued strongly and steadily afterwards. Wagoner compared the initial interest to an old UPS commercial where a pair of startup employees pressed a button on a computer to put their product on the market. As soon as the two made it available, the computer beeped to announce their first sale and the staffers high-fived and cracked beers to celebrate the instant success. Shortly thereafter, another sale registered to the surprise of the exuberant pair, who continued to celebrate. Then the beeping, originally resembling the pace of a heart monitor, began to sound more like a Geiger counter detecting highly radioactive material—everyone bought the product.

"And they're sitting there going like, 'oh fuck, we need to hire people,'" Wagoner said as he reenacted the commercial. "The same thing happened, I'm telling you. We went on sale with this thing, and leading up to it, we just weren't sure what was going to happen. I mean we're playing on football lines on a small field. No one knew our team. No one knows any of the players. We opened up against, was it Harrisburg? Who gives a shit about Harrisburg?"

For a group with the ambition of the Republic, 10,000 was doable. Maybe even easy. Hell, these were the same guys who set minor league baseball records with the Sacramento River Cats. "Back to my River Cats days, we didn't just blow out the attendance number, we killed it," Warren Smith recalled. "And so going back to 2000, we opened up Raley Field, and so we kept thinking why couldn't we do the same here?"

Perhaps that thinking was how Smith rationalized his next move.

# 20,000

With most of the front office stuck in a sales meeting, attempting to figure out how to draw a five-figure crowd, Smith and another front office employee arrived for a speaking engagement at Farrell's Ice Cream Parlor in East Sacramento. Never one to make controversial statements just to garner media headlines, Smith decided to go against the grain at Farrell's. The goal was no longer the internally discussed number of 10,000, but a very publicly voiced figure of 20,000.

"We had all our plans on how we were going to get to 10,000, and boy, we thought we could make it, because we sold 2,500 tickets on the first day," Wagoner said. "It was unbelievable. And then [Smith] comes in, and he goes, 'Hey guys, I just told all the people at Farrell's Ice Cream that we're going to sell 20,000 tickets.' I'm like, 'Warren, that's not what we talked about, by like half. We're not going from 200 to 400, we're going from 10,000 to 20,000.' You know, you gotta hand it to the guy, he looked at the group, and he and I talked, and he goes, 'What do you need? What do you need? It's not an option at this point. It's not an option that this is going to sell out...it will sell out.

"You will do it.'"

To help motivate his exhausted crew, Wagoner liked to remind everyone of their value by telling a story about *The Wizard of Oz* production he "starred" in as a child. The Republic co-founder first began sharing this anecdote when an employee expressed to Wagoner his job, in the grand scheme of things, wasn't that big of a deal because he just sold tickets. "You don't *just* sell tickets," Wagoner remembers responding. "Shit, that's the most important thing, it is the *single* most important thing that we do."

As a fourth grader, Wagoner held high hopes of landing the coveted Tin Man role at his school's production of the 1939 classic film. Whether due to his lack of acting chops or the school staff's penchant to select sixth graders for the larger roles, Wagoner didn't get the part. Instead, the drama department cast him as a flower in the background. "A strong supporting role," he said, sarcastically.

The play was scheduled to run three times and after the second show, because he lived in a small Midwestern town, all his family friends sent him cards congratulating him on his excellent performance. While flattered, there was one problem with the situation.

"I wasn't there," Wagoner laughed. "I wasn't even there, and [my friends' parents] sent cards about what a good flower I was standing in the background."

Ready to reprise a role he'd earned so much praise for, Wagoner arrived at the third showing only to find that it'd been called off. The actress playing Dorothy contracted pneumonia and without the lead, the production couldn't continue. According to Wagoner, the first time he repeated this memory to his employees, someone stopped him in the middle to ask, "Why the fuck are you telling this story?"

"Because here, we're all the leading role, man. We're all Dorothy," Wagoner responded. "The flower doesn't show up, no one notices. Dorothy doesn't show up, everybody notices. Every single person in this office plays a leading role, and it's important that they know that because when you only have twenty people to do the job of fifty people, everybody's critical."

From then on, the mantra "We're all Dorothy" became a common saying among Republic staffers. Wagoner even had coffee mugs made adorning that phrase alongside a cartoon of the character wearing the club's colors.

"Last year, the motto of the year was, 'We're all Dorothy,'" Wagoner said in 2015. "For people who didn't understand, it was like, 'What are they, transvestites? Are they crossdressers? What the hell are we talking about here?'"

Even staffed with an army full of Dorothys, 20,000 ticket sales would prove difficult, if not impossible. As Wagoner said, the Republic was a team full of unknown players playing a game against a small-market team that no one had heard of. The hosting venue featured a turf field with football lines and a racing track. It was hardly the ideal conditions for a task so large that no one in the history of United States lower-division soccer had attempted something of this magnitude. According to Smith, there was no longer any choice in the matter–it *had* to happen. Sacramento Republic FC needed far more Dorothys than flowers.

With the scope of the event greatly magnified, the Republic leaned on the community for all the support that it could offer, asking roughly eighty local businesses to send out messages using their email databases. According to Wagoner, not a single company mentioned taking a cut of the sales, which were successful. Extremely successful. "We sold something like, I want to say 6,000 tickets just through partnering with other people's databases," Wagoner said. "The whole community recognized that this was important."

Just as important was establishing person-to-person relationships between club executives and members of the community. "It was a lot of human interaction and a lot of sharing our vision, what we were trying to accomplish, and frankly listening to people," Smith said. "We needed to deliver, and we learned so much from that process. We're learning that it's not like any other sport, no gimmicks, no T-shirts being shot into the crowd, you know, stuff that we're used to. So, we learned that it's got to be about the event, and to Sacramento's credit, we really enjoy events. We do. Whether it be sports facilities, TBD Fest,[122] State Fair, we really do participate in events. I knew that in my heart, frankly, that it was capable. If we're selling 14,000 for baseball, why couldn't we sell 20,000 for a sport that is frankly hitting an age group really that hasn't had people pay attention to them, and that's the 18–40-year-olds."

Even though the Republic staff had grown by roughly a factor of four since Sacramento Soccer Day, sleep hours again came at a premium ahead of the game. To reach their magic number, the front office tried everything from cold calls to group promotions. Sales representatives established partnerships with local youth soccer clubs to help drive interest. Perhaps most important though, according to Wagoner, remained the work they'd put in while attending the American Outlaws' World Cup qualifying watch parties.

Drinking beers with the local die-hards allowed the Republic to discover an established, passionate fan base, communicate with all the important figures in local soccer, and to get to know the people who would likely become their biggest customers. It was at those parties that the foundations were laid for the Tower Bridge Battalion. The supporters' group revolution was still in its infancy in the United States, but the Republic wasn't going to miss out on helping its club establish an organic brand of support to help drive home its goals in the community.

"I think probably somewhere around the 12- or 13,000-ticket mark, we just kind of got together [and said], 'Hey, we've got 7,000 tickets to go, this is going to

---

122 A local three-day concert held in late September.

happen.'" Wagoner said. "'We're not selling a soccer game anymore; we're selling a movement of the community to make its mark.' And the people bought into it."

The final ticket sold the day before the game, but the work wasn't finished–Sacramento still had to actually host the event.

# Gameday

Track 7 Brewery isn't so much a bar as it is a converted warehouse. Situated six miles from Downtown in a light industrial block featuring drab views of blue auto body shops alongside the aptly named mustache wax supplier Cock Grease Hair Pomade,[123] it seems an odd place to brew arguably Sacramento's most popular beer. On a typical night, table space is rare, but the last call comes as early as 8:45 p.m.

Yet dog-toting couples, men sporting well-coiffed hipster beards, and twenty-something singles sipping on the flagship Panic IPA beer perpetually pack the facility to the brim. The intoxicating smell coming from the rotating assortment of food trucks the bar books nightly catches the light Delta Breeze on hot Sacramento evenings and wafts over the patrons.

Track 7 operates on a minimalist vibe–the brewery would rather focus on creating quality products with few distractions preventing patrons from actually talking to each other. There are no TVs, no live music, no arcade machines, simply benches, barrels, and beers provide the entertainment for a generation that can't seem to pry its eyes off pocket-sized super computers.

Employees brew their popular beer on site in the six giant metal vats behind the dozen or so taps that flow to the ten-person deep line that inevitably appears during the busy hours of the night. Parking always proves abundant for Track 7's patrons as the bar typically operates during the hours that the block's other businesses close shop. In the parking lot, the cars and bicycles that transport customers from any of the three surrounding residential neighborhoods all belong to those imbibing.

Named for the seventh line of railroad tracks that run parallel to the watering hole, Track 7 harkens back to a past time in the city in which trains operated within Sacramento on a regular basis. By 2014 there's hardly any activity left in the industry that the city was once known for. In 1852, the Sacramento Valley Railroad became the first in California to file papers of incorporation, bringing industry and prosperity to the region.

While the railway gradually faded from prominence in the new millennium, it had served as the main source of transcontinental transportation in the early twentieth century. Today Track 7's name pays homage to the apparatus many used to start a new life in what's now the most populous state in the Union.

---

123 Actual website: www.cockgrease.com

Already established as a popular destination for beer enthusiasts, Track 7 had hosted large crowds on weekend nights before. But no one could prepare for what was coming on April 26, 2014. Hughes Stadium stands just across the street from the brewery–The Tower Bridge Battalion began its invasion midday.

Two hours before gametime, around the same moment that Wagoner broke down in tears, the line for a beer at Track 7 stretches nearly 200 feet across the street. It takes forty-five minutes to travel from the back of it to the front–many fans purchase the maximum allowed two beers and then walk directly to the end of the queue again to wait for two more. By the time they'd again reach the front, they'd be finished with the brews and ready for another moderately priced pair of libations.

The demographics of the crowd appear split between soccer lifers wearing Republic kits and those preparing to attend their first professional match. Some come simply as fans of the beautiful game, others venture out to support something local. But nearly everyone, whether they'd return to another Republic game or not, sports at least one article of clothing in a shade of red while they intermingle in the jovial atmosphere.

About an hour before the game, it's finally time for the Battalion to commence its first home march to the match. A 100-strong group of maroon-clad supporters begin the two-block trek to Hughes Stadium, clogging Sutterville Road. The throng belts out songs, drawing confused looks from pedestrians who aren't used to the sight of a mob of grown men dressed in the same colors walking and singing their love for a soccer team and its five-game history.

As the Battalion marches west towards the stadium, two men rapidly approach Hughes heading east. One rides a bike, pulling along the other, who balances on his longboard just behind. When the pair turn onto Sutterville, the mass of pedestrians forces them to slow their pace. By the time they reach 23rd Street, they've come to a complete stop. On their right, a crowd of maybe 200 blocks traffic from bustling down the normally busy road. The second man steps off his longboard, jaw dropped in awe. He's attended countless World Cup and Euro matches, but this stops him dead in his tracks. After taking a moment to comprehend the madness, the man with the longboard turns to his friend with the bike.

"Holy shit, dude," says Jeremy Field. "This is a proper soccer game."

# Going National

The 2-1 loss robbed the night of its storybook ending, but the event put Sacramento on the map as a viable soccer market. "That next day, [MLS commissioner] Don Garber tweeted, 'Gosh look what's happening in the USA,'" Smith remembered. "He wasn't in particular saying, what a great job Sacramento, he said look what's happening in the sport of soccer in the United States, 20,000 people in Sacramento."

Added Wagoner: "It's one of those nights you think, we're going to get totally loaded after this thing and celebrate. That was the biggest disappointment of the whole thing. I wanted to go drink a ton of beer and celebrate, I think we had a couple of beers over at New Helvetia and then, literally everyone was just too tired. [I'm thinking], 'What the hell is this?' We're supposed to go out, but we're tired because we had to return banners in the morning or something."

If they were tired then, though, the Republic staff had no idea what type of exhaustion was headed their way. The club's planned home schedule involved hosting two more games at Hughes in the following three weeks before it opened Bonney Field on June 7 against Arizona United SC. Seven days after the Harrisburg City Islanders loss, 17,414 attended a 2-1 victory over Orange County SC in which Jahn bagged the club's first home-game winner in the seventieth minute. It wasn't a second consecutive sellout, but the attendance figure still represented a number nearly 7,000 higher than the USL's previous record.

"The haters came out right away," Wagoner later said, shaking his head. According to Wagoner, internet trolls and those who didn't understand the American soccer landscape claimed that the crowd for the second Hughes game represented a failure. That group called the opener a coincidence, hypothesizing that fans only showed up for the novelty.

"We got 17,000 people," Wagoner said. "That's when we started posting the MLS attendances in the office because people were like, 'Oh, they didn't sell out.' But hold on, we'd be ninth in MLS right now.

"Shut the fuck up."

Wagoner and the rest of the Republic staff took the comments personally. Instead of responding on social media, though, they chose to make a statement through their actions. The Monday after the game, they gathered at the club's headquarters and made a pact to silence the doubters. The club vowed to sell out every USL game for the rest of the season.

"At this point [from the outside perception], 20,000...it's a fluke," Wagoner said. "You were seeing all over the MLS boards, 17,000, but people were still like, 'Ah shit, that's a lot of people, but it wasn't a sellout.

"I believe the next game was two weeks away and we said, 'Listen, we can't show any chinks in our armor for USL games, there are going to be some friendlies that pop up that we find out about late,'" he added. "'But we're going to sell out every fucking game for the remainder of our livelihood in this league, don't give a shit what it takes.'

"Everyone just kind of buckled down and went, 'Okay, this is where we make our mark. If this is 10,000 people, we're off the map. Everyone recognized that, if this is ten, we're done. If it's seventeen, it still sounds good, but nothing says strength or market viability like 'Sellout.' It's the best word in the whole world from where I'm sitting, minus 'MLS.'"

The Republic again hit their target for the May 17 classico against LA Galaxy II. An announced 20,231 packed the stands to watch Rodrigo López win the match with a late free kick *golazo* that foreshadowed the two clubs' playoff match-up. By that point, construction delays had pushed Bonney Field's debut back a further two weeks, necessitating one final Hughes match. On June 7, the club earned a third consecutive positive result in a 1-1 draw against Arizona in front of the season's third sellout crowd. Chad Bartlomé's stoppage time header[124] earned the hosts a point in the club's final USL game at the stadium in 2014.

The staff pulled out all the stops for both matches. While the number of Republic season-ticket holders gradually increased, the sheer size of Hughes forced sales reps to think creatively to fill the venue. Sacramento employees pitched sales to relatives, relatives of relatives, youth soccer teams, adult soccer teams, and anyone else located within 100 miles who possessed any semblance of interest in soccer or the city's community.

"It was all these folks that came together, and again, it was a legit sellout, and we nailed it, and that was the Bartlomé header," Wagoner said. "I remember, you can see it on the video, we were standing behind the goal on this side of the stadium, and I jump into Brett [Reitter's] arms like, this is going to fucking happen...the implications, if you did it once, it's not legit unless you do it again, and then it's not legit unless you do it again. Everyone was looking for those reasons not to believe."

Sacramento Republic FC employees certainly believed. The club found the correct group of people–more Dorothys than flowers–who drove three sellouts in four games over a six-week period. In all, 78,107 attended the Republic's first four home games in 2014. Third division soccer somehow became the hottest ticket in town that spring despite streaming failures in Sacramento's first game and a loss in the home opener.

"It's the city, man," Wagoner said. "We gotta keep on remembering it. We're not the fucking smartest people in the world, we're just people that, I think, found the right time to bring it to the market.

"The market was ready."

---

[124] When asked after the game how it felt to score that goal, Bartlomé replied, "it felt great," and then stared at the group of reporters on hand.

# NINE
# BONNEY FIELD:
# A PROPER HOME[125]

"Hubert Rotteveel looks out his window from his Arco Arena office and sees his field of dreams," Debbie Arrington wrote in *The Sacramento Bee* in 1999. "The barest steel and concrete bones of a stadium crop out of the North Natomas dirt next door. To the general manager of the Sacramento Knights, that site represents a future on the outside. 'With the right stadium, outdoor pro soccer could bloom in the valley,' Rotteveel says. 'It comes down to a respect for the game. If you're professional, give it the professionalism it needs. Create a professional atmosphere. Then the fans will come.'"

Arrington's article continued by discussing numbers–how much such a venue might cost and how many people it would seat. "'We're not talking huge money,' [Sacramento Geckos CEO Yan Skwara] said. "'A new professional baseball stadium costs $400 million. We could do it for $3 million to $4 million. Our focus is to identify some land and build a soccer venue to hold 10,000 people.'"

The article hit the press in June of that year. The previous month longtime soccer supporter and investor Lamar Hunt unveiled Crew Stadium, Major League Soccer's first soccer-specific facility, to the public in Columbus, Ohio. Hunt financed the 22,555-capacity arena for just $28.5 million and in doing so provided the blueprint for soccer executives like Skwara to draw inspiration from. Two weeks after the Geckos CEO spoke about constructing a potential stadium in Sacramento, he stepped away from the club, sending it spiraling toward its predictable and inevitable death. Skwara never came close to building a soccer facility in the city.

---

[125] I recommend pairing this chapter with "Short Skirt/Long Jacket" by Cake.

Nearly two decades later, Skwara existed as a minor footnote in Sacramento's sporting history. He'd since moved on to run the fourth division United Premier Soccer League while coaching the competition's flagship L.A. Wolves FC franchise. Rotteveel exited the public eye in the summer of 2010 when his legal troubles designated him a *persona non grata* in Northern California. The pair who started the movement to construct Sacramento's first soccer-specific stadium have long since departed the local soccer scene.

But their idea lived on.

# If You Build It...

If there was one trait that stood out among the Sacramento Republic FC brain trust in 2014 compared to similar startups elsewhere in the country, it was its uncommon ability to exist in a state of constant self-awareness. The Republic front office was often the first to acknowledge it didn't always have the right answers to every question. Instead of approaching each of the many unforeseen problems that consistently popped up with a holier-than-thou attitude, Smith, Wagoner, and Co. openly acknowledged they had much to learn about the intricacies of soccer.

Or as Joe Wagoner sometimes said, "We don't always know what the fuck we're doing."

Speaking to fans in the lead up to Sacramento Soccer Day taught Wagoner and Warren Smith differences between soccer and "mainstream" American sports. The pair quickly ditched plans for in-game music, T-shirt guns, and the standard game-time promotions they'd become accustomed to during their years in baseball. But they only came to this conclusion after listening to complaints and feedback from soccer fans in other markets whose owners refused to listen to their expert supporters.

Those responses formed the basis of the Republic's philosophy to eschew "traditional" pro sports marketing strategies and focus on the needs and wants specific to soccer in Sacramento. Sometimes just asking your consumer what they want is the simplest and best decision a professional sports franchise can make. Depending on who you spoke to, Major League Soccer didn't understand this concept for its first ten to fifteen years, or it still hadn't grasped it around the same time Sacramento Republic FC started making national headlines.

As quick learners, Wagoner and Smith possessed this knowledge from Day One. So, despite Wagoner's earlier premonition of bringing soccer to Hughes Stadium, the venue was never seriously considered as a full-time home for the Republic. The fan feedback clearly indicated that Hughes wasn't what the supporters or players wanted.

The stadium's location, standing in close proximity to two major freeways and a light-rail station, certainly qualified as a positive, but nothing else would foster an authentic or high-quality soccer experience. Artificial turf covered the playing surface at Hughes, which already featured tight confines due to its original intended use as a multipurpose facility. Stretching roughly 116 yards from goal to goal, the length wasn't the issue. However, Hughes measured around sixty-four yards from sideline to sideline, making it ten yards narrower than most professional soccer pitches. The resulting area proved to be almost 15 percent smaller than the Republic's preferred dimensions. And this is before bringing into account the permanent American football markings on the turf which everyone, especially Graham Smith, despised.

Lastly, the racing track surrounding the field kept even front-row supporters more than a first-down's distance away from the action. No matter how many fans packed inside Hughes Stadium, the intimate, but intimidating, atmosphere Sacramento desired wouldn't be possible.

Another issue came with the sheer size of the venue—the Republic may have sold out three of the four home games at Hughes in 2014, but doing so over the course of a season would present major challenges. That same year, six MLS teams averaged more than the 20,231 fans Hughes could seat at full capacity. While it's impossible to know for sure, it remained unlikely that the upstart lower-division club could maintain those lofty attendance figures after the first four games.

Furthermore, the Republic planned to schedule relatively high-profile friendlies against European clubs like West Bromwich Albion and Rangers FC, neither of which would ever agree to playing on an artificial surface. Drawing a modest 10,000 a game would easily shatter USL records, but 10,000 fans in Hughes still left more than 10,000 empty seats. The scariest image in the minds of Republic brass was that of a half-full stadium. Half-full stadiums kill atmospheres.[126]

Then there was the other group that didn't love the idea of the Republic playing at Hughes: Major League Soccer. "I think the quote was, 'If you want to be taken more seriously, it would be better that you play on a pitch,'" Smith recalled MLS officials telling him. "And I didn't know what a pitch was."

After learning a new vocabulary word, Smith scouted properties from as far away from Hughes as West Sacramento (where he had experience from pushing through Raley Field), to the Railyards (Downtown Sacramento's white whale for literally everything). According to Smith, though, neither of those potential sites led to any advanced conversations, but there was a third option: the Cal Expo State Fairgrounds. Dormant for much of the year, the northeast Sacramento-based facility featured a water park, a horse racing track, and vast swaths of land to stage a state fair massive enough to jam up traffic lanes and turn a simple five-mile drive across Sacramento into an hour-long affair.

The first proposal involved converting the horse racing track into a soccer stadium, but an assessment determined that modifying the facility wouldn't be feasible. However, the eighty-acre fairgrounds included an expansive area of

---

[126] Just try going to literally any weekday MLB game.

undeveloped land adjacent to an endless gray parking lot sometimes used for RV shows. For fifteen years, the site had previously housed an outdoor amphitheater, but Cal Expo closed it following noise complaints in 1998. With the Republic's inaugural USL season on the horizon, the club hastily brokered a deal with Cal Expo and its concessions provider, Ovations, to erect a stadium on the vacant site.

Wagoner and Smith looked at the agreement as a win for all sides. With a new stadium, Sacramentans would flock to the fairgrounds more often, generating more revenue for Cal Expo and Ovations. While the new facility would prioritize Sacramento Republic FC, it could also host other sporting events, such as rugby, and serve as a concert venue. Cal Expo and Ovations would fill some of the off-season's dead days, while the Republic would help finance the $4 million project and enter the USL with a stadium to call home.

"You have to realize, the challenge of building a new stadium is the overall cost," Smith said. "At Cal Expo we didn't have to put gates up, we didn't have to build parking. They had some restrooms, [and] they had some stands. So it lowered the overall project cost, to make it feasible…If you look at building stands, if you look at building parking lots, they're immensely expensive, just because of the amount of space you need for the cars. But to have some gates, to have some restrooms, to have the infrastructure, sewer, water, electrical, that was huge. We had to run some lines to tap in, but we didn't have to create new infrastructure.

"Honestly, that project, if we had to do all of that, would have been over $10 million."

According to Wagoner, Cal Expo and Ovations might not have fully grasped Sacramento Republic FC's potential draw—the two companies reportedly focused on earning new streams of revenue by pulling concerts away from ARCO Arena. Even farther northeast of Sacramento than the fairgrounds, ARCO rusted in the suburb of Natomas, sitting on its last legs next to a strip mall. Public transportation didn't service the rotting facility, which consistently ranked as one of the worst stadiums in the National Basketball Association.

"Soccer was their trojan horse to get their concert venue, and they haven't held a concert yet," Wagoner laughed in 2015. "They're actually making more off of soccer games than they ever would have off of concerts. Ideally, they'd be able to do both and make a ton more money."

In addition to pro rugby and a 30,000-strong Bernie Sanders presidential rally, concerts would eventually arrive at the venue. In 2016 the company that owned and operated the facility, Spectra, acquired a stage for the field's south end, finally giving the green light to musical events. But that was still two years away in early 2014 when Cal Expo, Ovations, Spectra, and the Republic agreed on a deal to construct an 8,000-seat stadium on the former amphitheater grounds.

The contractor's first draft produced a few road bumps as the plans included low-grade, high-school style bleachers with each row barely rising above the one in front of it. Wagoner and Republic director of club partnerships Sean Morrison acted quickly to gather evidence showing why the plans wouldn't suffice. The pair drove around to high schools in the area, taking photos of themselves sitting in similar stands and some of the site lines from the bleachers. The two Republic staffers convinced the contractor by showing what it might look like for a fan if another supporter sat just six inches below—creating an authentic soccer atmosphere was paramount in the process.

As Sacramento hit the road to begin its inaugural USL season, construction workers back home put shovels into dirt on the site of the unnamed future stadium in March. The Republic aimed for a grand opening during the June 7 match against Arizona United SC. Local company Bonney Plumbing, Heating, Air, and Rooter Service signed a multiyear naming rights deal on April 19 but by then the project had experienced a few unexpected delays. Sacramento would play the Arizona match at Hughes and open Bonney Field on June 20 against the Colorado Rapids Reserves.

# They Will Come

By mid-June, Sacramento was ready to show off its brand-new, sparkling facility. Featuring three medium-sized grandstands, a VIP section behind the south goal, and a full-sized video replay board, Bonney Field immediately became the envy of the rest of lower-division soccer in the United States and Canada. Fans queued at the entrance hours before kickoff on a typically sunny summer Sacramento evening. As the heat dissipated into the cool night sky, a buzz in the crowd emerged. For once in Sacramento's sporting history, the quality of play on the field equaled the enthusiasm of the boisterous fan base.

The match served as the Republic's second and final contest against an MLS Reserve League team, but many of the players in the Rapids' starting lineup hardly qualified as reserves. Panamanian international Gabriel Torres led the forward line alongside former No. One overall MLS SuperDraft pick Danny Mwanga. Charles Eloundou, capped at the senior level by Cameroon, supported the pair from the wing and one-time U.S. international Gale Agbossoumonde anchored the visitor's back line.

While Mwanga opened the scoring with a fourteenth-minute sucker punch, the strike came against the run of play. Sacramento captain Justin Braun equalized six minutes later before a late first-half brace[127] from Rodrigo López sent the Republic into halftime with a 3-1 lead. Torres and Eloundou each scored in the first ten minutes of the second frame to level the match before San Jose Earthquakes loan player Mike Fucito stepped up to provide a storybook ending for the hosts.

An MLS journeyman already on his fourth club in a six-year professional career, Fucito hardly saw the field in San Jose as the Earthquakes preferred Chris

---

[127] Two goals.

Wondolowski up top. The future all-time leading MLS goalscorer had tied the MLS record for goals in a season in 2012 and showed no signs of slowing down to allow Fucito more time on the field. The Earthquakes hoped to resurrect Fucito's career three years after he'd shown promise with the Seattle Sounders. Rendered expendable for most MLS league games, San Jose still wanted to get Fucito a run on the field, loaning him to the Republic near the beginning of season. Fucito came into the Bonney opener with a solitary goal in four previous appearances for the Republic but was relegated to the bench to start the match against the Rapids.

Looking to make a halftime change for Portland Timbers loan player Steven Evans, Republic head coach Preki inserted Fucito into the lineup at the break. Dormant in terms of influence for most of the ensuing thirty-nine minutes, the speedy Harvard alum received a perfectly weighted through ball from reserve Republic forward Chad Bartlomé behind the Colorado defense in the eighty-fourth minute.

Though Rapids goalkeeper John Berner rushed off his line quickly to cut down Fucito's angle, the forward arrived just in time near the top of the box to deflect Berner's attempted clearance towards the opposition goal. Fucito finished off the play in acrobatic fashion from just one yard out with his weaker, right foot. Nearly crashing into the post and subsequently falling over the endline almost into the VIP section, Fucito somehow managed to stab the ball into the back of the net for a 4-3 home lead.[128] It wasn't the prettiest of goals, but it was the first game winner in Bonney Field history, predictably sending the sellout crowd of 8,000 into pandemonium. Only the referee's final whistle elicited a similar response from the jubilant crowd as Fucito's goal.

After the match, every home player strutted around the new stadium sporting boyish grins on their faces. The Republic had just played aesthetically pleasing soccer on an immaculate pitch in a soccer-specific stadium constructed in fewer than three months. Of course, the response wasn't all positive, Wagoner recalled hearing some say, "I wish we were back at Hughes."

The genial Wagoner laughed off those complaints, "It's like are you fucking kidding me?" he said. "Our team plays way better on this field at Bonney. [When] you're staring at it, you actually get to look right at the field as opposed to being on a curve. There are so many positives to that field. You have people, I don't know…" The normally animated Wagoner trailed off for a moment, here, shaking his head in disbelief when remembering the criticism the Republic received.

After a few seconds, Wagoner collected himself and continued his thoughts. "There are always those negative things, maybe that's part of social media," he said.

---

[128] Oddly, Fucito would never play for the Republic again due to a dispute between Preki and the Earthquakes. Citing dwindling numbers caused by injuries, San Jose reportedly called back Fucito to training sometime after this game. Fucito thus missed Republic training and upon return to California's capital was left off the Sacramento eighteen for the next game. The Earthquakes angrily called Fucito back, never to loan him to Sacramento again. He was out of pro soccer just one year later.

"If you love it, you're not going to say anything. If you hate it, you go, and you've got a forum there. That bugged me, that really bugged me, how many people were frustrated that...we went down from [20,231 capacity] to [8,000 capacity], and we left *the jewel* of Hughes Stadium. It's like, have you been there? They re-did the bathrooms[129] and that's about it. Not to dig on Hughes Stadium and this *crown jewel*. Yeah, it's an iconic place and there's a lot of great things about it. We love it but come on. It's not the palace you're making it out to be."

# Fortress

In the twelve games that preceded Bonney Field's inauguration, Sacramento Republic FC established itself as a solid USL squad that didn't easily give away results regardless of what Preki told the press. Despite playing eight of those matches on the road, the Republic picked up twenty points to go into its match against the Colorado Rapids Reserves as the joint fourth-place team in the league alongside Wilmington Hammerheads FC. Not bad for an expansion team, but the club Sacramento aspired to be, Orlando City SC, was running away from the competition. City had yet to record a loss and led the table with thirty points.

Though the Republic had already played the majority of its fourteen away contests and garnered a respectable seven points from four home games at Hughes Stadium, nothing had really clicked quite yet. Most teams would consider that start in an expansion year as a positive, just to be in the top half of the table this early in the club's difference would qualify as a success. Most teams, however, didn't employ Preki as their manager. And most teams didn't unveil a fortress of a home venue like Bonney Field.

With the United States Men playing in a World Cup with favorable West Coast kickoff times, a new soccer-specific stadium, and the first local international friendlies of consequence since Sacramento Pro Soccer Day, the summer of 2014 was Sacramento's coming-of-age moment as a soccer city.

Following the victory against the Colorado Rapids Reserves, the Republic braced for a jam-packed slate of games, most of which would come in its new fortress. Starting on June 26 against Arizona United SC, the Republic prepared for nineteen fixtures in the next seventy-two days, an average of one match roughly every four days. Of those, thirteen would come at home, nine in July as the adjacent Cal Expo State Fair provided several logistical and parking challenges, not to mention levels of traffic yet unseen for a USL game anywhere in the country. Somehow Sacramento not only progressed through the gauntlet unscathed, but the Republic became the hottest team in the league.

---

[129] During renovations before the 2014 season that made the venue viable for the Republic for USL play.

While carpooling to that first match against Arizona, Ivan Mirković told his roommate, outside back Emrah Klimenta, that Klimenta was going to score that night. It hardly made sense–Klimenta had only a few months as a professional under his belt after making the Republic from an open tryout. He had never played outside back in his life and still hadn't registered a USL goal or assist. Mirković's words proved prophetic, though–Klimenta's thirteenth-minute header was the only goal in a 1-0 victory.

Still, according to Preki, the performance wasn't good enough. In the fifty-eighth minute, United midfielder Widner Saint-Cyr was sent off for his second yellow of the night and though Sacramento had a man advantage for the next sixteen minutes, it couldn't capitalize by hitting the back of the net for a second time. The hero in the previous match home against Arizona, Chad Bartlomé, evened up the numbers by drawing a red card in the seventy-fourth minute for serious foul play. Both the scoreline and the red card, Bartlomé's second of the month in all competitions, enraged the Republic FC manager, who didn't hold back in his comments after the match.

"It's frustrating because the game should have been three, four to zero for us," he said. "We get a red card. It's just an unbelievable decision because when you see the replay, our guy plays the ball. The referee just decides to give a red card. Right now we're getting red cards for nothing. It's disappointing. Every game we're struggling with injuries, red cards out of nothing. We're clearly the better team, we clearly had more possession, more chances. At the end of the day, we're happy with taking the three points, but I thought the game should have been closed in the first half. I thought the final play in the final third should have been sharper."

A 2-0 road loss to OKC Energy FC in the following match was met with shrugs before the Republic returned home to host the club's first summer friendly on July 6 against Liga MX's Club Atlas, before welcoming in Orange County Blues FC fewer than twenty-four hours later for a league game. While the USL tried to get away from its policy of forcing teams on back-to-back nights, this scheduling quirk was self-inflicted–the front office wanted to build interest in the team by attracting top-level opponents that could draw additional eyeballs to the local upstarts.

For the Atlas match, a 2-1 loss, Preki fielded a makeshift lineup featuring reserves and loanees from the Portland Timbers and San Jose Earthquakes. However, Granite Bay High School graduate and San Jose Earthquakes homegrown player Tommy Thompson started against Atlas and came off the bench against Orange County. While Thompson would feature irregularly for the rest of the season, Jesuit High School alum Adam Jahn mostly stayed in Sacramento for the rest of the campaign, at times giving the Republic two key attacking pieces from the Earthquakes affiliation.

Meanwhile, the Timbers' Steven Evans played ninety on the sixth in the center of the park while his club mate George Fochive did the same from the same position on the seventh. Goalkeeper Jake Gleeson was Preki's first choice whenever he was healthy, and Timbers didn't require his services. Additionally,

Jamaican international Alvas Powell came down from Portland for three games in this tough stretch of matches.

It was a player on a Republic contract, though, who made the difference in the back-to-back gauntlet. Midfielder Octavio Guzmán popped off the bench for a cameo appearance versus Atlas before replacing Powell against the Blues and hitting a low twenty-yard winner past future teammate Patrick McLain in the ninety-second minute. The locals then split games with Richmond and Charlotte on the road while the State Fair began at the Cal Expo Fairgrounds. Sacramento returned home on July 17 to close out the final eleven days of the event with five matches.

The first of those games: a contest against Orlando City, who arrived on the back of a seventeen-game unbeaten streak. Trinidad and Tobago international Kevin Molino would go on to lead the USL in goals and assists and claim the league's MVP trophy, but he failed to provide a spark at Bonney as the MLS-bound club was held scoreless for the first time all year. The 0-0 draw between the two sides marked the fourth time Orlando had dropped points all season.

While the Orlando match became the first time Sacramento failed to garner all three points at Bonney Field, most of the storylines involved the club's off-the-field ambitions as it hosted a club it hoped to emulate by making the jump to the top division. New York City FC would join Orlando in MLS in 2015, but Sacramento looked towards the Floridians for inspiration. Never considered a soccer city previously, Orlando entered the USL in 2010 and promptly set attendance records while capturing a pair of titles. The two cities shared similar populations and took a back seat to other, more glamorous locations in their home states.

As the Republic built on Orlando's previous USL achievements, and neared 6,000 season ticket holders, Warren Smith candidly spoke about the club's goals. Yes, Sacramento wanted MLS from the outset, but how serious was the effort and what did the timeline look like to garner a precious spot in the league? At that time, MLS publicly had plans to expand to twenty-four teams, twenty-three of which were spoken for. There were rumblings, but nothing official, as Sacramento emerged as a second contender for that final spot alongside Minnesota. The Midwestern city, however, was thought to have the upper hand in several key areas: market size, market location, funding, and history.

"We're in this for Sacramento," Smith said when asked about the club's MLS prospects before the Orlando game. "[Soccer is] a great sport, we love it, it's been a lot of fun, but we deserve more in Sacramento. We want the best. The best league in the country is MLS so we want that for Sacramento."

The other key need was a new stadium–Bonney Field was downright luxurious for the USL, but it wasn't located downtown like Major League Soccer preferred and its capacity sat more than 10,000 below the smallest MLS venue. Smith said the club had already inquired about expanding Bonney, applying for permits for up to potentially 14,000 seats to drum up better home support and prove the city's quality in the eyes of MLS. Selling 20,231 tickets generated headlines, but moving to Bonney provided the club with a home. Drawing 8,000 fans per game was still great, but the underdog that was the city of Sacramento needed to think bigger, according to Smith.

"At the MLS level, you need to have at least 18,000 seats. [Bonney Field is of] great quality, but at the same time, [stadium location] is just as important as the team you put on the field," Smith said. "We will need to build another facility. We've been in conversations with the city about what we might be able to do and where we might be able to build, but that's a longer-term objective right now. Even if we were awarded the franchise next year, we're not starting play until 2018."

It was still early in Sacramento Republic FC history, but after just a few successes, how realistic did the former baseball executive think his club's chances of reaching MLS were? "I'm very confident that we will get there, to MLS," Smith said. "I was asked recently if I could put a percentage [on] it. I'd love to say 100 percent, but you know I can't do that, it's not our decision, but I'd say 75 percent."

However confident Smith felt, Preki's charges at least equaled that level of self-belief in league play. The Republic lost to Glasgow Rangers and then in two matches against EPL side West Bromwich Albion but closed out the State Fair overlap with a game on July 27 against the lowly Pittsburgh Riverhounds. That match would be the twentieth of twenty-eight USL fixtures and the Republic entered it sitting in fourth place in the standings. The pace Orlando City set to start the season made it unlikely anyone would catch it, but Sacramento stood within striking distance of the third-place L.A. Galaxy II and the second-place Richmond Kickers.

Sacramento was a shoo-in for the playoffs at this point—the focus of the season shifted to earning the best seed possible given that the higher seed would host each round of the single elimination eight-team postseason. The early returns in four USL games at Bonney Field proved excellent with a 3-0-1 record. But if the Republic finished fourth, it would only be guaranteed one home playoff game.

Facing a Pittsburgh team averaging one point per game and playing in its second game in three days, helped start a memorable late season run. On the night the Republic broke the single-season total USL attendance record by pulling in 118,107 fans, it broke its own single-game club scoring record in league play. Tommy Stewart bagged a first-half brace, while Rodrigo López [130] added a second-half double. Local boy Adam Jahn also scored in the 5-0 thrashing of the Riverhounds. The result put Sacramento just one point behind the Galaxy in the standings.

---

[130] López was rounding into such good form that the San Jose Earthquakes offered him another shot in MLS according to reports that the player later confirmed. "I didn't sleep for a week," he said about the interest. "They weren't offering me more than the rest of the season, if they [did], maybe I would have taken it. But things were going so well here in Sacramento. My family was happy, we didn't want to move anywhere. To be honest, I think I made the right choice. Obviously the fanbase had a lot to do with it. The front office and the way things are run here in Sacramento, I think, is what made me stay."

After the match, Republic FC vice president of marketing and communications spoke about the new attendance record. "I think this record, No. One, just reaffirms something we've kind of said from Day One: Sacramento has some of the best sports fans in the country," she said. "The Kings led for years with one of the longest sell-out streaks and records, not once but twice. The River Cats have led attendance in all but one of their seasons.

"This is just one more goal that this region has reached as far as sports," Bjork added. "It also demonstrates that this is a very under-served sports community. Many of our sell-outs have been on the same nights that the River Cats have sold out. I think it shows that this region has amazing sports fans who love to support their local teams."

The victory extended the Republic's unbeaten streak to three, a run that it would later further extend to a then-club record ten games. During the following seven matches, the lackluster play in the final third that enraged Preki at the beginning of the summer, became a clear strength—the Republic hit the back of the net twenty-one times during that run.

In an August 17 away win against Orange County SC, Stewart scored Sacramento's first league hat trick. The Northern Irish forward entered the match in the sixty-first minute to tally three in the last half hour of the game as the club again bested its record single-game goal total during a 6-1 trouncing. In that same stretch, the Republic allowed four goals—the club conceded the second fewest in the USL all year with just twenty-eight.

In addition to its unstoppable play on the field, Sacramento Republic FC continued to thrive off it. Just a few hours ahead of the September 4 home match against OKC Energy FC, the club unveiled its first true headline investor. Known for helping save the Kings from relocation through his minority stake in the club, El Dorado Hills-based pharmaceutical magnate Kevin Nagle[131] diversified his sports portfolio by committing to take over the city's new soccer club.

While estimates surrounding his net worth proved difficult to accurately pinpoint, the club proudly reported that Nagle led his company, Envision RX, to $4 billion in revenue the prior year. In what seemed like a coup, the Republic convinced Nagle to lead the club's prospective ownership group.

Talks had progressed for a while leading up to this moment—the prior month Nagle represented both the Republic and the Kings during mayor Kevin Johnson's meeting with MLS officials at the league's 2014 All-Star Game in Portland. Now he was officially in and tasked with securing additional investment and spearheading the construction of a privately financed downtown stadium for the club.

"I love Sacramento—its community, resilience, and potential," Nagle said in a release. "Early on, I admired Republic FC's success and efforts to galvanize this region; its bid for MLS is not only about sports, but also a shared vision for

---

[131] At the time, Nagle was the Kings' largest local shareholder.

Sacramento. I am honored to work side-by-side with Mayor Kevin Johnson and Republic FC president Warren Smith to procure MLS for Sacramento and demonstrate why this region is built for MLS."

Added Smith in the same release: "Kevin's leadership and investment in Republic FC positions us as one of the top ownership groups in the sport. His success, credibility, and financial wherewithal provide us the capability to succeed with our MLS bid. But what first endeared me to Kevin, and what I love most, is his passion for Sacramento."

Sacramento duly dispatched OKC 1-0 that night thanks to a López penalty. Two days later, the Galaxy traveled north for the regular-season finale, but by that time, the match couldn't impact the standings. The Republic's solid play saw it leapfrog into second place, a position it couldn't improve on or fall from. A team of reserves fell 2-1 to *Los Dos*, the first competitive home loss in Bonney Field history.

No one appeared too upset with the loss,[132] which dropped Sacramento's final inaugural regular season record to 17-7-4, good for fifty-five points from twenty-eight games. The club's great run of form ensured that it would host every playoff game it played through the semifinal, starting with a September 13 matchup against the seven-seeded Wilmington Hammerheads. Before kickoff, the Republic received another boon–in a match that began three hours prior, the eight-seed Harrisburg City Islanders shockingly ended Orlando's stint in USL with a 1-0 win. Should the Republic make the final, Bonney Field would now provide the backdrop.

Bolstered by the late-season acquisition of left back James Kiffe and the knowledge that Earthquake's forward Adam Jahn would play out the rest of the season with the Republic, confidence was riding high in the city. Wilmington finished seventeen points behind Sacramento and compiled one more win than loss on the season, but the first playoff game in Republic history began with both teams sending waves into the attack. Sacramento created most of the chances after kickoff, but the Hammerheads counterattack forced a pair of early saves out of Gleeson. When Tommy Stewart hit the crossbar midway through the first half, it brought to mind memories of the city's previous well-documented postseason failures.

It took an unlikely source to break the deadlock as center back Nemanja Vuković stepped up five minutes before halftime. The skillful Montenegrin defender didn't head Max Alvarez's corner kick cleanly, but he got enough on it to give the hosts a 1-0 lead before the break. Early in the second half, there was something of a scare for the home crowd as Gleeson hesitated to come off his line for a ball that Wilmington forward Sammy Ochoa pushed by Vuković. Gleeson's early indecision turned into a quick decision to go to ground and trip up Ochoa,

---

[132] My newspaper editors even sent me to a high school soccer game at the same time, deeming it more important than the Republic's meaningless regular-season finale.

who slotted home the ensuing spot kick in the fifty-eighth to level the game, 1-1 with more than thirty minutes to go in a city known for its playoff collapses.

No one recalled this game being close, however, because six minutes later Vukovic's center back partner, Mickey Daly, headed home a López corner off the bottom of the Hammerhead crossbar for the eventual winner. The pair then combined for a goal on another set piece in the sixty-seventh minute, with Daly heading to a wide open Vuković, who flicked a head ball of his own into the back of the net from six yards out.[133]

With the victory already secured, Sacramento continued to attack and put a fourth in the Wilmington goal for good measure. Kiffe, showcasing some of the skill that would make him one of the best attacking defenders in the league, found himself facing two defenders near the side of the box in the eighty-eighth minute. The freshly minted starter left both in the dust and crossed to an unmarked Jahn, who capped the scoring with the club's fourth headed goal on the night.

Bonney Field morphed into party central once the final whistle blew. Several players sprinted towards the Battalion and hopped in the stands to embrace the fans while beer showered down from above. The win improved Sacramento's USL record at the stadium to 9-1-1, with all 11 of those contests sold out.

The Republic simultaneously continued with plans to expand the facility, while looking to construct a new one. Each successive home match at Bonney in 2014 added to the facility's budding reputation as a fortress. With each of these moments, and the more to come, Bonney Field stood as the backdrop for Sacramento's first truly sustainable professional soccer team. And if that MLS stadium did, in fact, end up rising from the dirt wasteland in the Railyards, it would have its predecessor to thank. Both figuratively, and literally, that pitch at Bonney Field laid the roots for the success of Sacramento Republic FC, something that the loyal fans of the club wouldn't soon forget.

Thanks in part to its new fortress, the Republic was on its way to the semifinals and would host rivals LA Galaxy II a week later. For almost any other expansion team in any sport in any professional league in this country's history, the upcoming elimination match would dominate both newspaper headlines and water cooler conversations around the city. Locals certainly felt excited about the upcoming game, sure. It's just that the prospect of another development intrigued local sports fans as well.

Only a Titanic-sized news development could distract those quickly falling in love with their first-year soccer team from the Republic's actual play on the field. Yes, the players would contest a home semifinal match the following weekend, but first, the club's front office staff would play host to Major League Soccer officials during the week.

---

[133] In fifty-two career regular season USL games, Nemanja Vuković scored one goal. In four career USL playoff games, he scored two.

# TEN

# MLS VISITS[134]

Locals crowded the streets and watering holes of Midtown Sacramento, bringing the district to life like any typical Thursday night. As the sun set, music blared from watering holes, partially drowning out the background noise typically provided by pedestrians mingling with each other. As was typical, young working professionals packed bars to imbibe after work, single adults conversed over tacos with their dates, and shoppers perused boutique stores that neared closing. It wasn't game day, but the Tower Bridge Battalion pregamed at Alley Katz, where several of its members typically watched U.S. games.

That night, the Battalion would prove its worth, as the events that unfolded would prove anything but typical–Major League Soccer officials were in town and Sacramento Republic FC decided to throw them an impromptu block party.

The meeting had come suddenly but Republic officials pulled strings to close traffic on 20th Street between J and K, a trendy block featuring elongated patio seating outside many of the watering holes and coffee shops that sat open for business. Hundreds of Sacramentans packed the block to the brim, waiting for Warren Smith, mayor Kevin Johnson, and the Tower Bridge Battalion to arrive. The crowd was in no particular hurry, though. Most danced blissfully to the live music, sipping on Rubicon Monkey Knife Fights while the sun set behind the Midtown skyline. A few Republic players mingled about while a DJ worked a turntable mounted on a wooden box engraved with the club's logo.

Unbeknownst to the mass of care-free locals, Smith, Johnson, and the MLS crew of Deputy Commissioner Mark Abbott, special assistant to the Commissioner Charles Altchek, and the Executive vice president of Communications Dan

---

[134] I recommend pairing this chapter with "The Distance" by Cake.

Courtemanche, dined just a few blocks away.[135] Over a dinner at the upscale Mulvaney's Building & Loan, the group began introductions and discussed details of a possible formal MLS expansion bid.

As the rally continued into the night, the conversation inside Mulvaney's grew more and more serious. What started as a pleasant set of greetings morphed into discussing numbers and logistics. MLS wanted to know who it was dealing with, so Abbot leaned into the dinner table to pose a question to Smith, Johnson, and Republic lead investor Kevin Nagle: Why, exactly, do you want MLS to come to Sacramento?

Before any of the Republic backers could respond, an ear-splitting sound shook the tables at Mulvaney's. While the rally was likely audible a few blocks away, this noise sounded different. This thundering cacophony was much louder and the noise kept growing as it moved closer and closer each second. Marching over from Alley Katz was the Battalion, fully lubricated as if it was another march to the match. The rowdy supporters trotted on their way to the party while singing in unison, eventually passing by Mulvaney's.

Johnson, seizing the moment, pointed to the boisterous group of fans. "That's why," he said.

"It just showed how passionate people were," Smith later recalled. "When the march started, that was the organic thing…they must have found out where we were. But again, it was organic in nature, and it was just perfect.

"It couldn't have been scripted better."

At the same time, Republic vice president and co-founder Joe Wagoner fidgeted nervously among the throng of supporters at the block party. Every few minutes, he checked his watch, wondering when the MLS contingent would make its way three blocks north to witness the massive show of support. For him, what followed the picturesque moment of Johnson's response didn't turn out as perfectly as he had hoped.

"What I remember, and I was so furious because there was a high point in this thing," Wagoner said. "The folks were supposed to show up, call it nine o'clock, I forget what the exact time was. But the crowd had reached a roar, I mean it was insane at some point because the band had stopped, people were out there getting fired up, and it hit this high, and I kept calling [Smith asking], 'Where are you? The crowd's hyped. We're here, everything that's supposed to have happened, happened. The team's here, like where are you?'

"They hadn't started walking from the restaurant and they showed up about thirteen minutes [after the peak]," he added. "I was just sitting there watching my clock after it peaked. It still worked out great, but in my mind the whole time, I'm like, 'If [Abbott] had walked out here at the right time and seen, the crowd was going absolutely insane, there's no way he could see that and not let us in…but they

---

[135] MLS Commissioner Don Garber was unable to attend the visit to Sacramento as he was battling cancer at the time.

showed up, and it ended up being a really good event. But there was an energy in that place for about twenty minutes that was unlike anything I've seen in sports. And they missed it. I just kept on thinking, 'We missed it. That was our chance and we missed it.'

"Maybe we did. Who knows?"

# Welcome to Sactown

Earlier that day, the MLS delegation of Mark Abbott and Charles Altchek[136] arrived at Terminal A of the Sacramento International Airport to find one of the best assets Sacramento had to offer MLS: a built-in, passionate fanbase. Dozens of Battalion members and other Republic supporters had called in sick from work to flock to the normally quiet facility. They greeted the pair of decision makers with a standard blast of Republic chants and songs as soon as the MLS officials touched down from their flight.

Though the fans showed MLS what it could expect in the stands, what the league really desired to learn was whether the other aspects of Sacramento Republic FC could be a good fit for U.S. top division soccer. MLS officials wanted to know what corporate sponsorships might look like. They hoped to learn more about Sacramento's downtown and nightlife. They wondered where the team might construct a stadium, and *if* it could do so in a downtown, urban core area. They were curious about local hotels and potential visiting team accommodations. None of the league's front office members had ever visited California's capital in an official capacity, so they could only go off things that they'd heard about the city. And other than the headlines the Republic had made over the prior few months, nothing else MLS staffers could have heard was likely to paint Sacramento in a positive light given the city's status as a national afterthought.

"[MLS needed] to go around the city and make sure it's not a giant shithole," Wagoner laughed in an interview nearly a year later. "There's actually things happening downtown. Because so much of our story is that the city is rising, not just this club."

With assuring MLS officials that Sacramento wasn't a "giant shithole" as the main goal, Nagle began his quest to woo league staffers with a city tour. The group lunched at the Grange restaurant alongside Johnson and met Republic sponsors such as UC Davis Medical Center, AT&T, and The McClatchy Co. Then, back at the club's 17th Street digs, Sacramento delivered a forty-five-minute presentation on its MLS business plan.

"The deal was we had to show [MLS] how we were going to get to 15,000 season tickets, $12 million in corporate sponsorships, how Erika [Bjork] is going to grow

---

[136] Dan Courtemanche flew in later.

the community," Wagoner said. "What was memorable to me was that I've never been so nervous in my entire life."

Added Smith: "There was a whole bunch of stuff that they needed to learn about. And there's a lot of conceptions that they had about Sacramento, and we wanted to make sure that the information they had was correct."

Without a Fortune 500 company based in the city, MLS wondered where sponsorship dollars would come from, so Smith and Nagle presented examples of the strong corporate market in Sacramento by pointing to the city's only major professional sports team as an example. According to Smith, the Sacramento Kings ranked in the top-five in the NBA in sponsorship, providing a prelude of what MLS could expect.

"But the main goal was, when people come to Sacramento, they fall in love with it, so the goal was to get them here, let them experience it, and we knew that they would fall in love with it," Smith said. "And I think we accomplished that."

## The Difference a Year Can Make

More than a year before unveiling the Sacramento Republic FC brand, Smith traveled to Kansas City to attend meetings at the 2013 MLS All-Star Game. Smith introduced himself to league officials and described his plan to bring an MLS franchise to Sacramento, a mid-sized city eerily similar to Kansas City in terms of demographics and potential corporate sponsorships.

"They were very nice and cordial," Smith said. "But I felt like that little kid they were patting on the head, saying, 'Good job, Warren!' But we did share with them what we were trying to accomplish, and we were very strategic with following the model that has worked in Portland, Seattle, Montreal, Vancouver, and now Orlando, and that is USL to MLS. Build a brand, build a fanbase, then evolve it. It just so happens to be, if you look at some of the highest performing teams [in MLS], many of those are [former] USL teams, with downtown, urban core stadiums. Portland, Seattle, Montreal, Vancouver, and Orlando. It's not brain surgery. I shared with them that we were going to do the same thing. I shared that in one year [we'd average] 6,750 people per match. That would have been a USL record. Orlando was just over 6,000. Year three, acquire an MLS franchise. Year five, open up a downtown, urban core stadium."

Smith showed ambition, no question about it, but MLS officials remained skeptical. Fast forward to the spring of 2014 and 20,231 packed Hughes Stadium for Sacramento Republic FC's home opener. After garnering national headlines with the sellout, the Republic proved it wasn't a fluke as it began smashing all the USL's attendance records. The club wasn't succeeding, it was exceeding all its expectations on and off the field. Amidst the publicity and success, the Republic front office eventually shrugged its shoulders and said, "Screw it, the worst that can happen is they say no." So, Smith picked up the phone and called MLS.

When he got through to the league's New York office, he asked MLS officials if they wanted to visit. Smith knew more than likely, Minnesota would earn the league's coveted twenty-fourth, and final, expansion spot. But he reached out anyway, and MLS agreed to come.

League officials flew to Sacramento, dined, partied, and the following day toured a site in Elk Grove. The city of strip malls fourteen miles southeast of Sacramento had made headlines before the Republic debuted by announcing its aspirations to garner an MLS team by building a massive, sixteen-field sports complex, along with a 9,000-seat stadium that could be expanded to MLS standards. The bid was never taken seriously by the league, journalists, or fans due to the small size of Elk Grove and the MLS initiative to build downtown stadiums. Still, MLS felt an obligation to at least listen, jetting over to the city before heading out to inspect Bonney Field.

Finally, the Republic and MLS concluded the visit with a press conference at the Railyards. On the eve of the trip, Sacramento announced the long-ignored district as its desired location to construct a privately financed $150 million stadium. Once a prosperous area in the city that played a huge role in the strength of its economy, the Railyards spent years decaying into an afterthought despite featuring prime real estate. The proposed soccer facility would serve as the main attraction of a $300 million redevelopment in one of the country's largest urban infill projects.[137] The fact that local businessman Larry Kelley, a Republic investor, owned much of the land in the Railyards served as a boon to Sacramento's chances.

While it was unclear after all the meetings, dinners, and parties if the league would grant Sacramento an MLS franchise, the visit generated positive headlines locally and nationally. Nagle, Smith, and Johnson proved that Sacramento wasn't a "giant shithole." The Tower Bridge Battalion and Republic fans demonstrated the city's love for soccer. California's capital was no longer the kid that MLS patted on the head and said "good job" to. Sacramento officially earned the status as an MLS expansion favorite. Not *the* favorite, but *a* favorite.

Amidst all the buzz and hoopla, it appeared as if some forgot Sacramento Republic FC still had a game to play that weekend. A potential MLS bid brought excitement Thursday and Friday, but rival L.A. Galaxy II awaited the USL side on Saturday. With a trip to the championship game on the line, the match easily qualified as the biggest in the club's young history. And as fans dreamed of a top-division future, they hoped that the new heroes of their lower-division present wouldn't be distracted by this whirlwind of newsworthy developments.

---

[137] Essentially one of the biggest holes inside of any major American city's downtown area.

# ELEVEN

# THE MIRACLE AT BONNEY: AN ORAL HISTORY[138]

"That game, that match against Los Angeles, just resonated with people who had never cared about soccer in Sacramento before. That kick...all it took was one kick, and a game winner, and Sacramento seemed to be hooked from that moment on."

- Rob McAllister, Sacramento Republic FC play-by-play announcer

As Sacramento Republic FC continues into its second decade of USL play, it brings with it hundreds of memories that have defined the club on and off the field. Yet, in ten full seasons, the 2014 USL semifinal still lingers fondly in the memories of Sacramentans as arguably the best game in club history. The images stick like blind spots from staring at the sun: from Galaxy defender André Auras taking down the Republic's Ivan Mirković in the box as rain began to fall to Rodrigo López's stoppage time free-kick winner. The ink of Sacramento Republic FC's history is still wet, yet that night of September 20, 2014–the Miracle at Bonney–marked a heart-palpitating early chapter. One that will be read for decades to come.

Riding a wave of positive energy after a 4-1 playoff quarterfinal win over the Wilmington Hammerheads, all the stars aligned for the Republic's semifinal to prove itself a watershed moment in the Sacramento sporting landscape. Fresh off a visit from the MLS front office to discuss possible expansion in California's capital, the Republic had a chance to host the USL championship game if it could get through this semifinal.

---

[138] I recommend pairing this chapter with "Modern Day Cowboy" by Tesla.

In its path was its biggest rival in L.A. Galaxy II. The fellow expansion side was coming off a fine run of form, including winning at Sacramento in the final regular-season game. That match was the first time the Republic had ever lost at Bonney Field, where it posted an 8-1-1 record in the regular season after playing its first four games at nearby Hughes Stadium. Unlike the semifinal, that final regular-season game was meaningless—both sides had already secured their position in the playoff standings. But like the semifinal, the Galaxy came out of the gates as the stronger side and went up two goals.

For seventy minutes in the do-or-die semifinal game, it appeared as if the Republic was going to lay a typical Sacramento playoff sports egg. But after ninety minutes, the game would go down in the pantheon of sporting events in Sacramento history. For the people of the city, it was more than just a game, it was the moment when the Republic truly broke through to the mainstream in Sacramento.

It wasn't until the following day that then-Republic color commentator Kevin Goldthwaite realized the impact of the 2014 USL semifinal. According to Goldthwaite, multiple casual soccer fans—the type who generally tune in for the World Cup and not much else—in his life approached him to talk about what already qualified as an instant classic. "This is a top-five greatest sporting moment in Sacramento history," he remembers some telling him.

"That gave me chills," Goldthwaite said. "[These] big sports fans, casual soccer fans…saying that the game meant that much and was such a great game for the city of Sacramento. For me, personally, that was one of the best games I've ever been a part of, 100 percent."

The final twenty minutes of the game served as some of the most dramatic, exciting, and confusing moments in a Northern California market starved for top-level sports. What follows[139] is an oral history, recorded from interviews with roughly twenty players, coaches, and other figures involved in The Miracle at Bonney.[140]

# The Build Up

*Both USL expansion clubs in 2014, the Republic met L.A. Galaxy II in the first game in club history.[141] In this first season, scuffles and skirmishes punctuated their two encounters in Sacramento, but the Republic eventually edged Los Dos in their series with a 2-1-1 record. The first two matchups came and went without incident, played in Southern California in front of sparse crowds before Sacramento's first home game. It was the Republic prior to the version that we know it to be today.*

---

[139] All persons interviewed in this chapter are identified by their job titles on the night of the match.
[140] Some of the quotes have been lightly edited for clarity.
[141] L.A. Galaxy II played its inaugural game one week earlier against the Orange County Blues.

It wasn't until the third match, one of the four home games at Hughes Stadium, that supporters got a taste of the rivalry to come. In a move that Sacramento fans would soon become accustomed to, Ivan Mirković displayed some of the first hints of gamesmanship that would come to define the series in that third game. The diminutive Mirković, his in-game personality rough around the edges from the scars of two Balkan Wars in his native Serbia, constantly looked for any advantage possible on the field.

During a stoppage in play in the second half with the game tied, Mirković confronted Galaxy II captain Rafael Garcia, baiting the Los Dos midfielder into an error in judgment. For a moment, the two stood face-to-face, close enough to smell each other's breath. Garcia responded as many would, by shoving Mirković, who immediately crumpled to the ground as if a rooftop sniper had taken him out. Before center referee Nestor Chavez had time to react, the entirety of both teams sprinted to the middle of the field. Tempers finally settled down in the mob of Republic red and Galaxy blue, but one hand rose above the mosh pit on the Hughes turf. That hand belonged to Chavez, and it clutched tightly to a red rectangle of plastic, pointed towards Garcia. The Galaxy player slinked off the field in front of the now rabid sellout crowd of 20,231. Sixteen minutes later, Sacramento's Rodrigo López slipped a free kick past keeper Cody Laurendi to wrap up a 2-1 victory that left the Galaxy players with a bad taste in their mouths.

Two weeks before the semifinal match-up, the two teams faced off in their final USL regular-season fixture, this time at Bonney Field. Neither team could change its playoff seeding, but the Galaxy fielded a first-string starting lineup to contest mostly Republic reserves. A brace from L.A.'s Jack McBean gave the Galaxy a 2-1 victory, the first time a visiting team claimed all three points at Bonney. The win extended the Galaxy's unbeaten streak to five games, a streak they would further build on the following week with a 2-1 comeback victory over the Rochester Rhinos in the first round of the playoffs. Garcia again saw red in that game, forcing him out of the semifinal against the Republic. Garcia's suspension contributed to the revolving door of players who would come and go from L.A. Galaxy II during the season,[142] but the side that traveled to Sacramento contained enough regulars such as Oscar Sorto, André Auras, and Alejandro Covarrubias to make sure that any match-up would retain the intensity of past meetings.

Meanwhile, the Republic advanced to the semifinal to play the Galaxy, thumping an overmatched Wilmington Hammerheads side 4-1 behind a pair of goals from center back Nemanja Vuković. The midweek focus in the city then shifted to a visit from MLS officials, culminating in a block party in Midtown Sacramento two days before the semifinal. Many of the Republic players attended, perhaps taking their mind off the big game. MLS disappointed some of the more optimistic fans who expected the league to announce Sacramento as an expansion franchise immediately. Still, the league merely acknowledging Sacramento as a potential candidate generated hype in the days leading up to the match. According to the Republic, the semifinal sold out two minutes after Sacramento released single-game tickets for sale to the public.

---

[142] As the reserve team for the first division L.A. Galaxy, players were constantly jettisoned between the MLS squad and the Galaxy II, leading to a lack of continuity in the lineup. For the Galaxy II and other MLS reserve teams playing in the USL, the goal wasn't just to win games, but to develop players for the first team.

**Warren Smith (president and co-founder, Sacramento Republic FC):** Our belief has always been, if we can get them here, they'll understand what a great market it is, so it was a big step up for us to have MLS here. So many things that week went so well. First of all, Orlando lost the weekend before. If we were going to win [the semifinal], we'd be hosting [the final]...to have MLS and the block party and just to celebrate soccer and what we had done that year was really something special.

**Bill Paterson (Sacramento Republic FC beat writer, *Sacramento Bee*):** It just seemed like everything was going Republic FC's way. There was a lot of buzz, obviously, about MLS. Here they were playing in the semifinals, sellout crowds. There was a lot of excitement.

**Rodrigo López (midfielder, Sacramento Republic FC):** I think it was a little too early [for MLS to visit], in my opinion, just because we were still in the playoffs and focusing on L.A. Galaxy.

**Rob McAllister (play-by-play announcer, Sacramento Republic FC):** I do remember the whole week being very geared towards MLS and little focus on the actual match itself. I think it was one of those things where like, yeah, it's great and we want to keep winning, but it wasn't the Number One thing everyone was focused on.

**Emrah Klimenta (defender, Sacramento Republic FC):** I don't know about the rest of the team, personally I didn't come out distracted or anything. Yeah, it was great that MLS was in town and all that, but I think most of the players were letting the staff take care of all of that.

**Max Alvarez (midfielder, Sacramento Republic FC):** We definitely had momentum entering that game, just kind of on a short spurt of time, kind of building it up, with L.A. We knew ahead of time how competitive it was going to be. It was a semifinal match. We had the crowd pretty excited about the game. To have that kind of ceremony before the game, the game was a lot more high stakes.

**Ivan Mirković (midfielder, Sacramento Republic FC):** I don't think we were distracted.

**Charlie Rugg (forward, L.A. Galaxy II):** They were definitely our nemesis for the year, for that season, so we're always going to be wary going into games against them. We know we're going to have a tough time ahead of us, especially at that venue. [But] with Curt Onalfo as a coach, we had a pretty confident team in general.

We weren't scared to go in there, play in the semifinal game, but we [knew] it was going to be a tough game.

**Joe Franco (defender, L.A. Galaxy II):** After that first season, we knew what a good team Sacramento was. We kind of had that battle, back-and-forth, them beating us at our place and at their place, so after we won, I think it was the last regular season game at Bonney Field, it definitely gave us confidence. It proved that we were able to do it.

**Brian Perk (goalkeeper, L.A. Galaxy II):** I thought it was between us and them for the best team in the league. I think we knew it was going to be a battle...we knew the atmosphere was going to be pretty crazy,[143] but that's enjoyable.

**Charlie Rugg (forward, L.A. Galaxy II):** In every game that we played in Sacramento, the atmosphere was definitely one of the best in the league—probably the only one rivaling it would be Orlando. But Sacramento...it's a hard place to play. If you're playing away, in that league, it was the hardest...I played at Boston College, and we had away games at Maryland, so that was kind of my first introduction to rowdy away crowds. I think I've always handled away crowds well, but I can't speak for everybody on the team.

**Bill Paterson (Sacramento Republic FC beat writer, *Sacramento Bee*):** I really thought it was a toss-up game. Even though the Republic wasn't playing all their starters [in the last regular-season game], I thought the Galaxy II looked pretty good in that match. It really seemed like they'd improved. They were on a roll, winning some matches, so I really saw it as a toss-up.

**Joe Franco (defender, L.A. Galaxy II):** During the season, they kind of had our number. Being on the Galaxy, we're dealing with a lot of changes. The team that's going to play on the weekend usually doesn't even play together until maybe that Friday before. Sometimes during the season, it was rough because we couldn't get that continuity. But during the playoffs, we kind of had it set on who we were going to be playing. We built that rapport, and got on the same page. After we won that last game, we were positive, we were feeling confident, and then the whole week of training, building up to the game, it was high quality.

---

[143] When speaking about the crowd at 8,000-capacity Bonney Field, Perk remembered there being 20,000 people at the stadium that day. It's possible that he'd confused the game with the Hughes Stadium match, but Perk didn't play at Hughes.

# The Game

*Whether or not the Republic players felt distracted, L.A. Galaxy II dominated the game from the start. Tommy Meyer, on loan from the Galaxy first team, headed an André Auras corner kick on frame just three minutes into the match. The defender didn't generate much power on the attempt, but it beat Republic goalkeeper Jake Gleeson and appeared primed for the back of the net until Rodrigo López headed the ball off the line to keep the match scoreless.*

**Rob McAllister (play-by-play announcer, Sacramento Republic FC):** That said a lot to where [López] was mentally the entire match. What makes great players great is not their physical abilities, it's their mental capacity to stay in a match and not give up before that final whistle is blown. I think you could see in that moment that he knew the team was off, but he was going to ensure that he could impose his will any way he could, and he started on the defensive end. I think that speaks a lot to RoRo's character.

*In one of the Republic's rare first-half forays into the attack, Octavio Guzmán sent Max Alvarez in behind the Galaxy II defense with a clever, one-touch flick in the eleventh minute. Near the top right corner of the Galaxy penalty box, Alvarez beat sliding Galaxy defender Daniel Steres to the ball. He continued forward into the box, using his trademark cutback to move the ball to his stronger left foot for a better angle at the target. As he pushed forward, now well into the Galaxy penalty area, defender Jason Bli slid towards the ball from behind Alvarez.*
*The Republic midfielder was too quick in his cutback for Bli to contact the ball, but not quick enough to prevent the Galaxy defender from sliding through his right foot. Whether or not there was contact, Alvarez fell face first into the Bonney Field grass and immediately sprung back up, palms open at his side, pleading for center referee Baboucarr Jallow[144] to point to the spot. Three Republic players surrounded Jallow, who stood just ten feet away from the tackle, but the hulking figure waved away the protests and simply awarded a Sacramento throw-in. Close-up replays on the broadcast failed to catch Alvarez in frame during the incident, leaving only one, inconclusive, wide-angle shot of the alleged foul. Three minutes later, Curt Onalfo substituted Joe Franco for the injured Bli.*

**Kevin Goldthwaite (color commentator, Sacramento Republic FC):** Preki[145] was irate. I remember that. Definitely wasn't a good replay. From where we were

---

[144] Much of the conversation following the match came down to the performance of Jallow, who, while normally a fourth official in MLS, moved down to the USL to take charge of the match that night. PRO, the Professional Referee Organization, didn't respond to repeated attempts to contact Jallow for an interview. PRO assigned MLS veteran center referee Ricardo Salazar to officiate the final.

[145] Preki was scheduled for an interview regarding this chapter early in the summer of 2015, but travel delays for the Republic on a road trip prevented the Sacramento head coach from speaking to the

initially, up in the booth, it absolutely looked like a penalty, but I mean, there's a lot that could have happened within five feet of the play. It looked like a penalty, but there's no clear evidence to support that. I remember seeing Preki's face, he was yelling at the fourth official. He thought the same thing, and I think that's a justifiable shout by Preki to complain about that penalty.

**Max Alvarez (midfielder, Sacramento Republic FC):** It was a tough play because it was kind of a counterattack, and it was a one-v-one situation. Maybe the referee didn't have a good angle. I was able to cut in front of [Bli], and he clipped me a little bit and that was enough to take me down because we were both going at full speed. It's just unfortunate the play wasn't called. It's just one of those things where it's pretty difficult for the referee. I understand that. It happens. It's part of football.

**Bill Paterson (Sacramento Republic FC beat writer, *Sacramento Bee*):** It [looked like a penalty] to me, but it wasn't called and that happens. You're thinking that all of a sudden, things aren't going the Republic's way because they don't get the call.

*And things didn't go the Republic's way shortly after the non-call. The Galaxy silenced arguably the loudest crowd in the USL in the twenty-sixth minute with an opportunistic goal to take the lead. Top attacking prospect Bradford Jamieson IV, just 17-years-old at the time, found himself free on a counterattack after a sloppy pass from Sacramento center back Mickey Daly near midfield. Though Daly stopped Jamieson's initial run with a timely sliding challenge at the top of the box, the Galaxy forward recovered possession and played a crafty outside-of-the-left-foot pass through to midfielder Dragan Stojkov.*

*Picking the ball up ten yards inside of the corner flag, Stojkov sent a first-time cross into the box that was so poorly defended by Sacramento that either Charlie Rugg or Jaime Villarreal could have finished it off. Rugg ended up with the goal, ghosting between Daly and center back partner Nemanja Vuković to rifle a snapdown header into the back of the net. The noise coming from the previously raucous crowd faded into a deafening silence as Sacramento fans braced for yet another postseason disappointment against a team from Los Angeles.*

**Charlie Rugg (forward, L.A. Galaxy II):** Part of the reason I think the Galaxy II was really good [in 2014]—and we were such a confident team—was because we had a specific playing style. Part of that was getting the ball wide and getting a lot of crosses in. That was something that was automatic for me by that time of the year, and for a lot of people on the team. We knew if the ball was coming outside, they were going to get a cross in.

---

author. A few weeks later, before the interview was rescheduled, he seemingly disappeared off the face of the planet after accepting a mystery job in the U.K. that would never come to fruition.

**Bill Paterson (Sacramento Republic FC beat writer, *Sacramento Bee*):** He split [the Republic center backs]. Daly and Vuković had been so strong, and it's just like he cut through there and found a seam, and you're thinking, "Wow." It just seemed at that point the momentum really started turning L.A.'s way.

*Like many high-stakes soccer games, play on the field devolved into a sloppy mess in the middle of the park, with neither team wishing to take unnecessary risks going forward. No one truly threatened to score the second goal of the match until the forty-fourth minute. There's not really a way to describe the next Galaxy strike other than "weird."*

*Daniel Steres started the play left of the center circle five feet into the Republic half. The defender launched a seemingly harmless free kick over the head of Republic right back Emrah Klimenta, finding a streaking Jamieson near the corner of the Sacramento six-yard box. The young forward beat Klimenta to the ball and smartly squared it across the six to the onrushing Rugg.*

*Though Rugg found himself in an excellent position to double the lead, the Galaxy II goalscorer scuffed his initial chance off the side of his right knee, sending the ball straight up into the air a few inches above his head. By that point, Daly and Vuković had recovered to come within an arm's length of Rugg. However, the Republic center backs appeared confused and stopped running towards the ball a few feet in front of Gleeson, who already dove to the ground in anticipation of saving the first Rugg effort.*

*As Daly, Vuković, and Gleeson ceased their movements, seemingly freezing in time, the ball fell back down to Rugg's left foot. The forward awkwardly poked the ball over the prone Gleeson and into the back of the net. Other than a shrug from Vuković in the direction of Daly, none of the Republic players reacted to the goal. Likewise, their Galaxy counterparts stood confused as Rugg didn't celebrate the strike.*

*Five seconds of on-air time passed on the Republic broadcast before McAllister informed viewers that L.A. had, in fact, doubled its lead. "It was a goal? They're saying a score?" a confused McAllister said on the broadcast, himself attempting to confirm the information. "So it did find the net? Sacramento now down by two?"*

**Kevin Goldthwaite (color commentator, Sacramento Republic FC):** I remember Rob didn't even react to it and then five seconds goes by, and we see the referee pointing to midfield, signaling a goal, and all the Galaxy guys running back, and he's like, "Oh, looks like they scored a goal."

**Charlie Rugg (forward, L.A. Galaxy II):** Maybe it looked like the ball didn't go in or something. I don't know. It was just one of those weird plays that nobody really knows how to react right away, I guess.

**Kevin Goldthwaite (color commentator, Sacramento Republic FC):** Very weird play. I remember Gleeson was falling down and his momentum and his weight were on his heels, and he just didn't make a strong play on it. Rugg had two touches within like three feet of the goal line and just tapped it in, so definitely a weird kind of surprising play. It took the wind out of everyone's sails, that's for sure.

**Rob McAllister (play-by-play announcer, Sacramento Republic FC):** No one signaled anything, and [the Galaxy] barely celebrated. It happened so quickly and from the vantage point where we were at, I couldn't see whether or not it hit the side net or did it dribble inside? Jake Gleeson's reaction, everyone's reaction was almost flat, little emotion. Just like, "Eh, okay." It was weird. I had never seen that. I mean no one was fired up. I think the back four just didn't even respond. It just goes to speak volumes about where everyone mentally was at the time or at least most of the team was. Even the crowd was in a state of bewilderment because even without the goal, the team was...I remember them just being a step behind.

**Bill Paterson (Sacramento Republic FC beat writer, *Sacramento Bee*):** The way Gleeson fell down, it seemed strange from where I was standing. I didn't think it was a goal. I thought it hit the side net and he just kind of reacted late, and all of a sudden, we find out it's a goal.

**Charlie Rugg (forward, L.A. Galaxy II):** It was a little bit of a goalscorer's goal I guess. I just kind of hit it off my shin, and it went in. I was surprised, mostly because I kind of expected the goalie to get the ball before I was able to shoot it.

**Emrah Klimenta (defender, Sacramento Republic FC):** I think they were as shocked, as surprised as we were, that that goal went in.

*The halftime whistle blew, and Sacramento Republic FC headed into the locker room down 2-0 as the broadcast panned to a silent and shocked crowd before breaking to commercial. When the images returned to Bonney Field, McAllister and Goldthwaite appeared on camera on either side of Warren Smith, who they'd previously arranged to appear for a segment detailing Smith's experience during the MLS visit.*

**Kevin Goldthwaite (color commentator, Sacramento Republic FC):** As Warren's walking up, [I said to Rob], "This is going to fucking suck."

**Rob McAllister (play-by-play announcer, Sacramento Republic FC):** I remember at halftime, we interviewed Warren then, and he was just down. I mean, he was [acting like] the game was over and we missed our chance.

**Warren Smith (president and co-founder, Sacramento Republic FC):** Honestly, we didn't expect to get as far as we did. If we had ended that night, I still would have been just as happy. It was really for the boys at that point. We had accomplished everything that we needed or wanted to accomplish from a business standpoint and making our case [to MLS]. At this point, it was just for them. We wanted it for them. We felt bad for them at halftime.

**Kevin Goldthwaite (color commentator, Sacramento Republic FC):** Warren put on the right face. [He] needed to do what he needed to do, and said what he needed to say, but it was kind of a very odd and unique interview to say the least.

**Rob McAllister (play-by-play announcer, Sacramento Republic FC):** I remember Kevin saying, "2-0, that's a dangerous score because it gives teams a false sense of security."

*Meanwhile, in the Republic locker room, Preki admonished López in front of the entire squad, telling him that he needed to step up and carry the team.*

**Ivan Mirković (midfielder, Sacramento Republic FC):** [Preki] was pissed because [of] the way we were playing, just in the way [we] reacted after they scored the goals. He felt that we were down and we kind of gave up, so he woke us up in the locker room. I remember him yelling at RoRo, telling him, "You want to be a superstar? Now is the time to shine!"

**Rodrigo López (midfielder, Sacramento Republic FC):** What he said to me woke me up. He told me I needed to act like a leader and play like a leader and turn things around because I wasn't doing anything good for the team. As a player you don't like hearing those things, but as a player and a leader, as one of the veterans, you want to hear it because you want to turn things around. You want to be the guy who your teammates can depend on when needed. Obviously, I was still working hard, but things weren't going well for me with the ball. I think [the] second half just changed everything. Preki actually did wake me up.

**Emrah Klimenta (defender, Sacramento Republic FC):** The buzz around the locker room was as if we knew we were going to come back and we were going to win the game.

**Ivan Mirković (midfielder, Sacramento Republic FC):** I didn't feel for a second that we were going to lose.

*At least one shared the Balkan duo's optimistic mindset. While waiting to use the restroom during the break, Republic season ticket holder Ryan Cox created the moniker that Republic fans now use to refer to this match, tweeting, "At least we know @SacRepublicFC can score 3+ goals in a half! #MiracleAtBonney #BuiltForMLS".*

*Just before play resumed, Preki subbed on captain Justin Braun, who hadn't played in the previous five matches due to an injury, and Gilberto, a midfielder whose technical skill and passing ability allowed the Republic to unlock bunkering defenses.*

**Rodrigo López (midfielder, Sacramento Republic FC):** Gilberto came in as a sub and turned things around.

**Kevin Goldthwaite (color commentator, Sacramento Republic FC):** Ball at his feet, he's probably one of the most skilled and technical players on the field, and probably the best attacking mind to see things and how things are going to develop to make sure he plays someone in, or whatever the right ball is going to be. I think he's a guy that you want with the ball on his foot if you're going forward. Once that new energy was infused into the Republic, Gilberto was the catalyst for that. I think Preki absolutely made the right decision personnel wise.

*With Braun occupying defenders up top and Gilberto pulling the strings from deep in the midfield, the tide of the game began to turn, but it was in one of the most unlikely ways possible that the Republic pulled a goal back. Twenty-three minutes passed in the second half before left back James Kiffe found himself with the ball at his feet, double teamed in the attacking corner of the field. Though five Republic players flooded the Galaxy box, Kiffe cut the ball back onto his right foot, dribbled away from the goal, and played a square ball near the top corner of the penalty area to Mirković, who sprinted towards goal.*

*The defensively minded midfielder, who played forty-one league games for Sacramento before registering his first goal or assist, took a touch forward into the box as French defender André Auras closed him down from the side. Moving in from the left, Auras clumsily shoulder checked Mirković, who flew to the ground as rain began to fall at Bonney Field. With the entire state in the midst of a massive drought, it was the first time it rained in Sacramento since late April, nearly five months before the match.*

*Unlike the alleged foul in the first half, Jallow immediately pointed to the spot to signal a penalty kick. Two Galaxy players sprinted up to argue with Jallow, who appeared to have a clean look fewer than ten feet away from the incident, but most of the other visiting players stood with their jaws dropped in disbelief that the Republic possibly found itself back in the game with just over twenty minutes to play.*

**Joe Wagoner (co-founder and vice president, Sacramento Republic FC):** When it started drizzling during the second half...everyone in attendance knew something special was about to occur. The rain washed away any doubt. I remember looking at [Republic camps and clinics manager Kenny Cooper] and saying, "Some awesome shit is about to go down."

**Max Alvarez (midfielder, Sacramento Republic FC):** I never see Ivan going forward. When I saw that happen, I was like, "What is he doing? That doesn't look right." But I tell him, every time he goes forward, something magical happens.[146]

---

[146] In the interview, Alvarez joked that Mirković had only ever gone forward four times in the history of the Republic.

**Emrah Klimenta (defender, Sacramento Republic FC):** It was like it was written in the stars. Ivan, who I don't think once went into the penalty box [in the regular] season, finds himself in the penalty box, takes a great touch, gets taken down.

**Kevin Goldthwaite (color commentator, Sacramento Republic FC):** How often is Mirković going forward like that?

**Ivan Mirković (midfielder, Sacramento Republic FC):** That's my role in the team. When I have RoRo in front of me, then I stay a little back. But I felt in the moment, I was like, "I have to do something for my team."

**Charlie Rugg (forward, L.A. Galaxy II):** If you look at the replay, 95 percent of the time, I think nobody's going to call that a penalty.

**Rodrigo López (midfielder, Sacramento Republic FC):** I think he went down a little soft.

**Joe Franco (defender, L.A. Galaxy II):** I'm obviously on the opposite team, on the Galaxy, so I'm going to have a bit more of a biased opinion of what events occurred, but from where I was, it was just kind of a soft foul to give. And given that it was at Bonney Field, with the fans, and the kind of situation that it was in, maybe the referee didn't feel like it was that big of a deal [to give the penalty].

**Oscar Sorto (defender, L.A. Galaxy II):** He went down easily.

**Brian Perk (goalkeeper, L.A. Galaxy II):** I think the ref just had a bad vantage point because it looked like [Auras] was directly behind him, so I think he thought there was more contact than there was. I mean, it's so tough for refs like that. It just looked like he had a bad vantage point and kind of missed the call.

**Ivan Mirković (midfielder, Sacramento Republic FC):** I saw the ball coming and made a touch forward and saw [Auras] coming so my intention was to protect the ball, put myself in front of the ball, between the ball and the defender. The defender just came at me. It was obvious contact. I went down the right way. It wasn't too soft, but could I have stayed on my feet? If I wanted to, maybe I could, but it was the right moment to go down. After the game, Preki [asked] me, "Why was he fouling you?" Preki was like, "If I was the defender, what were you gonna do inside the box? He should just let you go." I was like, "Probably, yeah."

*The Republic finally created a golden opportunity, but the spot kick still needed to be dispatched. Up stepped López, who had only taken one penalty in the regular season, a blast straight up the middle sixteen days earlier against Oklahoma City Energy FC. With the rain continuing to fall, the Sacramento attacker confidently stepped up to the spot and blasted a low shot towards the bottom left corner of Perk's net. The netminder guessed correctly, diving full stretch to his right side as 8,000 fans held their collective breath. Perk's fingertips graced the edge of the ball, but López hit his shot too hard in too good of a spot. After spending seventy minutes as spectators, the hosts were back in the game.*

**Brian Perk (goalkeeper, L.A. Galaxy II):** Right as he struck it, I thought I was gonna have it. It snuck in, but it was a good PK. I thought RoRo's a good, crafty player, so I figured he would kind of open his hips [to feign like he would shoot it to my left] and close them [and go right], which is usually what good players, good finishers of the ball do. And that's what he did. He was just a little better than I was. He put it right in the corner.

**Rodrigo López (midfielder, Sacramento Republic FC):** Once we scored the goal, it just felt like everything turned around.

*Two minutes after the penalty, tempers rose when Jallow whistled Kiffe for what appeared to be a hard foul on Oscar Sorto near the edge of the Republic box. First López stepped up to confront Sorto, but Mirković quickly bisected the pair. Unnerved by Mirković's presence less than an inch from his face, Sorto awkwardly pushed the Sacramento midfielder in the face.*

*Like the earlier game in May when Mirković found himself head-to-head with Raphael Garcia, the diminutive Republic midfielder acted as if he had been shot and threw himself into the ground as a twenty-player scuffle ensued. Literally, every field player from both teams surrounded the massive Jallow, nostrils flared in anger.*

*"And there's going to be a red card[147] thrown against the Galaxy, no question about it," McAllister said on the broadcast, the volume of his call rising in excitement. But after a comically long period spent separating players and conferring with his sideline official, Jallow showed Sorto just a yellow card. Play stopped for nearly five minutes while Jallow attempted to sort out the issue.*

**Kevin Goldthwaite (color commentator, Sacramento Republic FC):** Mirković goes down really easy, but anytime you're touched in the face, you're going to go down, just try and draw a red. It was weird, and then the melee broke out a little bit and only one yellow card was given.

**Bill Paterson (Sacramento Republic FC beat writer, *Sacramento Bee*):** In a semifinal, do you want to give a red card in that situation? I don't know. If it's a regular-season game, yeah, you can understand, but in a semifinal?

---

[147] When asked about the incident, Brian Perk thought that Sorto had been given a red card on that particular play.

**Kevin Goldthwaite (color commentator, Sacramento Republic FC):** [Sorto] goes for his face and makes contact, whether it's a push, a slap, a hit, I don't know what you're going to call it or classify it, but any given day could be called either way, could have been given a red card any day of the week.

**Joe Franco (defender, L.A. Galaxy II):** Mirković is one of those players that's always kind of antagonizing, he really knows how to play the mental side of the game as far as getting into your head. The very first time that we played Sacramento was at [Hughes Stadium], our guy, Raphael Garcia, got a red card because of Mirković, and because of [Mirković] getting in our head and then kind of doing the flop thing where he made it look like [Garcia] hit him. But if you go back to the replay, there was no contact at all, and he just kind of sold it. That's kind of what the deal is with him, and we knew that going into the game. But the referees don't really know the histories of the teams, and so when Mirković goes down in the box and the crowd's screaming, I mean, what are you going to do?

**Oscar Sorto (defender, L.A. Galaxy II):** I just tried to push him away, but he overreacted and acted like I hit his face. That's his game plan all the time, just try to get into the player's heads. For me, if someone else fouls me, I don't think he has a reason to go up to me and start talking smack to me.

**Ivan Mirković (midfielder, Sacramento Republic FC):** My intention wasn't to go jump on Sorto and start a fight with him. I came [in] and I knew he was going to push me. It was obvious. When I came, my hands were down. When he pushed me, I threw myself [down]. I was just waiting for a moment to maybe get him sent off, get a caution, something.

*After those five long, confusing minutes, the players from both sides cooled down and Jallow seemingly allowed play to restart in the seventy-fifth minute with a dangerous Galaxy free kick near the edge of the Republic box. As André Auras, a dead ball specialist, whipped in the set piece, Jallow again whistled play dead when Nemanja Vuković crumpled to the ground in the six-yard box while clutching his face with both hands.*

*Replays showed that while Vuković wrapped both of his arms around Daniel Steres, the Galaxy defender made little, if any, contact with the Republic player's face. Play finally resumed in the seventy-sixth minute with Jallow resetting the ball for Auras to re-take his attempt. Because Jake Gleeson elected to construct a two-man wall in front of Auras, the last Republic defender stood parallel with the six-yard box line, a relatively close-to-goal defensive set-up for Sacramento. Spying the Republic's deep-lying position, Auras drove a ball across the six that Gleeson may have been able to corral if he wasn't obstructed by players from both teams standing directly in front of him.*

*Instead, the athletic Jamieson rose above Vuković just inside the six-yard box. The Galaxy striker powered a header towards the goal, thinking he'd restored his club's two-goal advantage.*

*But the ball smashed off the crossbar and Jamieson covered his mouth with both hands, shocked that he hadn't put the game away right then and there.[148]*

**Charlie Rugg (forward, L.A. Galaxy II):** That was just unlucky.

**Kevin Goldthwaite (color commentator, Sacramento Republic FC):** It just goes to show once and again how thin of a line it is for the Republic in that game in particular. You get the penalty, things are looking good, some scuffles are going on, [there's] momentum, it's heated and everything, and it could have quickly and easily been out of their reach if Jamieson just nods that in, but [the Republic was] saved by the crossbar.

**Joe Franco (defender, L.A. Galaxy II):** I felt like that would have sealed the deal for us. That would have drained their confidence and kind of taken the air out of them. But we're unfortunate it hit the crossbar. I remember just saying, "Oh, okay, back on our heels again, because they're going to come."

*That's exactly what happened as the Republic sent both outside backs bombing forward into the attack, desperately attempting to find the equalizer. For the ensuing seven minutes, the two rivals went back-and-forth down the field at breakneck pace, each trying to score the next goal in the match.*

*In the eighty-third minute, Gilberto picked up the ball just behind the midfield stripe and burst past three Galaxy players with his second touch. In under five seconds, the Brazilian advanced the ball forty yards upfield before a sliding challenge knocked it away to López outside of the L.A. box. López played the ball wide right to Klimenta, who stood in acres of free space as the entire visiting team had collapsed on Gilberto. The future Montenegro international took a touch, looked up to survey the field, then drove in a cross near the top corner of the box.*

*Joe Franco, who was forced into an unfamiliar left back role when he entered the match in the fourteenth minute as a sub, jumped and turned his back just five feet in front of Klimenta. Crucially, Franco was inside the boundaries of the box as the ball ricocheted off his arm. Everyone's eyes turned to Jallow, who stood at the top of the penalty area.*

*The referee decisively pointed his left arm towards the spot without hesitating. Gilberto turned towards the west stand, pointing to the sky as if the call was the result of divine intervention.*

**Joe Franco (defender, L.A. Galaxy II):** We knew [Klimenta] flies up the right side, and he serves in crosses. I usually play as the right back, but our left back had gotten taken out and they switched me to left back, so I kind of knew [what to expect]. When I saw him going down the line, I knew he was looking for a cross. I was like, "Okay, I need to get up in the air." So, I jumped as high as I could and kind of turned my back, which I shouldn't have done. I should have just faced the

---

[148] The majority of the people interviewed for this chapter didn't remember Jamieson's chance, and most who did recall it weren't able to provide many details of what actually happened.

ball because then I could have put my head on it, or whatnot, but I turned, and it hit the back of my elbow which was tucked into my body. And then again, the crowd's gonna be yelling, screaming at Bonney Field. There's thousands of fans there. Maybe that has a little bit of swing for the referee to call the penalty.

**Emrah Klimenta (defender, Sacramento Republic FC):** I got a great ball outside, took a touch, looked up, saw two men in the box, tried to play it early to surprise their back line. [I crossed it], Franco jumped up. Yes, his hand was tucked into his body, [he] couldn't really do anything. Yes, it hit his hand. For me, looking back at it now, after all this is said and done and all that, I don't think it was necessarily a PK. I think the referee saw that he went up, turned his body, his hand was out, called it for a PK. At the time I didn't care if it was not a PK or whatever, I was yelling, "PK! PK!," as was eight, nine-thousand fans, however many we had that night. We were fortunate to get that call.

**Rodrigo López (midfielder, Sacramento Republic FC):** I think it was a PK. [He] kind of had his elbow out a little bit.[149]

**Joe Franco (defender, L.A. Galaxy II):** I'm coming from a biased position as a Galaxy player. You'd have to ask one of the Sacramento players to see what their take on it was, but no, I didn't think it was a penalty. Like I said, the arm was in, on the body, and it wasn't extended away from my body to make me bigger or anything. My back was to the ball, so it wasn't like I acted towards the ball, to stop the ball from going anywhere. It's just unfortunate that it hit my elbow.

**Bill Paterson (Sacramento Republic FC beat writer, *Sacramento Bee*):** I think it strikes his hand, but [his hand is tucked] in on his body, so for me, it's not [a penalty]. But it happens so fast that I can understand. The crowd's probably got into [Jallow] a little bit, you know, because there are definitely calls for it, and he gives it. Sometimes you get them yourselves, sometimes they go the other way. It's just one of those things. Unfortunate at the very least.

**Warren Smith (president and co-founder, Sacramento Republic FC):** I think the only real questionable [call] was the handball. It hit his arm. It's just a [matter] of if it's inadvertent or not. And he was turning away from the ball, so you could make a case, but again, that's a call that goes either way. It just happened to go our way that night.

---

[149] Interestingly, López offered a different opinion directly following the match. When asked about the call during the post-game interview he said, "The second [penalty] was questionable, but what can I do? I can't tell the ref, 'Don't call it.'"

**Rob McAllister (play-by-play announcer, Sacramento Republic FC):** I think the Republic scored a big break on that one.

**Ivan Mirković (midfielder, Sacramento Republic FC):** It was an obvious handball.

**Kevin Goldthwaite (color commentator, Sacramento Republic FC):** After watching it a few times, that probably isn't a penalty as his elbow and arm were tucked into his body. Nothing was extended, no sort of movement was made to try to block it, but like RoRo said, "What are you supposed to do, tell them it wasn't a handball?" No, you're going to grab the ball, put it on the penalty spot, and get ready to take your penalty.

**Ivan Mirković (midfielder, Sacramento Republic FC):** Now they are talking about the positioning of his hand. Did he do it purposefully? Could the referee not call it? In soccer, it's everything about opinions, right? The referee's opinion at that moment was, that was a handball inside the box, that's a PK. Maybe somebody else who saw it in a different way, they think differently, but it was the referee's choice. Was it good or bad? That's his opinion.

**Charlie Rugg (forward, L.A. Galaxy II):** That's the play I remember most vividly. I remember the play live, and I remember seeing the replay. I remember Joe Franco jumped up to block the cross. His arm was tucked in, sort of like somebody was wearing a cast, like an arm cast. It was tucked in completely on his body.

**Kevin Goldthwaite (color commentator, Sacramento Republic FC):** In the heat of the moment, that is such a difficult call for a referee to make. I mean, you gotta make that decision within a split second, and it's all depending on what your view is. Franco ends up kind of turning his body a little bit. It is such a relative call for the official to make. It's so difficult for them to determine immediately, and you gotta make the decision within two seconds or three seconds, or whatever it is. I don't fault the ref for making that call. Maybe he could have been in a better position, but 100 percent if he sees the video and the replay, I don't think that's a handball, and we had the luxury of seeing that.

**Joe Franco (defender, L.A. Galaxy II):** They had a replay of the play,[150] and we're in the penalty box, and I [say to the referee], "No, please just talk to your assistant referee, just see what he saw." They showed the replay on the screen. The

---

[150] The side of the field the foul occurred in was right next to what was Bonney Field's only video board at the time.

referee admitted, he's like, "Yeah, you're right, I shouldn't have called the call, but you can't switch a play based on the replay."[151]

**Charlie Rugg (forward, L.A. Galaxy II):** I remember the referee said to one of our players, "I know it went off his arm, I know his arm was tucked in, but there's nothing I can do about it now."[152] You can take it back, as a referee, you can take it back. It kind of made the whole game into a joke to me, honestly. With the first call being questionable, and then that one, that one being even more kind of ridiculous, and then him saying that…what can we do? What else can we do?

**Joe Franco (defender, L.A. Galaxy II):** It is what it is, and he made the call.

*After waiting with the ball near the penalty spot for nearly a minute while Galaxy players argued with Jallow, López finally got the signal from the referee that it was time to take the spot kick. "Your second penalty of the night is way more difficult than your first," Goldthwaite said on the broadcast. "You already have a little mental game from the first penalty, you know, are you going to go the same way? Are you going to switch it up? Is the goalie going to guess? It just adds a whole other wrinkle to RoRo stepping up and taking another penalty here. It's a much more mental game, and it makes way more pressure built on top of this. If I'm RoRo, honestly, I'm just putting my laces through it and kicking it as hard as I can into the back of the net right down the middle."*

*Seemingly on cue, López tied up the game by driving the ball straight up the middle as Perk dove to his left.*

**Kevin Goldthwaite (color commentator, Sacramento Republic FC):** When you take the second [penalty in a match], the mind games start. As a player you start second guessing yourself…hence me thinking the easiest thing to do is just kick it as hard as I can down the middle and pretty much hope the thing goes in.

**Bill Paterson (Sacramento Republic FC beat writer, *Sacramento Bee*):** Rodrigo buried the shot, and this place was going crazy, and all of a sudden, you're thinking, "Who knows? They might win this thing."

*For the final five minutes of regular time, the Republic throttled up the pressure in the attacking third, while the Galaxy wasted several dangerous set pieces near the Sacramento goal. Then, as both teams prepared for overtime, Gilberto won a ball near midfield, immediately stepped forward, and looked up. Moving from left to right across the top of the Galaxy box was López, whom Gilberto found with a pass that threaded the needle past three L.A. defenders. With nowhere to go, López continued to dribble horizontally before Oscar Sorto tripped him up from behind about*

---

[151] The game took place long before the institution of video assistant referee (VAR).
[152] Both Franco and Rugg brought this point up without being prompted or asked about Jallow saying anything like this.

*twenty yards from goal. Jallow whistled for a free kick to be taken in the same spot that Alvarez had scored from a dead ball in the final regular-season game against the Galaxy.*

**Charlie Rugg (forward, L.A. Galaxy II):** That one was probably a foul. But at that point, with the crowd, they had a ton of momentum going and we were just kind of dumbfounded by the officiating.

**Joe Franco (defender, L.A. Galaxy II):** It's hard to say because some refs would call it a foul, some refs wouldn't. Like I said, maybe the fans had a bit of an influence, which shows the importance of home field advantage and fans really getting into the game, because you never know. I think even if a referee says that it doesn't influence what the call is, I have to say that we're all human.

**Oscar Sorto (defender, L.A. Galaxy II):** I didn't touch him.

*Even though Alvarez had scored from the same area three weeks prior, López elected to strike the dead ball after a short conversation between the two. The midfielder's shot was somehow able to get over the wall and back down again in time, curling perfectly into the upper right corner of the net. Perk read the ball well and leaped towards it, but like the first goal, he could only get his fingertips on it. As Perk crashed into the back of the net, López ran right past Smith on the western sideline and jumped onto the edge of the stands to embrace his family and the Republic fans in that section. After ninety minutes of play, the Republic enjoyed its first lead of the game thanks to a hat trick from the first signing in club history.*

**Max Alvarez (midfielder, Sacramento Republic FC):** I told RoRo, "I think you should take it, I mean you have two goals. You got the momentum going, you get your hat trick, I'll get you a drink later." I saw the confidence in him, I gave it to him. It was his moment. In training he knocks them down every time. He's the guy to take it, so I let him take it. He took the initiative and buried it. That's just the type of player he is. When it comes to crunch time, he's like Kobe. He's got ice in his veins. It's something special.

**Warren Smith (president and co-founder, Sacramento Republic FC):** I thought RoRo was coming over to see me, and he ran right past me. He saw his [significant other], gave her a big kiss.

**Rodrigo López (midfielder, Sacramento Republic FC):** At that moment, I didn't really see anything. I ran over because my family was on that side, my dad and my mom. It was actually my mom's first game since I played at Chivas. She gets really nervous [at my games]. She just didn't like going live and sitting next to my dad because my dad's really hard on me. She chose to come to that game, and that was probably the best game for me personally. But after the game, she said, "I'm never coming to another game again. That was it for me." It was just a special night all around. If I had seen Warren, I would have hugged him, but I didn't see him at that time. My head was everywhere.

**Warren Smith (president and co-founder, Sacramento Republic FC):** MLS came here on Thursday, they got to see the Railyards, got to meet the owners, got to meet our sponsors, got to talk to the mayor. Game time came, and two of the officials had to leave, one stayed back.[153] He was catching a flight that night. We got him an Uber because he had to run to the airport at the ninetieth minute. All of a sudden, the crowd roars, it's the [foul] call. I look over to the right, right as RoRo is taking the kick, and there he is. He had run back and was sweating. And then he saw the kick and just went, "Oh my god!"

**Bill Paterson (Sacramento Republic FC beat writer, *Sacramento Bee*):** Just an awesome goal. Unbelievable goal. I don't know what Galaxy II could have done. It was just a beautiful shot. It was the perfect shot, and you could just see the second half, as the momentum built, it was an incredible moment.

**Brian Perk (goalkeeper, L.A. Galaxy II):** RoRo just hit a really good free kick. I got a decent jump on it. It kind of looks like our wall, maybe ducks a little bit or leans back and [the ball] goes over. It's kind of a lower height than normally they [go over the wall]. So it wound up coming on me a bit quicker. I mean he hits it well, so all the credit to him, but [if the wall is] leaning forward, maybe they could have got a little deflection.

**Rodrigo López (midfielder, Sacramento Republic FC):** As soon as it left my foot, I knew it was a goal.[154]

**Rob McAllister (play-by-play announcer, Sacramento Republic FC):** I think that moment just sealed Sacramento's love for soccer and what it could mean for the city.

**Charlie Rugg (forward, L.A. Galaxy II):** I don't think we expected the game to be over in regular time. That was a great free kick.

*The celebrations lasted nearly 90 seconds, moving the clock deep into stoppage time before L.A. Galaxy II had the chance to resume play with the ensuing kickoff. Once Jallow signaled for the restart, Los Dos frantically attempted to push the ball forward, but couldn't find a way through the eleven Republic players bunkered in their own half. When the final whistle blew roughly 75 seconds later, both teams sprinted towards the middle of the field. The hosts rushed to blissfully embrace one another while the visitors angrily confronted the officials.*

---

[153] The official at the semifinal was MLS special assistant to the commissioner Charles Altchek.
[154] López said this during the post-game interview.

# The Aftermath

**Curt Onalfo (head coach, L.A. Galaxy II):** It's just one of those games that you just walk away shaking your head, and the league should be ashamed of themselves for such a poor officiating job. It's an absolute disgrace, and I'm disgusted by it. The sad thing is that we have a bunch of young men who have worked hard all year and positioned themselves to host the final, but it got pulled away.[155]

**Kevin Goldthwaite (color commentator, Sacramento Republic FC):** If you're [Onalfo], the one call that obviously had an effect on the game and changed it was the handball. I think that Curt's argument could have been you need to be in a better position to see it, and maybe a more skilled or seasoned official is going to be able to make that call correctly more times than not. But like we said earlier, if you see that replay, it's not a penalty, it's not a handball. If he's complaining about that and that alone, then I understand that, but everything else? The game wasn't the best officiated game; it wasn't the worst. There were some calls that were missed for and against both sides, but obviously the big piece of the puzzle is the handball in the box that drastically changes the complexion of that game.

**Jovan Kirovski: (technical director, L.A. Galaxy):** The calls that were made were things that I haven't seen in a very long time. We need quality officials to be able to handle a hostile environment [like Bonney Field]. The officials that were there could not handle it, and it killed the game. This has nothing to do with whether or not we lost the game, but I simply think that the officiating needs to be much better at this high level. Our kids played well and to have the officials decide the game was just not appropriate. Sacramento played well, but it shouldn't be the officials who decide the game. It's tough for referees in such a difficult and hostile environment, but now that there is more interest in this league, we need more quality officials in such important matches.[156]

**Kevin Goldthwaite (color commentator, Sacramento Republic FC):** In every game ever played, the officials have had an influence and an effect on the game for better or for worse for each side [and] that can drastically change the complexity of the game, the composition of the game. The handball in the box, that's a tough, tough call for an official to make. The way the rules are structured in soccer, there's no replay and the referees need to make on the fly decisions or judgment calls sometimes. That particular play, [the handball], it's a judgment call, the linesman may have had a better view of it. Maybe the linesman steps in and says something, but you rarely see that happen.

---

[155] Onalfo told LAGalaxy.com's Adam Serrano this after the game.
[156] Kirovski also told Serrano this after the game.

**Charlie Rugg (forward, L.A. Galaxy II):** I know officiating is hard; it's not easy to do. Players will complain about the referees all the time. Pretty much every game, players, coaches will complain about officiating. But I can honestly say that that was some of the most shocking decisions I've ever seen.

**Rob McAllister (play-by-play announcer, Sacramento Republic FC):** There's just so many calls that happen throughout a match, and I just think everyone's human. There's an emotion to it and that's what makes sports so great. There probably was some [talk of], "We should have called a few things here and there," but [the referees] didn't want to dictate the game. I think they were forced to because the energy and intensity kept growing throughout the match. And it's easy to swallow your whistle or just keep the flag down. It's hard to speak for someone else. Had it gone the other way, would we have been upset? Sure. But at the end of the day, they committed fouls where they shouldn't have, and that will kill you.

**Oscar Sorto (defender, L.A. Galaxy II):** I felt like [Jallow] didn't have a feel for the game. It affected us because we were fighting for every ball and then he was just calling easy fouls. At the end of the day we were just dealing with it, but I guess dealing with it wasn't enough.

**Emrah Klimenta (defender, Sacramento Republic FC):** Did he decide the game for us? No. I'd like to think that we worked our butts off to get back into that position and score those three goals whether it was off set pieces, or [in the] run of play. I think he played a big part in deciding the game, but ultimately, we could have missed the PKs. RoRo could have not made that free kick.

**Rodrigo López (midfielder, Sacramento Republic FC):** At the end of the day, we can't complain. I know for them, it's a little different. I know what they think, but I feel like we should have been given that PK at the beginning of the game. Obviously, we weren't, and things changed in the second half, it did go our way. [The referee] influenced a lot in the game. So be it. That game's over. It's passed. We can't do anything about it anymore.

**Max Alvarez (midfielder, Sacramento Republic FC):** There were a few calls earlier [in the first half] that he could have made that probably fell through. Maybe he might have made up for it in the second half. You never know. It's part of soccer. The referees make calls, and they see things differently than others. It's part of soccer.

**Joe Franco (defender, L.A. Galaxy II):** It's always easier to point the finger at someone else. The referee made some horrible calls from our perspective, from our standpoint. But then again, we were the ones that kind of let them in their situation. We were the ones that let Mirković into the box when, if we defended better, he wouldn't even get in the box. We were the ones that gave [Klimenta] time to get down the wing. If he didn't have time to serve it, then maybe it wouldn't have hit my hand. And then the third one, again, we were kind of slacking off and maybe missed a play or two, and [López is] on top of the box, and we go in a little too hard. As much fault it is for the referee making those bad decisions, some blame goes on our shoulders as well.

**Ivan Mirković (midfielder, Sacramento Republic FC):** The refs are a big part of the game. Without them, we won't be able to play the game, right? None of the games start without referees. Sometimes they make good decisions, bad decisions. But sometimes a good decision for me, maybe that decision is bad for you. Other decisions are bad for me, but good for you. They have to find some balance and always, there's gonna be someone who complains about referees. I feel like it was his opinion that he called two penalty kicks, and we are all just thankful for that. We're not going to complain about any PK that we get. From our point of view, yes, he made the right calls. From the Galaxy's point of view, he didn't, so who are we to say that it was wrong or not?

**Brian Perk (goalkeeper, L.A. Galaxy II):** You never want to say that the referee won or lost the game, but he definitely had an impact, that's for sure. If I look at it, maybe one of them you give, but probably not both. For me, obviously I'm a little biased I would imagine, but I didn't think either were actually [penalties], but those things happen in the game, and I'm not surprised. RoRo's still gotta convert that, and then they gotta score the free kick too, so I mean, there's a lot. They won that game. The ref didn't lose it for us. We lost it ourselves.

**Kevin Goldthwaite (color commentator, Sacramento Republic FC):** I don't think I could go to bed at night comfortably saying that the officials or the referees changed the course of [the game] or caused the Republic to win.

*Regardless of the controversy, Sacramento Republic FC moved onto the final, scheduled for Bonney Field one week later. The Republic's opponents would be the Harrisburg City Islanders, the club Sacramento lost to via a 2-1 scoreline in its record-setting home opener at Hughes Stadium in April. The match was set to become the first professional championship game played in Sacramento since the 2006 WNBA finals.*

# TWELVE
# RAISING THE STAKES[157]

In the same way that the 2001-02 Western Conference Finals served as the de facto championship of the NBA that season, whichever team won the penultimate playoff series between Sacramento Republic FC and L.A. Galaxy II in the 2014 USL playoffs appeared headed towards an anticlimactic title match. In 2002 the Los Angeles Lakers swept the New Jersey Nets, while in 2014 Sacramento faced the No. 8 Harrisburg City Islanders in an equally large mismatch. The City Islanders ruined the Republic's home opener in April, but hardly stood a chance five months later.[158] Not at Bonney Field, and not after the semifinal miracle.

According to *The Sacramento Bee*, the cheapest ticket available on the secondary ticket market StubHub was priced at $105 for the 2014 USL title match. The 8,000-seat stadium couldn't satisfy a demand that was already 75-percent sold out before each game thanks to the club's roughly 6,000 season ticket holders—some tickets went for as much as $300 on third-party sites. Recognizing that the final was the city's most anticipated professional sporting event in almost a decade, Franklin Productions scrapped together an impromptu local television broadcast for the match. For the first time, a Sacramento Republic FC game would feature live on local TV alongside the usual YouTube livestream.

For those who couldn't afford to attend the match, the Tower Bridge Battalion offered an alternative solution: anyone who inked the TBB logo on their body could earn a free ticket. Six members took the supporters' group up on its offer, including Jordan Hale, who already sported a Dallas Cowboys tattoo on his back.

"The Cowboys have been around since 1960, and the Republic FC have been around a year, but now I have tattoos of both teams so that tells you a little

---

[157] I recommend pairing this chapter with "Sextape" by Deftones.
[158] After beating Sacramento 2-1 in that matchup, Harrisburg finished the season 9-9-6, a rate of 1.375 points per game. Meanwhile the Republic went 15-4-3 in that same timespan, good for 2.18 ppg.

something about my love of Republic FC," Hale told *The Bee* ahead of the final. "We can't lose because we've already won. No one expected us to be playing for the title in our first season. We've shown we're built for [Major League Soccer]." According to Hale, president and co-founder Warren Smith spotted the new ink shortly before kickoff, leaned over, and kissed his new tattoo.

As the sun set and the air began to cool ahead of kickoff, none of the 8,000 seats at Bonney Field stood empty. The national anthem came and went and just before kickoff, the Battalion put on a show. The supporters' group simultaneously unfurled three banners that nearly engulfed the entirety of the bleachers behind Bonney Field's north goal.

On the western side, the supporters revealed a depiction of the iconic Tower Bridge with the words "Our City" written on its horizontal support. In the eastern section, the Republic's crest was re-created among a group of faceless supporters standing behind the words "Our Club." And in between stood a drawing of the trophy the two teams were playing for that night with one major alteration: the piece of silverware featured a giant red star on it. "Our Cup," it read just below.

When Octavio Guzmán scored the opening goal in the thirty-sixth minute from a feed from Rodrigo López, that was it. The title belonged to Sacramento. Most of the rest of the match played out in the middle third of the field before substitute Tommy Stewart struck from a tight angle in stoppage time to put the finishing touches on the victory.

When the final whistle blew, the entire team sprinted towards the Tower Bridge Battalion and jumped into the stands. Someone placed an oversized sombrero on López's head. Several players pulled their home country's flags from the stands, where all season the Battalion had draped one for each nationality represented on the team. Sideline photographers rushed to snapshot after shot of each athlete covered in their nation's colors.[159]

Defender Nemanja Vuković stood in front of the supporters draped in the red and gold of Montenegro. Next to the 2014 USL Defender of the Year was reserve forward Izzy Tandir, who proudly held up the blue and yellow of Bosnia and Herzegovina. The two champions embraced. Nearly two decades before, Vuković and Tandir's countries were locked in a brutal sectarian war rife with ethnic cleansing and war crimes. But that night in Sacramento, they celebrated together as teammates, friends, and champions.

In the center of the pitch, USL president Tim Holt began speaking over the PA system, delivering his prepared remarks to the still-packed crowd at Bonney Field. Unable to contain his excitement, mayor Kevin Johnson raced towards Holt and

---

[159] In addition to the American flag that represented the majority of the roster, the Battalion also displayed the colors of the following nations: Australia (Harrison Delbridge), Brazil (Gilberto), Bosnia and Herzegovina (Izzy Tandir), Mexico (Christian Gonzalez, Rodrigo López), Montenegro (Emrah Klimenta, Nemanja Vuković), New Zealand (Jake Gleeson), Northern Ireland (Tommy Stewart), and Serbia (Ivan Mirković).

interrupted the suited league official with a bear hug that sent the president's notecards flying. Luckily for Holt, he'd memorized his speech.

Club captain Justin Braun lifted the trophy as the sellout crowd chanted its desired goal: "MLS! MLS! MLS!" For Braun, it was the culmination of a somewhat disappointing campaign in which he struggled with a variety of different injuries. After scoring the club's first-ever goal, much was expected from the former MLS man, who only delivered three more strikes in league play. The towering striker revealed after the game that he'd suited up for the playoffs with a broken toe. "It's just a toe," he joked to the media. "You don't really need those."

To make up for losing out on the league's regular-season MVP award,[160] the media on hand chose Rodrigo López as the championship game's MVP. Overwhelmed with emotion from winning his first professional title, he immediately dropped his trophy, which broke into pieces on the grass. "It's amazing, man, it's something I can't explain," López said in the post-game interview. "When the whistle blew, I just teared up, just from joy because of the hard work I've put in, that we've put in throughout the year. It's very deserved by my teammates."

The inaugural season's title game captivated the local audience–those who couldn't find an affordable ticket watched in record numbers from home. In addition to the nearly 15,000 who tuned into the YouTube stream, Franklin Pictures' broadcast drew a 1.6 rating, including a 2.4 figure among MLS's key 18-to-34-year-old male demographic. The company won a California Emmy for its efforts, which outdrew two major college football games in competing time slots.

Head coach Preki, who won the USL Coach of the Year award earlier in the week, finally cracked a smile for the first time during his tenure in Sacramento. After spending three years away from the spotlight, Preki was finally back on top of the game. Dressed in a gray suit that he'd modeled during Sacramento Fashion Week, the manager strutted over to the press scrum to comply with his least-favorite part of the job. The coach's grin remained as he arrived to address the media. "I'm always happy, I just don't let you see it," he joked after a reporter brought up his demeanor.

The press conference began in standard fashion in every way other than Preki's joyful mood. "I told them before the game: 'We always play one way, go and get the result,'" Preki said. "Go forward. Play attractive. Play attacking. Believe in yourself. I said to them, 'Nobody's going to give it to you. You've gotta go out there and you've gotta go get it.'

"I give them all the credit in the world because they did, they wanted it, and they got it.

"[I'm] extremely excited for the city of Sacramento because I believe the city of Sacramento has proven that it deserves an MLS team," he added. "Look at the

---

[160] Orlando City SC's Kevin Molino deservedly won the award after scoring twenty goals and dishing out nine assists to lead his team to a 19-4-5 record and the No. 1 overall seed.

excitement, look at the support, look at the team we have on the field who plays attractive football.

"It would be a shame if we don't go to MLS very fast."

Near the end of the interview, a seemingly innocuous question struck a nerve with the head coach and what started as a jovial conversation quickly turned serious. "What does this mean to you, to win a championship?" a reporter asked.

"It means a lot," Preki responded. "I always knew that I could coach. I believe I was wrongly dismissed at my previous job at Toronto."

It was as if he'd been waiting all season to bury Toronto FC, which continued to struggle amid yet another playoff-less season while Preki's Sacramento set the USL alight. Leading up to the answer, no reporter prompted Preki to speak about any of the previous teams he'd coached. No reporter asked him how he had been treated before his stint in Sacramento. No reporter touched on any subject other than the championship victory and the 2014 USL season.

Regardless, Preki took the conversation to Toronto, the first time he commented on his stop in Canada after three years away from the game and one back in it in California. It had been more than four seasons since TFC dismissed Preki, and instead of celebrating a championship with his new team, he felt the need to express his displeasure over a perceived lack of respect from his previous employer.

## The Local Impact

While Sacramento had tasted sporting glory before, the Republic's victory *felt* different according to key figures surrounding the city and the team. "I've been involved in some championships with the River Cats [but] they're still the A's'[161] Triple-A team," Warren Smith said. "But this is truly our team, so it's really, really special. I'll cherish that ring a lot more than the River Cats rings that I have. [2014] was really a special time for our city."

Only a few months had passed between Sacramento Professional Soccer's lightly attended opening press conference and Sacramento Republic FC lifting a trophy in front of a sold-out crowd at a new soccer-specific stadium. Club officials went from begging for attention to turning away potential paying customers. The Republic became the talk of the town, even among casual sports fans.

"I just remember that it really galvanized the city," said Republic play-by-play announcer Rob McAllister. "Sports are so great because [they] bring people of all walks of life together. What I loved about [the championship run] is that it didn't just stay within that arena. It spread, and it just became this wildfire, like that was the center of this explosion. It just radiated out all over. I remember talking to

---

[161] Now Giants'.

Kevin, he was like, 'Everyone wants to talk about [soccer], I can't even get work done today. Everywhere you go, that's all people wanted to talk about. I would never have thought that I would be at work talking about soccer the way I am.'[162] I think that's fresh off the World Cup, I think that has a lot to do with it, that we had a lot of this great soccer being played. It was just a captivating moment for Sacramento at the perfect time."

Added *Sacramento Bee* Republic beat writer Bill Paterson: "This was a team of destiny. There were people who weren't real big soccer fans, they heard about it, they read about it, and all of a sudden, they're like, 'Wow, this is pretty fascinating.' I think it really caught fire, not just among soccer fans, but among sports fans in general."

# Celebration

For the first time in years, it was time for a championship parade to shut down Downtown Sacramento. The following Friday, the procession gathered at 4th Street on the Capitol Mall to begin the journey six blocks east towards the Capitol Building's west steps. Decked out in black championship T-shirts, Republic players climbed aboard the top of Sacramento fire truck No. 2 to relax with the local first responders ahead of the march. Goalkeeper Jake Gleeson had been recalled from his loan and was already back in Portland, prompting a club employee to print out a picture of his face. Fans were offered the chance to hold up his headshot and take a "Gleeson Photobomb" to ensure the netminder's likeness was immortalized in the celebrations.

By the time the players arrived, hundreds of fans had already been partying for four-plus hours. Food trucks offered sustenance and libations while local punk rock band City of Vain provided the soundtrack. Warren Smith and Kevin Nagle addressed the supporters in their trademark casual attire before Kevin Johnson grabbed the mic and pointed to the crowd. "They believe this team is built for MLS," he yelled.

When the Sacramento Republic FC office closed for half the day to finally relax and take in the scenes, it marked one of the first times employees were afforded to breathe since whenever they began working for the club. The rest of that Friday was for them, followed by another reprieve on Saturday and Sunday.

Come Monday, though, everyone was expected back in the office–the Republic exceeded every imaginable expectation in 2014, but the work was just getting started.

---

[162] At the time of the interview, Goldthwaite only moonlighted as the color commentator for the Republic, keeping a day job in the real estate market.

# Back to Work

Every major event in Sacramento Republic FC's short history had one thing in common: the staff planned a social gathering following each but had yet to actually follow through on those plans. No one ever made it to the party after any marquee celebration of soccer whether that be Sacramento Soccer Day, the Hughes Stadium opener, or the 2014 USL title game.

It wasn't because Republic FC employees didn't want to revel in their accomplishments, it was that they were often a victim of their own successes. The product they created proved of such high quality that each event opened new possibilities at a faster rate than possible. There was never time to relax—more work would always be required to achieve the MLS dream.

There would be no offseason for the Sacramento Republic FC front office in 2014. Instead of retiring to a far-off beach someplace warm, the group that had now spent the last two years putting in daily twelve-hour shifts, redoubled their efforts to make 2015 an even more successful campaign.

The prior August, Republic staffers traveled to Portland for the 2014 MLS All-Star Game alongside representatives from the Sacramento Kings and mayor Kevin Johnson. There, Kings minority owner Kevin Nagle stepped forward to agree to lead the group financing a possible MLS expansion bid. At the same time, the Kings, who showed potential interest in a majority stake, backed off and let Nagle take charge. Eleven other minority owners from the NBA franchise made small investments to bolster Nagle's capital.

But one major player in the local sports scene reportedly felt threatened by the Republic's success: Sacramento Kings principal owner Vivek Ranadivé. Just over a year after acquiring a majority stake in the Kings, helping keep the franchise in Sacramento, the successful business owner privately began expressing concerns to MLS officials about what he felt would hurt his recently purchased club.

According to *Sports Illustrated* and *ESPN*, Ranadivé thought that he would have to fight with an MLS franchise over fans, especially considering the Kings were just about to break ground for a new Downtown facility not far from the Railyards location the Republic set its eyes on. And if there had to be an MLS team in Sacramento, Ranadivé reportedly told MLS officials that he should take controlling interest in it.

By the conclusion of the season, though, Ranadivé changed his mind. Johnson, using the experience he gained while helping save the Kings from relocation, convinced Ranadivé that the Republic earning a spot in MLS wouldn't hurt the Sacramento Kings. The contrary would prove to be true, according to Johnson—the Republic would *help* the Kings. In addition to providing the city with a more vibrant major league sports culture, a top-division Republic side would allow for cross-marketing opportunities and potentially draw more investment to

Sacramento overall. Convinced by the mayor, the Kings officially joined as minority investors in a potential MLS franchise.

With a strengthened investment group, Sacramento Republic FC officials discussed three potential mechanisms to acquire an MLS franchise.

The first was the most traditional: formally submit a bid to join Major League Soccer. At the time, the league had publicly announced plans to expand to at least twenty-four teams. By the end of the 2014 USL season, twenty-three of those twenty-four were spoken for with MLS set to potentially vote on the final spot in December. While Sacramento had joined the expansion talk, MLS focused on developing a Minneapolis-Saint Paul bid that fit many of the criteria the league was looking for: a relatively large market with a good soccer fan base that wasn't located to any current franchises and featured potential Fortune 500 sponsors in the area. Hindering Minnesota were the multiple ownership groups that each wanted to be the one to bring top division soccer to the city, neither of which had secured a soccer-specific stadium deal. Still, the Twin Cities bid was the clear favorite, but the perception was that Sacramento wasn't far behind.

The second mechanism that could propel the Republic forward relied completely on the success, or lack thereof, of a rival expansion bid rife with turmoil. Earlier in the year, MLS had announced David Beckham's Miami bid as the league's twenty-third franchise. However, the deal came with an asterisk–MLS Miami couldn't begin play until it reached a deal for a downtown soccer stadium. The league had already failed in the city before with the short-lived Miami Fusion and wouldn't return unless success was all-but assured. Since the announcement, two Miami stadium proposals fell through, leading to rumors that another team could take Beckam's spot. Should the Englishman's ownership group falter, Sacramento Republic FC was thought to be ready to take its place.

The third option qualified as the biggest longshot and involved one of the most incompetent sports franchises in the history of top-division American professional sports. By early 2014, the worst kept secret in MLS was that 2005 expansion club Chivas USA would fold operations. What began as an ambitious project hoping to capture MLS's long-desired Latinx demographic, had morphed into a sparsely supported afterthought of a club that only remained notable due to a gaggle of scandals. After averaging nearly 20,000 fans per game in 2006, Chivas USA's 2014 attendance figures were generously listed above 7,000. Years of mismanagement, both on and off the field, turned the club into a joke that drew fewer than half the fans as the league's next lowest figure.

Owner Jorge Vergara had long cut corners and stripped the team for parts, but the club and league's biggest controversy involved Chivas USA's recently formed bigoted hiring and firing policies. "If you don't speak Spanish, you can go work for the Galaxy, unless you speak Chinese, which is not even a language," Vergara reportedly told a group of employees shortly before firing two non-Spanish speaking youth coaches.[163] Sensing the club's impending doom, the Republic launched an unlikely bid for Chivas USA's franchise rights. However, MLS rejected the move and instead awarded them to a Los Angeles-based ownership group that planned to relaunch a team in the same market at a date in the near future.

So, Sacramento Republic FC focused on the first option: beating Minnesota to earn the league's twenty-fourth spot. If MLS's September visit to Sacramento gave the Republic brass hope, the league's visit to Minnesota during the same months motivated them to take their bid to the next level. Sacramento may have lagged behind Minnesota in terms of desired geographical location, market size, and potential local sponsors, but Republic co-founder and president Warren Smith felt that his club held at least one advantage over its Midwestern rivals: the successful fight to save the Kings that resulted in Nagle becoming the largest local investor in the team's new ownership group.

"We've had the fortune of being in a battle before, so we know the intensity that's needed," Smith told *The Sacramento Bee*. "I'm not sure those other markets, with all due respect, understand that intensity because they haven't had that battle."

Quickly working following the conclusion of the 2014 USL season, Smith and fellow co-founder Joe Wagoner focused on improving the local product to further impress MLS. Not even a year old, Bonney Field would be renovated to expand capacity above 11,000. The 2014 campaign saw the Republic sell more than 6,000 season tickets, which, according to the club, were renewed at more than a 70 percent clip. Despite dwarfing the numbers of every other USL team, Sacramento pledged to increase this total. In addition, the club launched its "Built for MLS" website that allowed fans to put down a refundable fifty-dollar deposit for future MLS season tickets. The goal was to hit 10,000 deposits before the league's Board of Governors met in December to discuss the current expansion bids.

Following the script of his early 2012 effort to help save the Kings, Johnson hopped on a plane to New York to meet with the higher ups of an organization which would decide Sacramento's future in a top division sports league. Alongside several from the Republic's investment group, the mayor used the meeting to hype Sacramento to Garber and Co. Representatives from Minnesota and an unlikely Las Vegas bid also met with MLS officials that same day.

"This was a chance for us to tell our Sacramento story, and what we've done, and how committed we are to demonstrate that we are a city and community worthy and waiting to be in the MLS family," Johnson told *The Bee*, while also admitting that there was no clear indication of the what the league's next steps entailed. All that was known was that the three bids were invited back to that Board of Governors meeting, which would take place just before MLS Cup.

"We had productive expansion meetings [Thursday] with representatives from Las Vegas, Minneapolis and Sacramento," MLS commissioner Don Garber said in a statement released by the league. "We were impressed with the presentations

---

[163] Reported by *SB Nation*.

made by each group. Following our MLS Board of Governors meeting on December 6, we will provide an update on the expansion process and timeline."

Ahead of MLS Cup, Sacramento had sold roughly 9,000 MLS season-ticket deposits, surpassing the 2014 totals of nine of the top division league's franchises. To reward the fans for playing a major part in this, and all the inaugural season's successes, the Republic rented two buses to take forty of the club's most loyal Tower Bridge Battalion members down to the MLS title game in Los Angeles. Before the match, Republic brass traveled to the MLS headquarters hotel in Hollywood for their presentation. Alongside them were the forty, who provided their club leaders with visible fan support.

"We want to make sure [MLS executives] know there are fans behind the Republic," Battalion member Juan Aguayo told *The Bee*. "I don't see anybody here from Minnesota or Las Vegas."

While none of the three bids presented their case to the Board of Governors, representatives from each were present to show their interest in the league and join a private meeting with MLS. Afterwards they emerged to boisterous applause from the patiently waiting Battalion and a handful of Sacramento-based journalists. MLS deputy commissioner Mark Abbott addressed the reporters, revealing that the league hoped to meet again with each of the bids in the coming months. He also confirmed the speculation that the next announcement could include two teams if Miami continued to stumble in their efforts to secure a stadium deal.

"If we cannot move forward in Miami, does it create another opportunity? While it would, we're not contemplating not getting a deal done," Abbott told *The Bee*. Added Nagle: "They're going to continue to do due diligence, like any business would. We're prepared to answer any question that they have for us."

Sacramento still might have been the underdog, but the Battalion's presence ensured that the Republic would remain in the conversation as the national media speculated about future expansion markets. During MLS Cup, a small throng of red-and-gold in the stands provided Sacramento with visibility at American soccer's marquee yearly event. For the second time in three months, the Republic's largest supporters' group chanted for ninety-plus minutes at a title game, this time capturing the national broadcast's attention multiple times during the L.A. Galaxy's 2-1 victory over the New England Revolution.

The new year brought new investment as Sacramento finally announced the culmination of talks that had begun in earnest a few months prior. No, the San Francisco 49ers weren't investing, but 49ers CEO Jed York and six of his partners from the NFL franchise joined up as Republic minority owners, reportedly buying a similarly sized stake as the Kings. The addition pushed the number of club investors also involved in other major league franchises to eighteen. One of those, Kings minority owner Larry Kelley, provided the group with a boost by commencing negotiations for Sacramento's entire downtown Railyards plot, which the Republic hoped would serve as the location for a possible MLS stadium.

"We want to make it very easy for MLS to make a decision," Nagle said following the announcement. "We built an extraordinary ownership group. It's going to make a very strong, compelling case."

According to *The Bee*, Kevin Johnson originally approached the York family to introduce them to Nagle. York and Co. had already been looking to invest in a soccer club but had passed on partnering with the geographically closer San Jose Earthquakes, reportedly because they preferred to join an organization they could help build from the bottom up.

"We've looked at different soccer investments in the past, internationally and in the [*sic*] MLS, but the Sacramento opportunity looked the most promising," York told *The Bee*. "We have more 49ers season-ticket holders in Sacramento than we do in San Francisco."

Several national media reports covering MLS expansion noted the addition of 49ers officials to the Republic bid. Brian Straus of *Sports Illustrated* wrote that the involvement of the Kings and 49ers have "altered the MLS expansion landscape." Meanwhile, *ESPN* reported that Sacramento was "within touching distance of the expansion finish line."

## Expanding the Fortress

While MLS and potential Railyards stadium talks dominated the local media, Sacramento Republic FC began the process of improving its existing home venue in Bonney Field. Construction workers tore down the moderately sized supporters' section behind the north goal, replacing it with a towering monstrosity that effectively doubled the section in size.

Though he originally thought "it was going to be dumb," Republic co-founder and vice president Joe Wagoner later changed his opinion on the new stands. In 2014, Bonney Field's seating proved quaint and symmetrically idyllic. Wagoner described the new grandstand as "fucking big."

"You can hear [the fans] yell 'fuck' a lot louder because it bounces right off the metal," Wagoner said in the lobby of his club's headquarters in 2015. "That was the beauty of the old ones, they weren't as high, so the sound kind of went away. [The new seats] are solid, so the whole thing, it's just one giant piece of metal, and so when you've got a thousand people yelling 'fuck' at the same time…"

Wagoner trailed off after the word "time." He was speaking roughly ten feet from the open-to-the-public team store. He paused, checked nervously for a few seconds behind the wall separating it from the lobby, and when he felt satisfied no one would overhear him, he returned to the conversation about the new grandstand. "Just checking, I'm going to start yelling 'fuck' and I want to make sure I'm not yelling at kids," he said.

During one of the first preseason games at the renovated Bonney Field, Wagoner hosted a delegation from baseball's Triple-A Reno Aces alongside Zappos founder Nick Swinmurn. The former were researching the USL experience ahead of the league expanding to Reno, while the latter showed interest in investing in professional soccer. One of the parties inquired if the soccer game-day experience catered to families, to which Wagoner confirmed that the Republic featured a kid-friendly atmosphere.

"Right then, was the first 'fuck' in the new bleachers," Wagoner said. "It was so clear and crisp in the night, it was the 'We are fucking dynamite' [chant]. [Our guests looked] at me and I go, 'Hey, this ain't baseball, dude.'"

Overall, the renovations would see Bonney Field's capacity increased to 11,442, a figure that sounded larger thanks to the new stand's metal surface. The Republic also installed a second video replay board and constructed a beer garden behind the western sections. The hope was each improvement would enhance the gameday experience for fans, especially with the beer garden, which featured a stage for live music, space for food trucks, and multiple different drink service stations.

# Overlooked

Sacramento Republic FC's titanic progression on and off the field couldn't pull it even with the Minnesota bid. Four days after the Republic kicked off its 2015 campaign, Garber and MLS traveled to Minneapolis to make it official. The commissioner cited several factors in the decision, including the city's large population of young adults and the area's history of supporting local soccer in various professional leagues. The fact that the Minneapolis-Saint Paul metro market stood as the fifteenth largest in the country, and third largest without an MLS team, also helped justify the league's decision. As MLS pushed for a better television deal that would help infuse the league with cash to improve the standard of play, Sacramento's twentieth place standing in that statistic didn't particularly stand out. Furthermore, eighteen Fortune 500 companies called Minnesota home, eighteen more than Sacramento.

Republic officials later said they always knew their bid was a longshot for this round of expansion. When Minnesota finally secured a deal to construct a downtown soccer-specific stadium, MLS almost immediately confirmed that its next club would hail from the Midwest.

"We made their decision very difficult," Smith said. "They told us that and said we had to stick with our strategy. They said, 'Don't worry, we're going to announce expansion again, keep doing what you're doing, and you're in a good spot.' They didn't say you'll get [a team], but they did say you're in a good spot. The last few times we've talked to them, it's very consistent, [they say], 'Keep doing what you're doing. We haven't decided what we're doing yet but keep doing what you're doing and good things will happen.'"

Though MLS had then reached its publicly stated goal of twenty-four teams, few league observers expected the league to cease expanding. Instead of tailing off, Sacramento pressed forward as the new favorite to land a spot should MLS decide to further grow. Three weeks following the Minnesota disappointment, Johnson, Nagle, and Smith held a press conference at the Railyards to announce, "Operation Turnkey." The ambitious proposal outlined by the trio included several milestones that the club hoped to achieve by the end of 2015 to secure an MLS bid as soon as possible. Paramount among those milestones: breaking ground on the construction of a Downtown stadium suitable for Major League Soccer.

"The moment we get word from MLS, we'll start digging," Johnson said in front of the decaying rubble that the Republic had chosen as their stadium site. "By the end of the year, we'll be ready to put shovels in the ground."

When the club announced later that month that it sold out its season-ticket allotment for the 2015 USL season, it barely registered in the national news—it no longer surprised anyone that Sacramento could sell 9,500 season tickets for lower-division soccer. "Our fans continue to prove their passion for the city of Sacramento and Republic FC," said Republic FC president Warren Smith. "Sacramento is a soccer capital filled with fans that watch, play, and attend professional matches. Hitting this goal, something not even achieved by numerous MLS clubs, demonstrates our market's demand and growth for professional sports."

With a further 600 deposits from those who were only interested in MLS, the club surpassed 10,000 in total, cementing the Republic's place as the new expansion favorites.

Around the same time, *Sacramento Bee* columnist Marcos Bretón flew to New York to meet Garber for an exclusive interview at the league's Midtown Manhattan offices. During the sit down, the commissioner admitted to Bretón that MLS hadn't yet decided whether it would grow past twenty-four franchises. Given that information, the longtime columnist asked Garber if Republic fans should feel pessimistic about their chances. The commissioner's response would at first provide a source of hope for Sacramento soccer fans, but over time, become infamous.

"No," Garber said. "I want to reiterate what [Republic owner Kevin Nagle] said: 'It's less about if and more about when the Republic joins MLS.'"

# ACKNOWLEDGEMENTS

Writing a book is a painful experience and because this one took such an absurdly long amount of time, there's a massive list of people I must thank for helping ensure that this project became a reality. No matter how many years passed between its inception and its completion.

As I write this, I just returned from a trip abroad where my friend Cris mentioned that we're all a product of our environments—we're only able to move through life in a certain way because of the people and culture we have surrounding us. For that I'm grateful that I've always had such a strong community supporting me. If I hadn't grown up where I did, with the amazing friends and quality teachers influencing me, there's no way I would have had the chance to live the life I want to live.

I already mentioned Matt Ream at the start. Once we finally started to tolerate each other, we developed a mutual love for the beautiful game and there's no person who has had a bigger influence on so many different parts of my life than my older brother. Within my family, I also must thank my mom, Celia, who came to all my soccer games and silently supported me without understanding the sport's laws or caring about the outcome. Having a mother who legitimately didn't know which team won or lost the game, but still supported me regardless, ensured that my love for soccer was able to blossom without parental interference. Also she let me live with her for free until I was like 26. I bet that was annoying for her.

I must also acknowledge all the people I consider family: most of my tight-knit crew of friends I grew up with in Davis. I've known Billy and Wyatt since kindergarten. While they're minor soccer fans, they've still always supported my work. Thank you also to Laura, Murry, Dale, and Rob for treating me like one of your own kids for my entire childhood.

I don't think there's any friend who has helped me progress through my writing career more than Will, with whom I started a terrible blog in 2010. The reps we got together, and his feedback, were instrumental in me evolving into a non-terrible writer. Nick, my friend who kind of likes soccer, chipped in with said blog and we became good friends in the process. I can't thank Will and Nick enough for helping me through some of the worst times in my life and never giving up on me despite my years of struggles.

Danny, as promised, gets a mention for always keeping me motivated. And Russell, even though we live three miles apart and never hang out, I'm still glad that I can count on waking up to your ridiculous takes and that you send game updates whenever I can't watch live. Kenny, you're so sick, you shouldn't even be in this section.

I want to thank everyone who has ever been involved with Da Vinci Charter Academy, specifically Adela, Scott, and Tyler. DVCA gave me a community to call home during high school and later a steady job on several different occasions. Adela, Scott, and Tyler were there for both parts of that journey. I'm happiest when I'm at the school, and without it, I wouldn't have gotten anywhere. Also, shout out to my boys Joey and Justin, who make even baseball tolerable. At least compared to the Star Wars prequels. Kait, I have never not enjoyed interrupting your class for completely pointless reasons and Gretchen, your laugh makes me laugh. Debbie, you're one of the kindest people I know, thank you for always helping when I inevitably don't know how to do something. Leonie, thanks for always having me over to watch soccer with a bunch of idiot men.

I'm forever indebted to the tireless staff at *The Davis Enterprise*, most of whom have sadly moved on. Bruce, Chris, and Debbie gave me my first steady writing work and recognized how big Sacramento Republic FC was, allowing me to cover the club starting in 2014. In a newspaper world that was dominated by checked-out higher-ups who made up their mind on soccer 30 years ago, those three constantly evolved and gave me way more creative freedom than I deserved. I also must thank Kim and Owen for always reading my work and helping me improve.

This section would be incomplete if I didn't mention the good people at NorCal Premier Soccer, who have been most responsible for my soccer education and have helped me broaden my horizons through a series of international trips. Ben, Dan, and Robbo gave me the opportunity to truly learn the game even if I was always the least qualified person in the room. Andy and Jason have also helped form who I am as a thinker. I've made more mistakes working for NorCal than I can count but the company has always stuck with me and exists in my biased opinion on the forefront of this country's youth soccer evolution. Through chaperoning for Cris and Ian, I learned that I wanted to coach, and I'm glad we still keep in touch. Eric, you don't work for NorCal, but I met you on one of our trips and I'm glad that we roomed together in Germany because that began a great friendship.

Thank you to Davis Legacy Soccer Club for believing in me and giving me my first coaching job. When the newspaper laid me off, I didn't know what to do with my free time, which helped contribute to some of my troubles. I now consider my forced vocational change as a blessing in disguise as I love coaching more than I ever thought I would. I've already singled out Robbo, but Ashley, Brian, Didi, James, Janae, Janessa, Jesus, Jorge, Josh, Kevin, Paul, Sara, and Simon have all had a huge impact in helping me through a job where I frequently have no idea what I'm doing. I also can't offer up enough gratitude to every player I've coached and the parents who have supported me. Without my team managers, Jim and Marisol, I'd be lost. Thanks to my first-year captains, Holly and Marisela, for always setting the tone at training. And without Christina, Courtney, Olivia, and Madison, I wouldn't have been able to field a team my second year of coaching, which turned out incredibly. I can't believe I'm coaching younger boys now, which has been a steep learning curve, but I'd like to thank all of my 2014 boys and their parents for being patient with me as I've learned to work with an age group I've never coached before.

I would like to thank the friends I've become close with as an adult, most of whom I met playing in my local, co-ed, recreational soccer league. Andria, we miss your presence on the field in Davis. Also, the Lakers are trash. Benware, your friendship helped me through the bleakness of the pandemic–the Insanity workout is aptly named, and I hated every moment of it but needed something productive to do to stop me from throwing my life away. Connor and Izzy, sorry I wasn't the best roommate when we lived together, but I'm glad y'all are always still down for food and live games. I'd give Ehsan a shout out, but I know he's not going to read this. Hollay, please tell him and yourself thanks for helping me through those tough few years and for always being there when I've needed it. Jesse, thank you for letting me live in your house and for being a great roommate/blackjack/golf/sports gambling/leftist takes buddy. It's still funny that the Portland Timbers gave you, someone with no knowledge of photography, a photo credential for that game against the Sounders in 2016. And then you captured one of the best images I've ever seen during it. Juan Pablo, I'm not sure how we made it out of Russia unscathed, but I look forward to more strange adventures with you. Josh, I'm glad we still play together after what was by far the weirdest possible season of Southern Oregon University men's club soccer. Kortlin, I love that you stay in touch and I'm looking forward to hopefully reading your book soon. Sami and Trav, Nick Cage movies rule. Serge, I'm bummed you never moved back, but wherever you are, can you act out what you thought happened with that elbow in the Arsenal-Chelsea game again? Victor, let me tell you something...YAH SUSPECT! Vince, thanks for being that guy who, ever since I was 16, has always been willing to ask some dude fouling me if they'd "like to go to the parking lot."

There's no way I would have been able to complete this text without the help of my therapist, Clay. Simply, I struggled with mental health issues during most of my 20s and only really overcame them when I started therapy. I have a hard time doing anything unless I think it makes sense and Clay's data-driven approach that goes against conventional wisdom was exactly what I needed. Even my bad days now are far happier than any of my best from roughly 2016-2020. Seeking out help isn't a sign of weakness, it's a sign of strength. I highly recommend that anyone struggling with similar issues reach out to a professional as soon as possible.

Dad, you have really stepped up in my adult life to help me achieve some of my goals. I'd like to thank you, Denise, Nicco, Marco, and Macy for always supporting me when we've been in each other's lives.

I'd like to thank all of those who have directly helped me through the writing process. Wes Burdine and William Stenross originally green lit the project and many of Wes's edits survived to the final draft. Joe Wagoner, Warren Smith, and the rest of Sacramento Republic FC's original employees were incredibly generous to me while leading a massive expansion bid. They had a million better things to do with their time, but instead spent way too much of it with me. Erika Bjork, John Jacobs, and Eddie Ralph all helped connect me with people I needed (wanted) to interview. Terrie Martin, my motorcycle-riding, Pulitzer Prize-nominated journalism professor in college, taught me how to actually write and organize large projects. I still use some of her lessons in the journalism class I teach today.

Matt Pentz, Robert Andrew Powell, and Steve Sirk were always willing to answer my dumb questions regarding the writing process. All three wrote pieces that helped inspire me during various stages of my career. Powell's book, *This Love Is Not for Cowards*, is the text that made me want to become an author. I still use excerpts of it to teach my Honors English students how to write unforgettable hooks. I already thanked Kim Orendor in the newspaper section, but after I wrote that section, she graciously agreed to copy edit this book and provide me with valuable feedback for a small fee well below her deserved market rate. After leaving the paper, Kim became an author (twice!) and I've enjoyed both of her works. Like mine, both of her books are available for purchase with the click of a button from Jeffrey Bezos's evil online empire. You should buy 100 copies of each and leave five-star reviews for both. Well, definitely for Kim'. And please, if you can, check out the beautiful work that my cover artist, Dante, has created in his short time on this planet. If I ever write another book, there's no way I'm going to be able to afford him.

Finally, I only met the late Grant Wahl a few times, but my recollections of those meetings are similar to those I've heard described by other struggling soccer writers. At a hotel lobby in Port of Spain the night before *that* USA-Trinidad and Tobago game, he pledged his support for this book when it came out and told me to reach out if I ever needed advice. Grant was a pioneer in his field who we lost too soon. I still miss his work in my life. *The Beckham Experiment* remains a perfect piece of literature, especially all the Alan Gordon parts.

There are countless more people I'm sure I've missed, without whom this book would not have been possible. I'd like to thank them too, along with the city of Davis and its vibrant soccer community, all the Sacramento Republic FC fans who have followed my work, the Southern Oregon University communications department, and Logan Harrison.

Start writing again, Logan. Use Talkeetna as inspiration.

Or something.

Made in the USA
Las Vegas, NV
01 June 2024

90613095R00108